Martial Traditions of North East India

About the Editors

S. Dutta, formerly Dean of faculty of Social Sciences and Head, Department of History, Arunachal University, Itanagar, is an eminent historian of North East India. Besides publishing seven books, he has published more than sixty papers in various research journals of repute and has edited many volumes. He is member of various regional and national academic bodies.

B. Tripathy, currently the Head of the Department of History, Arunachal University, Itanagar, is a keen researcher in the history and culture of the North East and ancient India. He has published several research papers in various research journals and edited volumes. He is member of various academic bodies.

Martial Traditions of North East India

Edited by

S. Dutta

B. Tripathy

CONCEPT PUBLISHING COMPANY, NEW DELHI-110059

Cataloging in Publication Data—DK
Courtesy: D.K. Agencies (P) Ltd. <docinfo@dkagencies.com>

National Seminar on the Martial Traditions of North East India (2003 : Itanagar, India)
Martial traditions of North East India / edited by S. Dutta, B. Tripathy.
p. cm.
Papers presented at the National Seminar on the Martial Traditions of North East India, held at Itanagar during 18-19 November 2003.
Includes bibliographical references.
Includes index.
ISBN 818069335X

1. Military art and science—India, Northeastern— History—Congresses. 2. War and society—India, Northeastern—History—Congresses. I. Title.

DDC 355.009 541 22

The opinions expressed by the contributors of the papers are their own and neither the editors nor the publishers owe responsibility for this.

ISBN 81-8069-335-X

First Published 2006

Published and Printed by

Ashok Kumar Mittal
Concept Publishing Company
A/15-16, Commercial Block, Mohan Garden
New Delhi-110059 (India)

Phones: 25351460, 25351794
Fax: 091-11-25357103
E-mail: publishing@conceptpub.com

Preface

This book has grown out of a National Seminar on the "Martial Traditions of North East India", organized jointly by Maulana Abul Kalam Azad Institute of Asian Studies (MAKAIAS), Kolkata, and the Department of History, Arunachal University, Itanagar on 18-19 November, 2003. A number of eminent scholars and researchers from different disciplines participated in the seminar and presented their valuable papers. As many as twenty-two papers were presented, which dealt with various aspects of martial traditions like war mechanism, warfare, war-tactics, military history of tribes, cult of war goddess, forts and fortifications, war implements, village defence mechanism, martial arts, etc.

The work, perhaps is the first attempt to document the martial traditions of the people and of various ruling dynasties of North East India. The book, it is hoped, will prove useful for scholars as well as general public interested in the subject. The work is of regional as well as national importance as it throws light on the little known aspect of history and culture of North East India in particular and of India in general.

The volume would have not been possible without the help, support and cooperation from various persons, quarters and institutions. We are specially grateful to Prof. Devendra Kaushik and Prof. Mahavir Singh, Chairman and Director of the MAKAIAS respectively for providing financial aid for organizing the seminar. Prof. Atul Sharma, Vice-Chancellor, Arunachal University gave academic advice and material support in organizing the seminar. We are thankful to him. We are extremely thankful to

Prof. Imdad Hussain of North Eastern Hill University (NEHU), Shillong, for his learned Key Note Address. The learned contributors have spared their valuable time and precious researches, which have gone into the making of this volume. Thanks also go to our colleagues in the Department of History for their cooperation in organizing the seminar.

Itanagar

Sristidhar Dutta
Byomakesh Tripathy

Introduction

The history and culture of North East India, occupies an important place not only in the history of India but also in the history of Asia. The geographical location of the region, touching Bhutan, Tibet (China), Myanmar (Burma) and mainland India, saw the blending of various cultural traditions in this part of the country since early historical period. More specifically, the socio-cultural traditions of the indigenous people of the area are so diverse and unique that the anthropologists and sociologists refer to the area as paradise for the study of tribal history and culture. The martial traditions of the people of the area have to be viewed in these perspectives.

The North East India was consisted of three independent states like Assam, Manipur and Tripura, besides many tribal pockets in various hills of the area. Before independence Assam, earlier known as Kamarupa and Pragjyotishpura, has a chequered history of warrior traditions. From the time of king Bhagadatta to the Ahom rulers of medieval Assam, the people of Assam showed their bravery, heroism in the battlefield. The military organization was efficiently structured and that is the reason, we see that throughout the history of Assam (upto 18th century), hardly the soldiers of Assam tasted defeat permanently in the hands of the enemies. The epigraphs, the Ahom Buranjis, manuscripts and various folk traditions of Assam throw light on various aspects of warfare, war organization, espionage system, war tactics, and on various related aspects. Even the medieval Muslim historians have praised the warfare of the Ahom kings in a befitting manner. Adjacent to the plain area of Assam, a number of martial tribes inhabited the Northeast Frontier (now known as Arunachal Pradesh). These tribes are notable for their valour and courage and could challenge the mighty British off and on, which reveal their warrior traditions. The village defence system, the role of their dormitories and traditional political institutions in warfare, their war dances, festivals and rituals associated with war etc. are of considerable interest to study their warrior tradition. Here mention can be made of the Wanchos, the Tangsas, the Noctes, the Mishmis, the Adis, the Nyishis, the Tagins, the Akas and others, who used to show their valour in the battle fields, which can be known from a scrutiny of archival literature of the period. The number of actual forts and fortifications, noticed in the foothills of Arunachal and various parts of Assam, reveal their offensive and defensive techniques. Various kinds of tribal warfare can also be gleaned in the military report and political proceedings of the British period, of 19th and early 20th century concerning the region.

The Nagas, considered as a warrior tribe, have a glorious history of their warfare, which was associated with headhunting. Their mode of head hunting, warfare, war mechanisms, village defence mechanism and philosophical dimension of head hunting reveal one of their best socio-cultural traditions. The Nagas observe a number of war rituals, dances and festivals, which are reminiscent of their warrior tradition of the past. Various ethnographers, military reports and literature of the period reveal various aspects of Naga warfare.

The Mizos of Mizoram had a good system of military administration in the early Mizo society and their socio-economic and political life was also greatly determined by it. The role of the Mizo chiefs, their regular militia, zawlbulk (house of dormitory), types of village fortifications, methods of warfare, weapons, hair dresses are of immense and considerable importance in the military system of the Mizos. The role of Zawlbulk and the village fortifications, besides employment of intelligence services etc.

reveal their form of military system. Infact every village was a military cantonment of the chief in which the chief himself was the supreme commander.

The hill region of Meghalaya, inhabited by the Khasis, the Garos and the Jayantias, like their counterparts in Arunachal and other states, had their own indigenous mode of warfare and war organization. The history of Meghalaya is replete with a number of references regarding British-tribe conflicts/war, in which the tribes of Meghalaya, did create a lot of problems and difficulties for the British administration. So was the case with Manipur and Tripura. The historical literature of Tripura, like the 'Rajamala' provides a number of instances of the participation of tribal people in defence mechanisms of princely Tripura.

The State of Manipur is notable for unique martial art, throughout India. The art, known as 'Thang-Ta' is part and parcel of their culture. This martial art in fact not only deals with kicks and punches but also provides enlightenment.

Though North East India has a chequered history of martial traditions, no comprehensive work has been undertaken in this regard and we do not know various facets of the glorious traditions of the people till now. Again due to modernization and other factors, these traditions are almost dying out. Taking these things into consideration, the Department of History, Arunachal University, organized a National Seminar on *Martial Traditions of North East India* on 18-19 November, 2003. The aims and objectives of the Seminar were: (i) to know various aspects of history of war, military warfare, war techniques, defence mechanisms etc. of various ruling dynasties of North East India and (ii) to document the war dances, war festivals, rituals, village defence mechanisms, role of village chiefs, role of dormitory system and traditional political organization etc. in various tribal pockets of North East India.

The present volume is the outcome of the seminar proceedings. The essays are not uniform in their content, analysis, references or otherwise. But it throws light on various unknown facets of martial traditions of the region. We hope, this proceeding will be of immense use for historians anthropologists and laymen, who want to know history and culture of North East India.

Sristidhar Dutta
Byomakesh Tripathy

Contents

Preface v

Introduction vii

Sristidhar Dutta and ***Byomakesh Tripathy***

Key Note Address xiii

Prof. Imdad Hussain

1. Head Hunting and Warfare : A Critical Reappraisal of Naga Political Systems 1
N.K. Das
2. War Mechanism of the Nagas : A Case Study of the Tangkhul Nagas 28
A.S.W. Shimray
3. Mode of Naga Warfare : A Profile 43
A. Nshoga
4. Ahom Tactics of War : The Espionage System 70
Jahnabi Gogoi Nath
5. Koch-Ahom Tactics of War : The Guerilla Fighting 80
D. Nath
6. War Mechanisms: The Defence and Warfare of the Adis 87
Tai Nyori
7. War Weapons in Medieval Assam 97
Punyadhar Gogoi
8. Defence Strategy of Later-Medieval Assam 104
P.C. Sarma
9. The Martial Tradition of the Nyishis : An Overview 112
N.T. Rikam
10. Tai-Ahom Martial Traditions in Medieval Assam (1228-1682) 121
Romesh Buragohain

11. Military System in Early Mizo Society 125
Sangkima

12. Aspects of Military Organisation in Early Medieval Assam 138
Byomakesh Tripathy

13. Historical Importance of the Battle of Saraighat 1671: Saga of Medieval Assam 153
Bharat Kalita

14. Participation of Tribal in Some Selected Defence Mechanisms of Princely Tripura 161
Satyadeo Poddar

15. Technology and Society : In Pre-Colonial and Colonial Perspective of Arunachal Pradesh 170
Amrendra Kr. Thakur

16. Forts—Indicatory of Martial Tradition: A Case Study of Arunachal Pradesh 195
Sasikanta Dash and ***Ritu Bhatt***

17. Defence Technique of the Tagins' Traditional Villages 204
Ashan Riddi

18. Defence and the Cult of the War Goddess in the Formation of the Dimasa State 211
Sarah Hilaly

19. War Dresses and Weapons of the Apa Taniis 220
Pura Tado

20. Military Activities in North East as Uniting Force 228
Bharat Kalita

21. War and Art Tradition of the Wanchos of Arunachal Pradesh 237
Sarit K. Chaudhuri

22. Thang-Ta: The Traditional Martial Art of Manipur 251
Sristidhar Dutta

The Contributors 263

Index 266

Keynote Address

Prof. Imdad Hussain

I thank the organizers of the seminar for doing me the honour of inviting me to deliver the keynote address. This is the first of its kind in this part of the country that I know of and I congratulate Professor Sristidhar Dutta and his colleagues in the Department of History on their choice of the seminar problem and the several themes they have so carefully worked out. In its planning they must have noted the absence, and perhaps ran into the context of the region this absence would worthwhile frame of reference. In the context of the region this absence would have been even more striking. Such being the status of research in this emerging new area of historical enquiry, this seminar to my mind assumes a special significance.

1. In a map in the Simon Commission Report showing the number of combatants in the Indian Army drawn from various parts of the country and Nepal, Assam figures as a virtual blank. Recruits from the Punjab, the United Provinces and the North West Frontier predominate, the first two provinces alone accounting for 62 per cent of the total Army. They were the so called martial races, "fine fighting material", the Report said "while the other communities and areas do not furnish a single man for the regular army". This has been the view of Assam of a succession of British army commanders and a host of military writers. Did Assam or what today is called North East India lack a military tradition? This is perhaps the key question before the seminar.

2. I have argued elsewhere that the martial races theory wants a more critical looking into. Indian regiment involved in the process of imperial expansion in the subcontinent from the mid-eighteenth century onwards were always raised in borderlands and frontier areas outside formal control, the very areas that were likely to become scenes of military activity, either as a prelude to their incorporation within the extending political boundaries or as regions annexed but vulnerable to external aggression.

The peasant recruit's importance after the annexation of his homelands correspondingly shifted: from that of the bearer of arms to that of the holder of the plough. This was what made wars in India different from those fought in Europe. Unlike continental warfare, colonial warfare, as one French expert of the subject noted—

> aims not at the destruction of the enemy but at the organization of the conquered peoples and territories under a particular control. As far as possible it must avoid destructions during the campaign; first in order to preserve the productive potential of the theatre of operations and thus minimize the supply coming from more distant bases; but more important, because the country is to be integrated immediately after the conquest into the imperial whole, politically as well as economically.

3. British expansion east of Bengal and their recruitment policy follows this pattern in all its essential aspects. Early attempts to create buffer states and partisan forces along the Company's Eastern Frontier against the Burmese was given up once the entire region was brought under varying degrees of administrative control. Interest in recruiting local material gave way to indifference

once their territories were absorbed. It was only after the Second World War when experience had been gained of the northeastern soldier that opinions changed and at least one military officer, the author of the first volume of the *History of the Assam Regiment* (1959) was able to recognize that "Assam and her Military Traditions".

4. In poplar perception the golden age of Assam's military history lies in her pre-colonial days, and is best illustrated in the Ahom-Mughal conflict. These wars, however, do not enjoy any centrality in regional history that, for instance, the Thirty Years' War occupies in seventeenth century European history. Rather, it is still dominated by accounts of individuals. Some time ago the Department of History of the Gauhati University held a seminar on Lachit Barphukan and his times, because the Governor of the state, himself a former Lieutenant General, felt that in not adequately projecting the military exploits of the great Barphukan historians have neglected Assam. The river battle fought at Saraighat has become the *Locus classicus* of Ahom warfare and military system. That Lachit Barphukan was heir to a military tradition has all too often been overlooked. Saraighat was in reality the culmination of techniques and structures that had been evolving over the past centuries. It started with the early rulers of Kamata followed by new military technologies adopted by the Koch, and both of which were developed under the Ahoms. The main elements of that tradition were the art of fortification, use of firearms and the methods of riverine warfare.

5. Sir Edward Gait says that the use of firearms by the Ahoms dates from the close of the conflict with Hussain Khan in 1533-34. Did this lead to a transformation of Ahom

warfare from about the middle of the sixteenth century with corresponding changes in social and political organization? Major technological advances in arms in Europe in the seventeenth century is said to have led to what Michael Roberts and Geoffrey Parker have called the 'Military Revolution'. Some of the collections in Gomman and Kokff's Oxford Readings on *Warfare and Weaponry in South Asia* 1000-1800 (2001) discuss the relevance of this concept to India.

> did the Sultanate period see a military revolution? (Asked the General Editor of the series) How important was the development of artillery and firearms for Mughal Warfare? How far were new technologies of warfare devised in the immediate pre-colonial, the result of diffusion from the west or local initiatives?

6. There may not have been a military revolution in Ahom or Koch history comparable to what occurred in Europe but the impact of new technologies on their warfare seems to me quite discernible. To understand these one needs to go beyond the conventional periodisation into ancient, medieval and modern periods as in European history. This begs the question whether such periodisation is at all valid for military history. "Are not the real dividing lines in the history of a country based rather on social and material independent of the race or religion of the rulers"? Asked Susobhan Sarkar some years ago. Likewise, can we not build the chronology of military history around military technology or certain recognizable strategic or tactical concepts? The well-known military historian Major-General J.F.C. Fuller attempted just that in his *Armaments and History* (1945). He divided the period from approximately the fifth century BC to the post-Second

World War into six ages: the age of Valour, of Chivalry, Gunpowder, Steam, Oil and Atomic Energy. In his case, however, the result was a curious mix of social values and scientific developments. Yet such an effort would be much worthwhile than such narratives as Jagadish Narayan Sarkar's *The Art of War in Medieval India* (1984), which does not convey any sense of military dynamism.

7. Much of the difficulty academic historians have in writing military history lies in the confusion about definitions and terminology. The bulk of the writing on India or Assam have titles about military policy and military systems. An *Aide Memoir on the Science and Art of War* of the mid-nineteenth century defined military policy as "the habitual views of the Government regarding its ambitions or interests externally directed towards objects to be attained by force, or internally to be guarded by defensive means". Of the second, it says:

> the military system of a state denotes the nature and composition of the forces by sea and land; the militia and reserves; their organizations; laws, pay, recruiting, clothing, discipline, instruction, promotion, rewards and punishments; fortifications, fleets, ordnance, equipments and all elements required for war.

Thus considered P.C. Chakravarti's well-known *The Art of War in Ancient India* (1972) which deals almost exclusively on subjects enumerated in it could well have been entitled the Military System of Ancient India. I would, therefore, draw the attention of the seminar to the importance of understanding military terms, concepts and definitions. They help not only in categorizing and evaluating the existing literature but also provide the direction to further studies.

8. In the hill areas where the tribal peoples were organized into small village based polities rather than in large territorial units, warfare was materially different from that waged in the plains. What in the nineteenth century literature on the hill tribes was called tribal warfare consisted of two distinct categories. The first was the inter-tribal and intra-tribal conflicts. Why these so frequently occurred has not yet been satisfactorily explained. But around them was built what I would like to call the 'warrior tradition' in preference to 'martial tradition', with its elaborate rituals and ceremonies. This warfare took a variety of forms, each determined by circumstances of population, social and political organization, the physical features of the country and so on. Warfare among tribal societies under chiefs appears to be more organized than were those under a more democratic system. Sema Naga 'military' terminology would bear this out.

9. More important was the second, the armed response of the tribal people to British military expeditions and to the imposition of colonial rule itself. Tribal methods, often called in contemporary British manuals as "savage warfare" apparently did not differ significantly from those they adopted in the conflicts among themselves. But what was the impact of these encounters on tribal society? In the areas of psychology or their economic and social organization little is known. Among the Angami Nagas, however, the innumerable military expeditions had the effect of revolutionizing their warfare. The arms traffic of the 1860s and 1870s and the transformation of their village defences into masonry fortifications complete with loopholes for musketry is a clear indication of this change. Similar

developments are noticeable in the Lushai hills prior to their annexation. I have brought out these two categories in the hope that it will bring clarity to the discussions on warfare in the hill areas.

10. If we consider the trends and developments in recent historiography one deficiency in military history at once becomes obvious. This is the almost total lack of focus on the conduct of warfare at the lowest level of participation. How did the private or the common soldier face up to the battle, what were his fears, his thoughts or mental condition? Some insights have been gained from letters written by them from the front during both the World Wars and surveys conducted among survivors. In the context of the North East India I would like to draw our attention to a private diary of a sergeant (corresponding to a havildar) in the 1st Assam Light Infantry Battalion, which describes action during the expedition against the Adis in 1859.

> it's light enough work (says the entry) to climb up these hills with a rifle and ammunition through a tolerably level country, four days ration may be carried, but here (at Kebang) the climbing tries the wind and stamina too much without a load of provisions. Of Adi tactics, George Carter, the writer of the diary says: this noiseless peppering was very annoying: we could not tell where to aim at an Abor, but when any of our men fired, a dozen bows sent arrows towards the flash.

11. This makes interesting reading. But I would be more interested in the other side of the story. A nineteenth century authority on frontier warfare has called punitive expeditions into hills as "small wars" on the basis of the numbers of troops involved. Could a column of troops armed with modern rapid fire weapons marching against a village of a

few hundred defenders destroying houses, standing crops, livestock and stored grain have been to the small victims? One might ask. How then did the tribal people view these encounters? The answer would come from oral traditions. It will be necessary therefore to widen the source base of our research. Equally important would be the need to examine maps and topography sheets. Incidentally, the map on Guwahati and its environs prepared by Thomas Wood who accompanied Captain Thomas Welsh to Assam during 1792-94 provides the key to our understanding of how the war at Straight was fought.

12. I have placed before you some stray thoughts I have had on issues concerning this interesting if neglected area of research what then would be the core of my address. The chairman of the Indian Council of Historical Research wrote in October 1976 that "the study of military history, in all its strategic, tactical and logistic, as well as its economic and sociological aspects, has not received adequate attention from our historians so far." Twenty-seven years after those words were written I am making much the same point. Dr. R. Chidambaram, former Chairman of the Atomic Energy Commission, was said to be fond of the expression, "Velocity of Research". Velocity implies both direction and speed. If this is to be our *mantra* we need to be able to draw upon the resources of other disciplines, beyond our own Social Sciences. There must be cooperation between individuals, between institutions and between countries. This, after all is what our ancient scriptures have taught us. The Rig Veda feels us: *Let ideas come to us from every side.* The Taitireya Upanishad says: *Let us come together. Let us enjoy together. Let our strengths come together. Let there be light. Let there be no poison of misunderstanding or hatred. That way lies progress.*

1

Head Hunting and Warfare

A Critical Reappraisal of Naga Political Systems

N.K. Das

Anthropologists tend to include forms of treaties, warfare and reconciliation after feuds within the purview of political system. They are called the regulated interrelationships in the political field (Notes and Queries on Anthropology, 1951 : 135). Through such pacts unrestricted vengeance may be replaced by 'blood money' or other obligations of redress. Within the Naga tribes there were socially recognized measures for taking vengeance, particularly through 'head hunting'. The practice of cutting off parts of slain enemy's corpse, particularly the head, was a widespread feature of Naga warfare and persisted until even colonial rule. Besides the value of the 'head' as a trophy, there are a number of ritual or psychological motives behind 'head hunting' as practiced by the Nagas. After the head, the hands and feet are the most usual parts to be possessed and exhibited in order to gain the warrior's status and previlege to wear scarlet gauntlets. In Naga society the head (scalp) is also treated as a source of fertility. In all Naga tribes allable-bodied men (either recruited through *age sets* or membership of *morungs*) joined the war expeditions to obtain enemy's heads.

In this chapter we will discuss the mode of head hunting and warfare, war mechanisms, village defence mechanisms and philosophical dimension of head hunting in the backdrop of Naga social structure and political system. The chapter is mostly based on secondary source material including my own anthropological works.

The entire Naga inhabited areas may be described as one culture area. Despite their occupation of distinct hill ranges and a long history of inter-tribe warfare and feud, the Nagas show strong homogeneity in terms of their kinship and political systems, uniethnic settlement pattern over the hill summits, common house and dormitory (*morung*) type, tradition of log drum, identical dress and ornaments, common food habits, modes of agriculture, hunting, fishing and weaving and customs and laws.

In Naga societies kinship provides the principle of political relations and it also defines the territorial organization, which constitutes 'the tribe'. Through internal mechanisms of kinship lineage and clan groups take shape, who are often differentiated amongst themselves, and thus play distinct ritual roles. Lineages, clans, territorial divisions and age sets provide main fields of social relations in Naga tribes. Within the system, there are institutions of 'dormitory' and 'headmanship' which regulate and maintain the social cohesion, and political stability which in the past also implied the village defence…the honour of martial traditions of people.

The Nagas portray the model of 'the tribe' in excellent manner. Thus each Naga tribe has been a politically and socially coherent and autonomous group occupying a particular territory. In the precolonial era even a single village existed and operated as an independent unit with no centralized political hierarchy (Das, 1993 : 16). Such boundary formation in a way had been a logical outgrowth resulting on account of persistence of inter-village warfare (Das, 1993 : 15, 16). This author has critically discussed the question of tribeship in Naga hills (Das, 1982, 1989, 1993).

In Naga tribes persons of same sex and of about the same age are formally grouped into distinct 'sets', which are formed at successive intervals. Each age set passes through a series of stages, each of which in the past had distinctive status and role, associated with ceremonial, military and economic activities (Das

1993 : 92). There were also procedures of ceremonial initiation and formal military training. The age confers authority in matters of law and government and the seniormost of the oldest group has the decisive voice in all matters that concern the regulation of public life (Thus Pithi-Ketsami and Mehu-chu age sets in Zounuo-Keyhonuo Naga tribe have 'elders' who deal with religious, jural and legal matters. In the past they guided the military activities including village defence).

The Nagas: Origin and Identity

J.H. Hutton (1965) the colonial administrator, Furer Haimendorf (1939), a trained anthropologist and W.C. Smith (1925) have regarded the Nagas as representative of an archaic cultural stratum extending from North East Region of India to Indonesian islands and as far east as the Philippines. In their view there is a direct link between the Naga and the people of Malaya and Indonesia in sharing many common culture traits, some of which are head hunting, common sleeping houses for unmarried men, betel chewing, tattooing by pricking, absence of powerful political organization, the simple loom for weaving cloth and a crude form of agriculture. In his book *A History of South East Asia, Hall* (1901) provides a good description of Neolithic culture in Naga Hills.

Before their settlement, the Nagas had moved in small groups and they narrate about their origin in folk tales and songs. Most of the Naga tribes have own legends indicating the course of migration. All Nagas do not emerge as a simple 'tribe'. There is no single ancestor who founded this large group of Nagas. One may refer to two books *Nagaland* (1994) and *Manipur* (1994) published under the project people of India to get current ethnographic profile of Naga tribes (Das and Imchen, 1994). In his book *Kinship, Politics and Law in Naga Society* this author (Das, 1993) has discussed the method of law enforcement and pattern of uncentralized political system of a Naga tribe.

Naga Social and Political Structure

The Naga tribes, except Konyak, Sema and Tangkul, generally have uncentralized political system based on segmentary system of interlocking descent groups. The descent groups, which are strictly localized, confined to clan ward/village, are formed through a process of periodic splitting (Das, 1985, 1993). Besides clear-cut kinship rules and descent principles, there are definite customs and tribal laws recognized in society. Individuals have rights, jural obligations and moral responsibilities. These rights and obligations play a vital part in resolving conflicts and maintaining social order (Das, 1993: 2). Gluckman wrote that 'men quarrel in terms of their certain customary allegiance' but are restrained from 'violence through other conflicting allegiances which are also enjoined on them by custom' (1955 : 2).

Majority of Naga tribes such as Angami, Chakhesang, Lotha, Rengma etc. lack formal chieftainship or any organized political or governmental system. Thus all kinds of inter-group and inter-personal relationships serve significant politico-jural purposes. These tribes also possess well-recognized arbitrating institutions which are also often informal in character and through which the headmen and elders maintain social order and politico jural cohesion (Das, 1993 : 3). In addition to their distinct kinship statuses these elders also occupy specific positions in age sets operating in many Naga tribes. There is yet another type of elders particularly among the Zounuo Keyhonuo called as Zohdimi. They are called so far their generosity in giving feasts (of meat and rice beer) to villagers. These Zohdimi or 'big men' command respect and prestige for their age, wealth, integrity and wisdom.

In precolonial era the clan was a more significant unit politically. It emerged as a single peace group and was united for 'war and self-protection' against a common enemy (Das, 1993 : 5). Every clan was subject to the authority of its senior male members who derived their statuses through age set system. Age set systems functioned generally at the level of clan territory (Das, 1993 : 124). Writing about clan system among the Tengima Angamis, J.H. Hutton described the exclusive political status of clan territory in following words:

> "So distinct is the clan from the village that it forms almost a village in itself, often fortified within the village inside in its own boundaries and not infrequently at variance almost amounting to war with other clans in the same village. In almost every dispute between two men of different clans the clansmen on each side appear as partisans and ferment the discord" (1921, 1969 : 109).

This author observed similar clan level solidarity among the Zounuo Keyhounuo Nagas (Das, 1993 : 124). This author observed that clan as a social as well as a territorial unit fully shapes and regulates the entire life of the Nagas as the customary laws to be still followed are all based keeping exclusive character of clans. Even dispute settlement and law enforcement is clan affair. Being territorially intact and socially cohesive, a clan is considered to be the widest grouping within which there is a moral obligation and a means ultimately to settle intra-clan disputes peacefully. A clan may, therefore, be portrayed as a 'peace group' (Das, 1993: 125). Clan areas of the Nagas were called as Khels by the officials of British administration. In Zounuo Keyhonuo Naga society the clans emerge as compound clans. In contrast to lineage (*sarra*), a Zounuo Keyhonuo clan or Thenu is not a mere collection of individuals. It is an organization of well defined smaller social groups—Putsanu, Lokro and Punumi. A clan grows by continuous multiplication of its parts, following the fission and segmentary processes, and not by mere accreation of new members. This takes place by splitting of its cells into new segments in successive generations (Das, 1993 : 119).

Territorial organization is an important element of any political structure. Anthropologists have argued that 'the expression of the political and territorial structure is to be found in the field of law and warfare' (Redcliffe-Brown, 1940: XIV). Clan level territorial solidarity is an important characteristic of Naga life and this phenomenon is observable in all Naga areas (of Nagaland and Manipur). The Nagas may not be ready to organize today real blood feud or warfare but whenever there is a threat common to all clan members, it is difficult to suppress the anger of clan members. This author observed in 1977 a serious quarrel between two clans belonging to Viswema and Jakhama villages over distribution of water of a natural stream (Das, 1993 : 126).

In the past clan membership was coterminous with the political membership because the clan was the largest jural community. Help in inter-clan feud and inter-village war was a necessary prerequisite of clan solidarity. Indeed, the corporate lineages, clan localities and age sets in most Naga societies provided the main field of social relations and the arenas of political life. Since purely political or governmental system did not exist in many Naga tribes, the Naga elders remained primarily responsible for ordering relations (Das, 1993: 144-146).

The Naga-British Conflict and the Colonial Era

The British entered the Naga Hills for the first time in 1832. By 1850 as many as ten expeditions had been sent to the hills. After 1851 the British followed the policy of non-intervention in Naga areas, though till 1858 the Angami and other Nagas kept raiding British outposts. Before Naga Hills District was formed in

1866, some 8000 Kuki 'militia peasants' had been placed in Naga areas. In 1869 one of the major tasks of Captain Butler, the political agent of Naga Hills, was to interfere in inter-tribal disputes of the Nagas. In 1873 the Inner Line Regulation was passed and introduced. Thus, no British subject or foreign resident could go beyond a certain frontier that was drawn along the foothills of Naga Areas without a pass or licence issued by the Deputy Commissioner.

First Anglo-Naga War of 1879

In 1879 the Nagas had been equipped with hundreds of fire arms. In 1879 the Nagas had killed Damant, the British Political Officer with thirty-seven of his men. The Angami Nagas then besieged Kohima. Kohima and Khonoma remained impregnable for many months and its occupation was protracted owing to the strong defence lines led by warring Nagas. There are several instances of Naga raids of British outposts. During 1884-85 the Ao Naga had caused trouble. In 1885 Ao villages of Ungma and Longsa had raided British camps. In 1887 the Chang Nagas raided the British camps in Ao areas. As a result of Naga raids several punitive expeditions were sent to those Naga areas by the British. The Mokokchung sub-division was formed with the object of checking the Naga raids from Cis Diku and Trans Diku village. To check excessive occurrences of head hunting and warfare, Pangsa areas expeditions were sent during 1938-39. In 1952, Tuensang area was constituted as a sub-division of NEFA but it was merged into Naga Hills (Das, N.K. 'Introduction', Nagaland, POI). The last officially recorded case of head hunting was in 1958 (Elwin, 1961 : 12), although many head hunting like killings occurred in many areas afterwards also.

There are two broad phases of the Naga history of pre-independence era. At first there was a protracted war during which endemic head hunting and warfare prevailed among different tribes in the Naga Hill areas. Phase two began with the advent of the colonial British who brought 'warfare', blood feud and 'head hunting' to a gradual end (Das, 1993: 24). To ensure peace the British slightly modified the existing pattern of village political system and Naga headmanship.

In fact the British relations with the Nagas then were "one long, sickening story of open insults and defiance, bold outrages and cold blooded murders, on the one side, and long suffering, forbearance, forgiveness, concession and unlooked for favours on the other" (Butler, 1875). *The Nagas in the Nineteenth Century,* edited by Verrier Elwin (1969), is the best single ethno-historical source on the Nagas. Elwin provides extracted passages about the Naga people from printed books and articles covering the period 1827 to 1896. Elwin remarked that "there are many mistakes and misunderstanding of customs and institutions" (1969 : 1) in old British writings.

Naga Head Hunting : Practice and Tradition

Head hunting was something more than war. It inspired wonderful dances. Head hunters enjoyed great prestige. They believed that head hunting would result in a better yield of crops. Traditions and designs of weaving and wood carving were influenced by it.

The most elaborate textiles could only be worn by a successful head hunter and his relations. Small replicas of heads were carved to be worn almost like medals. Wooden pipes, with their bowls fashioned as heads, were made. Strong and vigorous human figures were carved and attached to baskets and the warrior's grave was the most splendid of all.

The practice of head hunting is based on a belief in a soul matter or vital essence of great power, which resides in the human head (Elwin, 1961 : 11). It was believed that by taking a head from another village, some kind of a vital and creative energy would enter the head hunters village. This was valuable for human and animal fertility. It stimulated the crops to grow better.

In view of Hutton [1921(1969):132] head hunting arises from a theory of the soul as the source of all, life existing as a quasi-material entity within the body which it pervades, and transferable to other bodies indirectly through the soil and the crops, the circuit of life being continued by the consumption of the crop by human beings. Among the Phom Naga the village headmen and rich persons had controlled the warfare and head hunting activities (Roypa, 1994).

Among the Chang, the men who had taken human heads, were elaborately tattooed. This author met several such former head hunters during fieldwork in Chang area in 1985-86 (Das, 1994). This author wrote in 1989 that "till recently dormitories (*Haki*) and log drum houses had functionally existed among the Changs and sleeping houses for the girls had helped the Chang boys to select their brides. While Hakis have almost died, in many villages log drum houses have provided sites of church buildings" (Das, 1994). An informal council of elders had traditionally been responsible for maintaining social order. The prominent warriors and head hunters were the members of such councils in the past (Das, 1994). A Naga warrior thus held a great advantage over his fellows in attracting the most beautiful girl of his village for marriage.

Because of head hunting practices, the Sema had no friendly relations with the neighbouring 'tribes' and even within the sections of the Sema community. The Sema often used to establish new villages by acquiring land from enemies (Raypa, 1994).

This author observed that among the Sangtam Nagas the skilful craftsmanship, woodwork and woodcarving were damaged on account of neglect of morung and log drum houses. House doors of former head hunters and richmen are also not decorated now-a-days with traditional designs (Das, 1994).

Head Hunting : Philosophy

Writing in early part of twentieth century J.H. Hutton (1921) observed that "Head hunting in one form or another is a wide-spread practice...the ultimate reason of its existence in a spot must be sought in some deep rooted characteristic of human nature". Hutton quotes O. Henry who said "Truly the head hunter...introduced art and philosophy to a simple code. To take adversary's head... to see it lying, a dead thing... Is there a better way to foil his plots, to refute his arguments...?" [Hutton, 1921 (1969) : 157)].

Hutton has argued that to show and produce the body of the slain is to give a definite assurance that the foe had been killed. This is the Angami explanation. Hence the Angamis preferred to bring the whole body, including head. The only difference between human head and animal head is teeth. If teeth are not cut they are not taken (Hutton, 1969 : 158).

Among the Lothas any human flesh brought into the village on return from an expedition is "vetted" by a group of old men to make sure that it is what is stated to be by the bringer. And until the trophy has been passed by this board, no ceremony can be performed for the success of head hunting [Hutton, 1921 (1969) : 157].

The killing of a man entitles the killer to certain distinctive articles of dress, so does the killing of a leopard or tiger. Among the Konyak Nagas it is common for a slave to be brought for the chief's son to kill in order that the boy may wear ceremonial dress without risking the dangers of war. Pieces of flesh are distributed throughout the young men of the Morung.

Quoting Major Butler, Hutton stated that "the Angamis would cut off the heads, hands and feet of anyone they can meet with, without provocation or pre-existing enmity, merely to stick them up in their fields and so ensure a good crop of grain" [1921 (1969) : 160].

A.W. Davis, Deputy Commissioner of the Naga Hills writing in 1898 said: "All the tribes in this district consider that by killing a human being in certain cases they are doing the most effectual thing towards averting the displeasure of some particular evil spirit (*terhoma*). Amongst the Angamis especially this idea is very prevalent", [Hutton, 1921 (1969):160]. Several instances of Kigwema and Jakhama villages are cited by Davis in which men were sent out to bring in heads as offering to '*terhoma*' in order that the plague or small pox might be averted. Further, according to A.W. Davis (also *vide Human Sacrifices in Ancient Assam* by Gait) "there is a very general superstition among the Angamis and Semas that to kill a human being and place a small portion of the flesh in the murderer's fields is a specific to ensure a good crop, and this is said to have been the reason that prompted certain men of Purobami to murder two men, a woman, and a child near the Sijju river towards the end of 1895. Murders like these partake of the nature of sacrifices, as their object is to avert disaster and so to ensure good crops" [Hutton, 1921 (1969) : 161].

A.W. Davis wrote in 1898 that "Before we annexed their country, the Aos were great slave owners, and these slaves were occasionally made use of for a semi-sacrificial purpose, e.g., two villages are at war and are desirous of making peace. It is found that one side has taken more heads than the other. To make things equal and as a sacrifice to the spirits of the dead, who have gone unavenged, an agreement would be arrived at that the village which had taken the fewest heads should receive one or more slaves from the other village" [Hutton, 1921 (1969): 161].

Davis cites another controversial practice of the case of slave burning. "In trans-Dikhu tribes, when the village Jhuns are ready for firing, a slave is tied up in the middle of them. The jhums are then lighted and the slave is burnt to death. A sacrifice like this ensures a good crop." Hutton has refuted that such practice ever existed. He says above report is incorrect [Hutton, 1921 (1969): 162]. Hanging of heads in chief's houses or Morungs is a widespread practice, particularly among the Ao and Konyak. But the Angamis buried the heads [Hutton, 1969: 162].

Head Taking Ritual

The successful warrior on returning to his village waits outside the village gate. One of his family members brings food for him. After that he enters the village escorted by the men of his clan singing and shouting, and goes first to the 'Kipuchie', the genna stone, of each clan in the village, and deposits at the foot of it the flesh of his enemy or enemies, shouting, "Wo, ho... Wu" for each man killed. Then he goes to his own house and deposits the head, limbs, or whatever flesh he has brought in front of the house, and his wife goes to make Zumho [Hutton, 1921 (1969) : 239].

War Mechanisms, Military Organization: Review of Colonial Ethnography

In numerous reports of the British colonial officers the custom of head hunting and methods of warfare are elucidated. Often ethno centric, these reports fail to provide any sociological explanation of these customs. J.P. Mills and J.H. Hutton, probably on account of their anthropological background, have dealt with philosophical basis of head hunting. Major Butler and W. Robinson are also generally sympathetic in their description of violence in Naga Hills in early nineteenth century. Captain Butler has also described about the Naga weapons.

Robinson (1841) wrote that "the maxims by which the Nagas regulate their military operations, are well suited to their political state...on approaching the enemy's territories, they collect their troops and advance with great caution. Even in their hottest and most active wars, they proceed wholly by stratagem and ambuscade...To surprise and destroy is the greatest merit of a commander, and the highest pride of his followers...they set on fire the enemy huts in the dead of night, and massacre the inhabitants as they fly... defenceless...they rush upon them with the utmost ferocity, and tearing off the scalps of all those who fall victims to their rage, they carry home those strange trophies of their triumph. These they preserve as monuments not only of their prowess, but of the vengeance which their arm has inflicted upon the people who were objects of resentment. On the death of a warrior, all the scalps taken by him during his lifetime are burnt with his remains" (1841, Elwin, 1969: 538).

There are several organized means to defend the village/ clan territory. Robinson (1841) wrote that they defend themselves with obstinate resolution, but attack their enemies with the most daring courage: The number of men in each tribe is so small... the life of a citizen is extremely precious, and the preservation of it becomes a capital object in their policy...But wherever their communities are more populous, so that they can act with considerable force, and can sustain the loss of several of their members without being sensibly weakened, the military operations of the Nagas more sensibly those of other nations... (1841: 390-394).

'The universal weapon of the Nagas is a javelin, which is usually adorned with coloured hair and ornamented with strips of rattan of various colours' (1841 : 390, 394). Their shield consists of a long mat, lined inside with leather or thin boards (1841, Elwin, 1969: 540).

J.K. Butler wrote that, "When the Nagas propose taking vengeance on a neighbouring tribe, the village elders assemble, and in accordance with established customs, the omens (being) consulted and proving propitious, a plan to cut up their enemies by surprise is decided on. Each man provides himself with a spear, sword, bamboo choong, a hollow joint of the bamboo filled with water, and a small basket of rice, and the party being formed, set out in the day towards the frontier of the enemy who is to be attacked. At night they cross over and occupy a favourable position in ambush...and when the cock first crows on the following morning, they rush, with great, shouting...cut up everybody they meet with: even the cows, pigs, and poultry of the foe are slaughtered. Sometimes the victors remain on the spot for two or three days, but generally return to their own village on the same day; taking with them the heads, hands and feet of those they have massacred, these they parade about from house to house, accompanied with drums and songs (Butler, 1847: 158, 164). They then sing dance and perform all manner of antics; pierce and mangle the heads of their enemies (Butler, 1847: 158, 164). One (Naga) who distinguished himself by evincing great ferocity in cutting off more heads than any of his party challenges the villagers to mark his deeds and with many songs he drags the heads of his enemies proclaiming his own triumph: "in the world I am the most powerful and courageous; there is none equal to me. I am the greatest of all men"... After this, the ceremony of tattooing the body is performed. For a whole month from the day of massacre, the Nagas daily sing the war song and dance and manifest the greatest excitement and delight (Butler, 1847 : 1581, 64).

Material Culture: Dress, Weapons, War Helmets

Writing about eastern Nagas, a group called Molamah Naga, R. Brown (1874) observed that 'of arms, they have a formidable and very strong cross bow, with a double barbed arrow about a foot long; the arrow head, or iron, is loose, presumably to be left in the wound; the feather of the arrow is of stiff leaf, so formed as to give a rotary motion, and consequently, greater precision to its flight, these weapons appear very hard hitting and straight shooters upto 200 yards; they are fired from the hip. The arrows were not poisoned' (Elwin, 1969 : 269). The spear (of Molamah Naga) resembles Angami spear, the head small and sharp, and the shaft ornamented with goat's hair. The Dao is worn behind over the hip, in a wooden case, faced on the outside with polished bone. They have also axes, some with iron some with wooden handles; these are evidently of Burmese manufacture (Elwin 1969: 269).

The Molamah Naga War helmet is of cane, and has a coronal of bear's hair at the base, and goat's hair dyed red and black, over it. These tribes are also tattooed on the breast across in stripes of a blue colour. These stripes have this pattern, and lines with marking between alternately thus. The extent of tattooing is about four or five inches in depth and is only on the front of the chest, extending from below the collar bone to just below the nipple (Elwin, 1969: 269).

Village Defence Mechanisms

According to John Butler (1875) "Naga villags are built on the summits of high tabular hills. Stiff stockades, deep diches bristling with panjies, and massive stonewalls, often loop holded for musketry are their usual defences. In wartime, the hillsides and approaches are escarped and thickely studded over with panjies. These panjies are sharp pointed bamboo skewers or stakes, varying from six inches to three and four feet in length, some of them as thin as a pencil, others as insignificant things to look at, they give a nasty and most painful wound, often causing complete lameness in a few hours. Deep pit falls and small holes covered over with a light layer of earth and leaves, concealing the panjies within, are also skilfully placed along the paths by which an enemy is expected to approach, and a tumble into one of the former is not a thing to be despised."

The approaches to the villages are often up through tortuous, narrow, covered ways, or lanes, with high banks on either sidelined with an overhanging tangled mass of prickly creepers and brushwood, sometimes through a steep ravine and along the bed of an old torrent, in either case admitting of the passage of only one man at a time.

These paths lead up to gates; or rather door ways, closed by strong, thick and heavy wooden doors, hewn out of one piece of solid wood. The doors are fastened from the inside and admit of being easily barricaded, and thus rendered impregnable against all attacks. These doors again are often overlooked and protected by raised look outs, on which, whenever the clan is at feud, a careful watch is kept up night and day; not unfrequently the only approach to one of these outer gates is up a notched pole from fifteen to twenty feet high.

The several clans, of which there are from two to eight in every village, are frequently divided off by deep lanes and stone walls and whenever an attack is imminent, the several roads leading up to the village are studed over with the stout pegs, driven deep into the ground, which very effectually prevents anything like a rush. On the higher ranges, the roads connecting the several villages, as well as the paths leading down to their cultivation are made with considerable skill, the more precipitous hills being turned with easy gradients, instead of the road being taken up one side of the hill and down the other as is usually the case among hillmen.

Their houses are built with a ground floor, the slopes of the hills being dug down to a rough level; no mat covers the bare ground. They are generally placed in irregular lines, facing inwards, and are constructed after a pattern. These houses have high gable ends whose eaves almost touch the ground on either side, to be a precaution against high winds. The gable in front, which, in the case of men of wealth or position, is often decorated with board, handsome weather boards, is from 15 to 30 feet high, and the roof slopes off in rear, as well as towards the sides, the gable at the back being only about from 10 to 15 feet in height. In width the houses vary from about 20 to 40 feet, and in length from about 30 to 60 feet. In many of the villages each house is surrounded by a stone wall, making off the 'compound' so to say, wherein the cattle are tethered for the night. Half the space under the front gable, is often walled in with boards as a loose stall, and bamboo baskets are tied up under the eaves of the house to give shelter to their poultry. Pig styes also in the corner of a compound, are not uncommon. The house itself is divided off into from two to three compartments according to the wealth or taste of its owner. In the front room, the grain is stored away in huge baskets made of bamboo from 5 to 10 feet high and about 5 feet in diameter. In the inner room, there is a large open fire place, and around it are placed thick, broad planks, for sitting and sleeping upon, and the back room of all generally contains the liquor tub, the most important piece of furniture in the house in the Naga's estimation.

In this they brew their 'dzu', a kind of fermented beer made of rice and other ingredients, composed of herbs found wild in the jungle. This liquor is the Angami Naga's greatest solace, for strange to say never indulging in either opium, or tobacco (as many of his neighbours do), he may be seen sipping this 'dzu', either through a reed (after the manner of a sherry cobbler), or with a wooden or bamboo spoon out of bamboo or mithun horn drinking cups, from morn to night (Elwin, 1969: 301).

The 'blood feud' of the Nagas is what the 'vendetta' of the Corsican was, a thing to be handed down from generation to generation, an everlasting and most baneful heir loom, involving in its relentless course the brutal murders of helpless old men and women, innocent young girls and children, until, as often happens, mere petty family quarrels, generally about land or water, being taken up by their respective clansmen, break out into bitter civil wars which devastate whole villages (Elwin, 1969: 302).

According to Johnstone (1896), blood feuds were common among all the hill tribes, but the system was carried to excess among the Angamis. Life for life was the rule, and until each of the opposing parties had lost an equal number, peace was impossible, and whenever members of one village met any belonging to the other, hostilities were sure to result. Sometimes attempt was made to bring about a reconciliation, but then it frequently happened that the number of slain to the credit of each were unequal. Mozuma and Sephema might be at war, and Mozuma killed five, whereas Sephema had killed only four. Sephema says, 'I must kill one more to make the balance, then I will treat for peace', so war continues. Someday Sephema has a chance, but kills two instead of one that was required; this gives her the advantage, and Mozuma refuses to treaty. So it goes on interminably. The position of a small village at war with a large one, was often deplorable as no one dared to leave the village except under a strong escort (Johnstone, 1896, Elwin, 1996 : 313).

No Angami could assume the 'toga virilis', in this case the kilt ornamented with cowrie shells, until he had slain an enemy, and in the more powerful villages no girl could marry a man unless he was so decorated. The cowrie ornaments were taken off when a man was mourning the death of a relation.

To kill a baby in arms, or a woman, was accounted a greater feat then killing a man, as it implied having penetrated to the innermost recesses of an enemy's country, whereas a man might be killed anywhere by a successful ambush. I knew a man who had killed sixty women and children, when on one occasion he happened to come upon them after all the men had left the village on a hunting expedition (Elwin, 1996: 314).

Slavery

This custom was universal throughout the Ao tribe. Writing for Census of India, A.W. Davis (1891) wrote that "since our occupation of the country, every effort has been made to suppress the custom, and the selling and buying of slaves is now, I fancy, very uncommon. Slaves were and are I believe, on the whole, very well treated, being considered almost as members of the family. Cases of harsh treatment, of course, most have occurred occasionally, but these must now be very rare, and the slaves who have remained with their owners know very well that, if treated, all they have to do is to run away. In old days slaves, unless they could get down to the plains, could not run away, it being etiquette for them to be caught and returned by the inhabitants of any village in which they took refuge.

Troublesome slaves were usually sold to people living across the Dikhu, amongst whom the custom of human sacrifices is not, I believe, entirely unknown. Amongst the Aos before occupation of the country, slaves were not infrequently paid by one village to another village with which they happened to be on bad terms, to make up a quarrel, and as a sort of set off against any head taken by them. Slaves paid in this way were invariably slaughtered by the village, which received them, as an offering to the spirits of the men on their side who had been killed (Davis, 1891).

Female slaves were not allowed to marry or have children. If they became pregnant, their children were killed immediately after birth, or else abortion was procured. Female slaves are not tattooed (Elwin, 1969 : 336).

Disposal of Heads

Among the Manipur's Kachcha Nagas any heads taken were kept in the village and afterwards exchanged for those of relatives, or redeemed by the payment of money or mithun. It was of common occurrence for two villages at deadly feud to agree to keep from the warpath for a period of two, three, or four months. During the truce the heads taken on either side were often exchanged, the two villages meeting and holding a big feast. At the conclusion of the specified time, the contest was renewed with fresh vigour.

In common with the Angamis, in old days the Kachcha Nagas looked upon no male as worthy of the name of man, unless he had taken at least one head. Any head was sufficient to stamp a warrior, an old woman's or a child's. In all probability the proud owner waited at the drinking place or one of the many paths to the village *jhums*, and smote some venerable dame toiling home with her basket of sticks. It mattered not, the head was just as valuable in the eyes of the people, and brought him as much in favour with the village belles (Soppit, 1885, Elwin, 1969 : 429).

Treatment of Prisoners of War

In former years all persons captured in war were looked upon as slaves of the captor. They could, as a rule, however, be redeemed by the relatives, on payment of a certain sum. The ordinary procedure in the case of disputes and quarrels is for both parties to be brought up before the Matai and the villagers, and a decision given. A cup of liquor is then produced by the Matai and each of the disputants drink one half. This is supposed to re-establish peace, and the quarrel is at an end (Soppit, 1885, Elwin, 1969: 432).

Arms and Mode of Fighting

Among the Tangkuls the only arm used in warfare is a long heavy spear; this is thrust, as it is too heavy to be thrown. On the left arm is worn an oblong shields of hide, ornamented with tresses of human hair and wool dyed in various colours. Amongst the

Luhupas, the headdress of the warrior is peaculier; hence the name Luhupa, which is formerly mentioned. The basis of his head piece is a conical structure of wicker work, about a foot high; over this a layer of fur and hair, black and red in colour; to the sides are stitched as wings round structures, filled in with coloured seeds in rings; in front is a disc of polished brass, with a button shaped knob in the centre; slips of bamboo, feathers, etc. are also attached to the head piece, and occasionally a long crescent shaped piece of buffalo horn scraped this is placed in front of the helmet. Warriors of distinction who have slain many people, wear the hair of their victims, depending from the side ornaments of the helmet in the first instance, and, as they accumulate, made into a kind of fringe worn round the face, like the mane of a lion. Women's tresses are preferred, as being longer. The rest of the warrior's dress presents nothing peculiar. When the villagers are desirous of fighting, notice on the one side is invariably given; and, as amongst the Angamis, the date may be given, and a stand up fight in the open agreed upon at a given place. In other cases, intimation is made to one village from another that its members from a certain time will be killed, whenever an opportunity is found. In fighting, the spear is thrust; two hands being generally used. When an enemy is killed, the head is immediately cut off by the edge of the spear; these heads are dried and hung up in the houses of the victors, and, as with the Angamis, may be returned, and the feud ended. Feuds are handed down from generation to generation (R. Brown, 1973, Elwin, 1969: 487).

Naga Offensive Weapons

The only national, offensive weapons, used by the Angami, are the spear and dao, but of late years they have managed to become the pround possessors of a considerable quantity of fire arms. "The spear is generally a very handsome one, and at close quarter, or when thrown from a ambuscade, is a formidable weapon, well calculated to inflict a most dangerous wound. At anything over thirty yards, however, it is but of little use, and is not very difficult to dodge even at two thirds of that distance. The spear head is of iron, varying from 18 inches to 2 feet in length, and from 2 to 3 inches in breadth. Its shaft is generally from 4 to 5 feet in length, and is usually very picturesquely ornamented with scarlet goat's hair, here and there intermingled with a peculiar pattern of black and white hair; sometimes, though rarely, the whole shaft is beautifully worked over with scarlet and yellow cane, and it is always tipped at the bottom with an iron spike of from three inches to over a foot in length, used for sticking it into the ground. A Naga would never dream of leaving his spear against a wall. It must be always kept in a perpendicular position, either by being stuck upright into the ground or by being suspended against one of the walls of the house, so as to keep it perfectly straight. On the war path every Angami carries two of these spears" (Butler, J. 1875). The dao is a broad headed kind of handbill, with a heavy blade about 18 inches in length and only edged on one side. This dao is invariably worn at the back of the waist in a rough sort of half scabbard made of wood.

Item of Defence

The only article of defence they possess is a large shield from 5 to 6 feet high, 2 feet broad at the top and tapering down to about a foot in breadth at the bottom. This shield is made of bamboo matting, and is covered with either the skin of some wild animal (elephant, tiger, leopard and bear being among the most common), or a piece of cloth, generally scarlet. In the latter case, or even without the cloth, it is decorated with pieces of skin cut so as to represent human heads, and tufts of scarlet goat's hair, whilst on the inside is attached a board, so as to make it spear proof. From each corner of the upper end of the shields spring two cane horns from 2.5 to 3 feet in length, decorated with the long flowing tresses of human hair taken in war probably the locks of some unfortunate woman butchered at the water hole intermingled with goat's hair dyed scarlet; and from the centre rises a plume about 3 feet long of scarlet goat's hair, tripped at the top for about 4 inches in depth with white goat's hair, and along the top edge runs a fringe of white, downy feathers. Along the inner edge, a string of lappets made of feathers of various hues, white, black, blue, and scarlet, wave to and fro most gracefully, at every motion of the shield. Besides the spear, dao and shields, when proceeding out on a foray, they invariably take with them several bundles of 'panjies', with which they rapidly cover the path on retreat, so as to disable and retard any party that may start in pursuit (J. Butler, 1875).

Head Hunting

The whole of the Naga and Kuki tribes are headhunters, and they all try and get heads in the same treacherous way. Any head counts be it that of man, woman, or child and entitles the man who takes it to wear certain ornaments according to the custom of the tribe or village. Most heads are taken, or rather used to be taken, not in fair fight, but by methods the most treacherous. As common a method as any was for a man to lurk about the water ghat of a hostile village, and kill the first woman or child who came to draw water. Sometimes expeditions on a large scale were made, several villages combining for the purpose of making a large bag. Even then if the village to be attacked was found prepared, the valiant warriors who had come against it would, as a rule, retire without striking a blow. If, however, it was found that the whole of the adult population was away in the fields, an attack would be delivered, and as many children and old people as could within a reasonable time be killed, a retreat being effected before the men of the village attacked could have time to receive the news and return from their fields (Davis, 1891, Elwin, 1969: 546).

Importance of Dormitory: Military Training

Dormitory, along with logdrum, is part of the oldest cultural stratum of the Naga Hills. The dormitory (*morung*) was the main institution directly related with the Naga military organization and warfare. The Naga morung was the centre of warfare in the sence of imparting to its members the required leassons for fighting the enemy and of guarding the village. Thus it served as a guardhouse. The dormitory was inseparable from the institution of 'head hunting'. After the 'local war' and 'head hunting', human skulls were hung in the dormitory.

As a result of British administrative actions and persuasion since 1923 in particular, the practice of head hunting gradually stopped and thus the morung houses were made partly defunct. Spread of Christinity also gradually ushered in a change of attitude. Gradual development of formal education also helped in eradication of dormitory institution. In Eastern Naga hills the rites and ceremonies centring around the dormitory disappeared, though morung houses continued to serve some purposes among the many Nagas, particularly in Tunsang and Mon district (Das, 1994).

Morung did not exist among the Angami, Chakhesang, and other western and southern Nagas. Among the Semas the chief's house served for all the purpose of a morung, both as a centre of gennas (rituals) and as a bachelor's sleeping place (Hutton, 1921: 37).

Among the Chang Nagas, Haki, the morung like structure was used as a logdrum house, repository for the 'trophies' or war and the skulls of the animals sacrificed (Das, 1994). In Haki, the head hunting raids were planned, discussed and celebrated. Heads taken in war were first brought to the Haki, followed by ceremonial functions and rite. The Lothas also brought the heads taken in war first to the bachelor's hall (Champo) and 'prisoners of war' were also detained here (Mills, 1992: 105).

To sum up it may be restated that practices of head hunting and warfare in Naga areas of Nagaland and Manipur did operate as the 'regulated interrelationships' in the political field. As we discussed clearcut kinship rules and descent priciples as also tribal laws regulated the rights, jural obligations and moral responsibilities among the Nagas. Blood feud, head hunting and warfare remained part of this system of rights and obligations.

NOTE

The view expressed in this chapter are those of author alone. The author is thankful to the authorities of Anthropological Survey of India for providing opportunity to work in Nagaland and Manipur.

REFERENCES

Brown, R. 1873, *The Tangkul Nagas*. In Statistical Account of the Native State of Manipur 1874. Narrative Report of the Progress of the Survey Party, Naga Hills, Season 1874, pp.36-38.

Butler, J. 1874-75, Report on the Exploration Survey of the Naga Hills, Shillong: Secretariat Press.

Butler, John 1875, Rough Notes on the Angami Nagas. *Journal of Anthropological Society* (London) XLIV No. 307-27.

Das, N.K. 1982, Tribe as a Segmentary Social System. Social Research, Vol.1:1-5.

---------- 1989, *Ethnic Identity, Ethnicity and Social Stratification in North East India.* New Delhi, Inter-India Publications.

---------- 1985, *The Politico-Jural Aspects of the Segmentary Social System of the Zounuo-Keyhonuo Naga.* Ph.D. Thesis Gauhati University, Guwahati.

---------- 1993, *Kinship, Politics and Law in Naga Society.* Menoir No.96. Calcutta: Anthropological Survey of India.

Das N.K. & C.L. Imchen (Eds) 1994, *Nagaland: People of India,* Gen. Ed. K.S. Sing, Calcutta, ASI.

Das, N.K. 1994 'Introduction' *Nagaland, People of India,* Das, N.K. and C.L. Imchen (Eds) Calcutta: ASI.

---------- 1994 'The Chang Naga' *Nagaland, People of India,* Das, N.K. and C.L. Imchen (eds) Calcutta: ASI.

---------- 1994, 'The Sangtam Naga', *Nagaland, People of India,* Das, N.K. and C.L. Imchen (eds), Calcutta: ASI.

Davis, A.W. 1891, *Census of India,* Assam, Vol. I, pp.241-245.

Elwin, V. 1961 *Nagaland,* Shillong: Research Department, NEFA, Administration.

Elwin V. (ed) 1969, *The Nagas in Nineteenth Century.* Bombay: Oxford University Press.

Furer Haimendorf C.Von 1939, *The Naked Nagas,* London: Methuen.

Cluckman, M. 1955, *The Judicial Process among the Barotse of Northern Rhodesia.* Manchester: Manchester University Press.

Hutton, J.H. 1921, *The Angami Nagas,* London: MacMillan and Co. (1969), Second edn. Oxford University Press, Bombay.

---------- 1926, The Mixed Culture of the Naga Tribes, *Journal of the Royal Anthropological Institute,* XCV.

Johnstone, J. 1896, *My Experiences in Manipur and Naga Hills.* London, Simpson Low Marsten and Co.

Mills, J.P. 1922, *The Lhota Nagas,* London: MacMillan and Co.

---------- 1926, *The Ao Nagas,* London: MacMillan and Co.

Notes and Queries in Anthropology 1951 Notes and Queries in Anthropology, London, Royal Anthropological Institute.

Redcliffe-Brown, A.R. 1940, *'Introduction' African Political Systems.* Fortes and E.E. Evans Prchand (eds), London: Oxford University Press.

Rayapa, R.S. 1994, *The Sema Naga, People of India,* Das, N.K. and C.L. Imchen (eds) Calcutta: ASI.

Smith, W.C. 1925, *The Ao Naga Tribe of Assam,* London MacMillan.

Soppit, C.A. 1885, *A Short Account of the Kachcha Naga* (Empeo) *Tribe in the North Cachar Hills,* 1885, Shillong: Assam Secretariat Press, pp.1-20.

Watt, George 1887, The Aboriginal Tribes of Manipur, *Journal of the Anthropological Institute,* Vol. XVI : 346-70.

2

War Mechanism of the Nagas

A Case Study of the Tangkhul Nagas

A.S.W. Shimray

The Nagas are a group of the Mongoloids living in a compact area with powerful neighbours—China in the North, Burma (Myanmar) in the East, Bangladesh in the South and India in the West. Most of the modern scholars believe that they migrated from the Upper Reaches of the Ho-angho and the Yangtse rivers in South-West of China. Their coming and settlement in present Naga homeland was a matter of long process in terms of time and space covering thousands of years and miles of geographical areas crossing rivers, mountains, oceans, continent and islands. Their settlement can be roughly dated as early as Stone Age period. They are the original native people in the land they are occupying today. Because, no legend, tradition and historical evidence ever stated that they dislodged any tribe from the place they are living today.

Since their settlement in the land, they lived an isolated life of their own, free from social, cultural and political connection of alien people. The independent life of the Nagas has much to do with the warlike and martial nature of the Nagas. As a matter of fact, the Nagas, being a branch of the Mongoloid race possessed warlike nature even before they reached Naga homeland. In this regard, Prof. Horam remarks, "It might, however, be surmised that in the distant past, many hundred years ago, some warlike tribes were pushed from the mainland China, and they had scattered among the forest shades and the Himalaya mountains and these wandering race eventually settled there. These tribes, therefore, possessed certain points of resemblance that bore witness to their common origin, but at the same time, they differ from the other Indian races of men; they are neither black like the dark Indians, nor brown, but their skin was yellow like most of South East Asian people..."[1]

There are certain conditions, which temper the Nagas to be warlike and martial people. First, they have intense love for free and independent life. In early days, every Naga village was an independent village state, and their love for their village was so strong that no encroachment could be tolerated and no life was so precious to sacrifice for the defence of their village. This made every Naga to prepare himself for any eventuality of war. Secondly, to kill an enemy in war and bring the head home is the highest honour every Naga warrior desired. Then, they will rise to the ladder of social recognition, and they are entitled to wear a certain type of shawl with special embroidery and decorate their war weapons with human hair. Thirdly, people who live in hilly region have hard life. Without hard labour, they cannot sustain which demanded strong and sturdy physique. Naturally, a strong man is more courageous than a weak person. Fourthly, the "Naga Dormitory" or "Bachelors' Chamber" which is indigenously called "Long Shim" was responsible to produce man of war in early Naga community. All sorts of training for livelihood, including martial art was given in the Long Shim with strict discipline. In this regard Christoph Von Furer Haimendorf makes an interesting remarks: "The bachelors' hall is an institution much like the English public school. One may agree or disagree with the principle of giving boys training in community spirit outside the individual family, but there can be no questions that the Morung was one of the main pillars of the Ao's social order. The bachelors' hall was the centre of the village".[2] Strict disciplinary training, courage and warfare trainings are given to the village boys without exception. A warrior, who takes the enemy head, is honoured and feared and he gets a due place in Village Assembly, Social gatherings and in marriage market.

War Mechanism and Organisation

Naga war mechanism was simple but effective. It began from the selection of site for village settlement, choosing a strategic place which has a commanding position against the attack of the enemy-village. Therefore, a hillock is normally chosen for the establishment of a village. Availability of water at a convenient place is taken into consideration which should not be far from the village settlement. The village is well secured with natural and artificial fortifications like cliffs, bullwarks of stone-boulder, thorny creepers, bamboo spikes and sound-producing materials around the wall to indicate the approach of the enemy. The village gate is well secured day and night with a huge solid beam. Some watchman and village warriors always stand by against the possible attack of the enemy.

In early days, the Nagas did not possess sophisticated weapons of modern time. Their war weapons were consisted of machet (Naga sword), spear, shield of hide, bamboo and wood, helmets of cane, bows and poisoned arrowheads. But the Naga arrow-poison is of two kinds. One for hunting games which is less poisonous, whereas the poison used against human enemy is so strong that it can kill a man instantly. However, it is interesting to note that some Nagas like the Konyaks, Angamis etc. made muskets and gun powder and used them since early days, with the help of which they could resist the British invaders for several decades.

Bachelors' chamber is the centre of Naga war organization. All unmarried youths—in some cases married men also to assist young warriors—sleep there always ready for war, calamity and other social activities. They are in constant watchfulness for the defence and security of the village with full combat stand-to. At the centre of the village, the Naga Log-Drum is placed which is beaten for the people to prepare themselves either for war or other social activities according to the sound of the drum. Naga village state does not have regular standing army. All the grown up men-folks should take part in Naga war. In those days, due to inter-village feuds and warfare, the movements of outsiders and wayfarers are well-interrogated and investigated and the security of the innocent travellers and visitors of the village is the responsibility of the host village within the village jurisdiction.

Nature of Naga Warfare

Most foreigners, writers, and journalists who contacted the Nagas have an erroneous concept to the nature of the Naga and Naga Warfare. To them, the "Nagas are head-hunters, and head-hunters are Nagas". Not doubt, like any other tribes of the world, the Nagas took human head as war trophies. However, the fact is that, "there is head-taking in the war, but war cannot be initiated for head-taking", that means to take human head cannot be the cause of Naga war. Because, they have a refined and elaborate customary code of laws, well tested and preserved for centuries, violation of which entailed war. J.H. Hutton vindicated the Naga war in the following statement: "What a man, or at least what a Naga, who has killed his enemy does not want to boast about it? And unless he can show the body, where is the proof? … if the slayer can produce the body of the slain, his statement is likely to be accepted as true and since retrieving the body would be a labourious, and not to say often dangerous proceeding, the head is the natural part of it to bring back as testimony as it gives a definite assurance that the foe had been killed, not scahotched… Most Britishers are head-hunters at heart, and to a Naga every sort of head is welcome"[3].

Regarding the wrong concept of the foreigners on the Nagas, Prof. Horam remarks, "The outsiders, the so-called civilized man very often arrives at the hasty conclusion that the tribes live a life of unbridled licence and youthful corruption. In their approach, they commit two errors, one of method and one of fact. Their method of approach is wrong, for they import their own ideas and standard into tribal culture and judge their culture by theirs"[4]. Earlier Christoph Von Haimendorf carried the same wrong notion about the Nagas, but later, he came to know the true picture of the Nagas. He said, "popular opion was inclined to imagine the Nagas as a fierce and warlike people, continuously occupied with head-hunting, human sacrifice, and other exciting customs. But the picture drawn by journalists who spent perhaps a week in the Naga Hills, have very little in common with reality"[5]. Y.K. Shimray quotes R.C. Nag, "We talk a welfare state, of social security and the like, but here is a society which they have been in practice long before the most progressive countries of the West got any such ideas"[6]. J.P. Mills came out with the same remark, "On the whole the life of the Nagas is completely better than that of a western city dweller"[7]. A.S.W. Shimray maintains, "...those who go deeper into the social life of the Nagas cannot but agree that they are a people, well organized, simple, happy, honest, one another ready to admit his own fault when one has wronged a person, but never a coward, rather ready to sacrifice his life for the society whose social structure is based on the principles of traditional customary laws, well tried and preserved for generations"[8].

It is known fact that head-taking is a global feature, and there are many instances of head-chopping over the world in human history. It is, therefore, erroneous to generalize that Naga war means head-hunting only. It would be more appropriate to call it a war rather than head-hunting.[9] There are certain wars of the Nagas where taking head of the fallen enemy is prohibited. Summing up all the facts stated above, we may safely conclude that the Nagas are not blood-thirsty head hunters, but a people who live a well refined moral life ready to give his best for the good of the society. Nagas are men of war as well as men of peace. They can be anyone when the situation so demands. This is evidenced from the fact that in the society of blood thirsty and war monger nature, the principle of "survival of the fittest" prevails. However, in Naga society, even in the earliest days when inter-village feuds were common, small villages could live peacefully with bigger and more powerful village without fear of war. This is possible where there is rule of law.

However, it is nothing exaggerated to say that the Nagas take human head as war trophy. Because, there are some deep philosophical meaning in taking head of fallen enemy home which they celebrated with dancing, singing and making sacrifices to their deities. First, according to their superstitious belief and religion, taking human head home will increase fertility of women and soil. Secondly, the Nagas believed that a warrior, who killed an enemy in war, the soul of the enemy will be servant of the one who killed him in the land of death. There are also other social factors for a warrior to take enemy head. A warrior who brings the head of fallen enemy could raise the ladder of social recognition. He was honoured in the Assembly of the Village State, worthy to wear a kind of embroidered cloth not entitled to common men. He also got the right to decorate his war weapons with the hair of the enemy. Thirdly, he becomes a readily accepted groom of the most admired lady of the village in the market of marriage in the belief that he was a person capable of giving protection and security to wife and children. Politically, he got the access to the membership of Village Assembly. Soon his fame will be spread far and wide.

Causes of War

War is as old as the existence of mankind, and it determines the formation and existence of a nation. Man is a social animal, and therefore, fighting instincts is in man as much as it is in animal. Nevertheless, human war has its own logic. So also the Nagas have their own logic of war—cause of war and end of war. There are certain causes for the outbreak of Naga war. In the first instance we may say that encroachment in the territory of other village state leads to inter-village war. In early days, a Naga village was an independent state known as village state having its own defined terriroty, population and government free from interference of other village state. Secondly, violation of an established treaty or trust and inter-village laws causes a war. Thirdly, divorce of a women without appropriate reason leads the two villages to war. Fourthly, encroachment of inter-village hunting and fishing ground, theft, robbery etc. draws the villages to war. Lastly, murder, illegal head-taking for desire of social recognition, fertility of women, soil etc. as stated above cause the outbreak of war. Then, the Nagas must fight out justice as "An eye for an eye, a tooth for a tooth and a head for a head".

Warfare of the Nagas

No writer has ever made an elaborate research on the warfare of the Nagas, except to brand the Nagas savage, head-hunter, blood thirsty etc. Therefore, the material on Naga Warfare is scanty and as such, we have to depend on tradition and oral history of the Nagas. Among the Naga tribes, the Tangkhuls waged four main types of war—Declared War, War of Challenge, Undeclared War, and Single Combat System or Goliathic War. When differences between two or more villages cannot be settled amicably, then they are in the state of war and any form of connection has been cut off. Then declaration of war is made known to the hostile village(s) through a messenger, mostly a neutral village. The indication of war varies from village to village and tribe to tribe. However, the messenger cannot be ill-treated and interrogated. Rather, he has to be sent back home peacefully.

Declared War

Declaration of war must be made known to the enemy village(s) days ahead of the actual war. They indicated the number of heads to be taken, duration of war and the kind of heads to be taken, whether the heads of the warriors only to be taken or to be included the heads of women and children. However, it is the convention of the Naga warfare that they must observe truce during agricultural season so that there may be enough food supply for the year, and both the parties honour the truce in letter and spirit.

Whatever a type of war it may be, before a man goes to war, a warrior must sanctify himself, observe certain taboos and divination preparing himself for war physically and mentally. According to Shimray, "First, he has to abstain from conjugal union with women, and not to touch anything pertaining to woman and keep food taboos. He performed rites and sacrifices and consulted dream and divinations."[10]

When war is declared, all kinds of war tactics are put into operation. Aggressive village takes the initiative to attack the enemy either at the village or in the field by day or at night. They attack the enemy in group or single convenient to them. Then a party has taken the number of human heads as decided earlier, the village is declared winner of the war. Then peace must be established between the two, because, war cannot go on unending.

Both the parties have to keep and observe standard of war in letter and spirit. Innocent and neutral persons should not be harmed or killed, and a pregnant woman should be spared. By the standard of Naga warfare, a warrior cannot kill his enemy when he is eating morsel and when he is sleeping, whether in the day time or at night and the body of the slain war hero must not be left unattended. Honour and respect must be accorded to the slain body. Violation of the law of war entails disaster, not only on the person who violated it but on the whole group and loss of war.[11]

Under no circumstances, a woman of the attacking village living in the village under attack by virtue of her marriage should be killed. Because such a woman acts the role of peace Emissary called "PUKHAREILA" (to be discussed later), and a neutral force who comes forward to bring peace should not be killed. They are well honoured and revered as "Man of God" sent for peace. When any party violated the law of war, then punitive expedition was launched by a combined villages of the range against the defaulter. Therefore, in Tangkhul war, there is order in the midst of chaos and bloodshed.

War of Challenge

In War of Challenge, ambushcade, way lay, surprise attack etc. are not in operation. Here both the parties make a certain point of date and place where they meet each other with full combat position and move forward. Such type of war was fought in open air, particularly in a plain grassland or terrace field after harvest. Here women and children of both parties can come and watch the war game cheering and encouraging their warriors, and by their loud shout, dishearten the enemy soldiers. There are also cries of weeping because of their fallen warrior in the hands of enemy. In this type of war, taking the head of fallen enemy is strictly prohibited. Both parties retreat to collect the dead bodies or injured persons of their fellow warriors. There is time for refreshment with rice, meat and country-wine prepared in plenty for the warriors.

Then full-scale combat is resumed again. When the day is well advanced before the sun goes down below the horizon, the Pukhareila and in some other cases, some neutral forces of other village will appear with a branch of "Green Leaves" as a sign of peace in between the warring groups. The two hostile groups have to comply with the intervention of Pukhareila or peace force. Or the non-compliance village will face dire consequences of punitive action of the range council. Then peace and formal relationship must be established and all former links are restored again.

Undeclared War

Regarding the Undeclared War, Shimray writes, "The Undeclared War of the Tangkhuls may be termed as 'War of Revenge'. It is rather individual, family or clan war against some other village. There are also cases where the entire village was drawn in it"[12]. Because, all Nagas are not angels, and to call Nagas as 'blood-thirsty' may be accepted to some extent with reservation. The desire of a Naga to climb the ladder of social recognition, under the philosophy of head taking stated above, there were some instances of secret chopping off human heads illegally. In this event, the family of the victim or its clansmen would act in the same way as their member had been killed. Thus, they fight out justice. Here, they will never be abated until they fulfil, 'a head for a head'. The undeclared war had the tendency to drag on for years, decades, even for generations.

Single Combat

Another interesting type of Tangkhul Warfare is 'Single Combat System' or 'Goliathic War'. In this type of war, the two warring villages agree upon to meet at an appointed place on an appointed date. Here the best, strongest and the most skilful warrior is chosen from each village in the some manners as the Palestine Giant Goliath did to Israelites and they were made to fight the war so that the whole villagers may not be drawn into the war. They are well equipped with full armour with one hand holding a spear and the other a shield. They came forward against each other with full war dance and war cry with measured footsteps and displayed their war tactics. *Theirs* is especially to disarm the opponent to make him helpless, jumping and kicking and pointing the spear on the opponent. Here again, opponent villagers stood around watching the war acts as they cheer and encourage their warriors.

The one who has the upper hand over the other will demand the enemy to drop or lay down his shield and spear and give in. Here the enemy thus defeated cannot be killed and his head cannot be chopped off. But if the defeated enemy refused to surrender and lay down his arms, he may do so at his own risk. Then the warrior who gains the combat and his village is declared winner of the war.

However, painful and costly the Naga war may be, to bring the enemy head home is the highest honour and glory. The victorious group comes back home shouting, hawling and ho-hoing all along the way and the people from the village will come out to receive them on the halfway with food and drink of dainty items. They joined the war group throughout the night; they spent with war song, dancing in tune with the sound of 'Log Drum', which its sound could reach for miles. Then, they deposited war trophy, which is different from tribe to tribe: either in public house, or in the house of clan chief or even in the house of village chief.

In the warfare of the Tangkhuls, a warrior is strictly controlled by their culture and customary laws. Rape, torture and theft is unheard. Because, during the state of war, sex is a taboo to a Naga warrior, and as such, he has to abstain from women and anything pertaining to women. They can touch the body of woman only in the time of chopping the head. Here R.R. Shimray remarked: "Head taking is a cruel practice, but torture or rape before actual killing is more appalling and beastly"[13]. Violation of the code of law of war brings disaster and defeat in the group of the violater.

In Tangkhul Naga society, whatever types of war may be, the war must come to an end and peace must be established. Because, good sense must prevail and it prevents them from further continuation of war to the suffering of mankind, and the neighbours should live peacefully for the bright future and prosperity of the generations to come. As W. Shimray says, "It may be of interest to note that in the history of Tangkhul war, the dominant village hardly reduced the defeated village into vassalage". Verrier Elwin, on the other hand, described about the nature of Naga war: "However, war like people may be, their quarrels are not fundamental to their lives, and unhappily the history books have little to tell of the real life of this enterprising and romantic people"[14]. During the state of war when a party of the war wants peace, it can take the initiative for peace, and approach the enemy village with peace proposal. If the security of the peace emissary is in question, they sent a man of neutral village. Whoever, the person may be, he approaches the warring village uttering the message: "I am as a peace Emissary. I bring a tiding of peace". Sometimes, even in the heat of the fray, a neutral village can take the initiative to bring the war to an end and negotiated for peace between the two villages.

In the initiation of peace, the service "PUKHAREILA" is eminent which commands obeisance of the warring groups. She is a woman of either attacking village living in the enemy village by virtue of her marriage. When the enemies are killing each other, she acts as a Peace Emissary. She enters in the battlefield with a branch of "Green Leave" as a sign of peace shouting—"No more war. Enough is enough. Now, there must be peace".

To make a peace treaty, both the parties of the two villages meet at the centre of the boundary of inter-village states each bring one or two animals, either Mithun or Buffalo, rice, meat and country-wine. The animals are divided into two equal halves from head to tail and share each other. There is exchange of food and drinks in a big feast. But the most interesting and important part of the peace treaty was exchange of war weapons as a sign of peace. Then they take solemn oath swearing in the name of God that they will raise their weapons no more against their neighbours. Heads of the slain enemies taken during the war may be retained or returned as per the terms and conditions of the peace treaty.

War Council

Since early days, the Tangkhul Nagas have their social organization called "TANGKHUL LONG". It is also called 'Longrei' meaning Great Long. This is the highest social organization of the Tangkhul Nagas living elsewhere. Under Longrei, there are a number of "Branch Longs" called "Longphang". The settled inter-village disputes when two or three villages of the issue concern could not settle the matter by themselves. As such, they acted as "War Council" of the Tangkhul Nagas. When war dragged unabated despite the intervention of peace forces, the War Council of Longrei or Longphang as the case may be, will exercise arbitrary power and impose peace on both sides. If any village does not obey or comply with the order of War Council, punitive expedition is launched against the disaffected village by combined villages of the range. As a matter of fact, Longphang is more effective than Longrei since it is an organization of a local region, which has better contact and knowledge to the local issue in detail. But there are also several cases where the Tangkhul Long issues certain directives to settle some issues of serious problems.

There is no written constitution of the Tangkhul Long, and the Branch Long, even in the village states of the Tangkhuls also. Yet they have their own unwritten constitution called 'Riyan'. Tangkhul 'Riyan' is composed of customary laws, traditions, conventions and religious practices. Based on Riyan, Tangkhul laws called 'Mayonrin', are made. Therefore, to keep the customary law in letter and spirit is the religious duty of every individual Tankghul Naga, violation of which entails curse of God not only on the violator of the law, but serious disaster on the whole village community since the Nagas live a corporate social and religious life. This made small Tangkhul villages to exist peacefully without being afraid and victim of bigger and more powerful villages. Rather, Tangkhuls are simple, honest, hard working people for which Grant Brown remarked, "As a people, they are neither insolent nor cringing, and if they think they are wronged by any order, they will say so plainly". It is these qualities of frankness, cheerfulness, hospitality and obedience which have endeared them to call these officers who have been stationed among them long enough to obtain a knowledge of them and their ways.[15] Their honesty is the same both to friends and foes.

NOTES

1. Horam, M., *Nagas Old Ways and New Trends,* p. 9.
2. Chistoph von Furer Haimendorf, *Return to Naked Nagas,* p. 47.
3. J.H. Hutton, *The Angami Nagas,* pp.157-158.
4. Horam, M., *North East India, A Profile,* pp. 92-93.
5. Christoph von Furur Haimendorf, *op. cit.*, pp. 93-94.
6. Y.K. Shimray, *An Introduction to Tribal Language and Culture of Manipur,* p. 29.

7. J.P. Mills, *The Effects on the Naga Tribes of Assam, of their Contact with Western Civilization,* p. 73.
8. A.S.W. Shimray, *History of Tangkhul Nagas,* pp.111-112.
9. R.R. Shimray, *Origin and Culture of Nagas*, p.71.
10. A.S.W. Shimray, *op. cit.*, p. 173.
11. *Ibid.*, p. 174.
12. R.R. Shimray, *op. cit.*, p. 87.
13. A.S.W. Shimray, *op. cit.*, p. 175.
14. Verrier Elwin, *The Nagas in Nineteenth Century,* p. 111.
15. Grant Brown, *Burma Gazetteer, Upper Chindwin District,* p. 26.

3

Mode of Naga Warfare
A Profile

A. Nshoga

The Nagas belong to martial race and their mode of warfare is based on guerilla tactics. Naga head hunting was not necessarily .involved in indiscriminate forms of killing or murdering but it is undertaken as indigenous fine sports to build one's status or bring fertility to the individuals and the village. Every Naga man is expected to follow the warpath to test his manhood, bravery and manoeuvre in warfare activities. Nagas know no distinction between heads but it does not meant that they did pride of themselves on the killing of a redoubtable enemy. The man who had taken a head, demonstrated his potency; and taking the head was a manifestation of their contact with fertility cult and through them the village share the fertility. The motive behind a head hunting raid is the development of simple idea in which explanation is centred round the beliefs amongst the Nagas that the soul exists in the head, just under the scalp. This soul-force and fertility strength is believed to have concentrated in human head which is transferable. When an enemy's head is brought to the village, his soul is transferred to the village and imbued the soul. The head is acted as fertility agent and brings prosperity to the village men in the shape of agricultural products and increase in population. Taking a head, therefore, has become a ritual to provide economic benefit of the people. The decrease of yielding in the crops was believed to be cessation of head-taking by the village men, and when the village resumes the raids, agriculture and cattles recuperate from low yielding and growth. This ritualistic belief clearly indicates the effects of agriculture, cattle and population growth from non-participation of head-taking. The entire idea is revolved round the belief that soul-matter resides in the human head. Probably, the idea of soul-matter which is located in the head might have developed from the sight of diminutive reflections in the pupil of human eye. This belief persistently stimulates and induces the village men to take heads without any hesitation and compunction. The soul-force commands the nature and environment of the people, which metamorphoses into fertility cult to the embryo of crops, cattles and human beings. The increase of mortality rate and decrease of cattle correspond to the demands of more heads to be sacrificed for the restoration of this rituals malaise. Sometimes, compensations for the loss of heads were imbalanced which resulted to increase the mortality rate and decrease of fertility cult in the village. The counter-attacks were, therefore, necessity to equalize the loss of heads, since it adversely affects the entire community of the village. Hence, the attacks and counter-attacks often becomes a sort of cannibalism. During the sanguinary days, when the sickness swept through the village, the village men took the enemy heads and brought into the village then the sickness stopped. Similar idea is established in the mind of the people that the enemy head was taken to maximize the crops. The belief of fertility, which lies in the human heads, is an underlying concept of head-hunting, practiced widely among the Nagas. Feasting and martial prowess was a central element brought under the concept of fertility, which gained by these activities and manifested in them. The Nagas believed that the wealth of a man is the direct contact and manifestation with fertility through the bringing of enemy's heads into the village. His wealth is believed to be the manifestation of fertility contact and which allows him to hold a feast of prestige to the village men. And this feast enabled him to obtain high status in the society. Human skulls, thus, act as the vehicle to bring fertility and enabled the man to inherit fame and reputation among the society. The practice of the head-taking has become a central figure to fertility complex belief.[1]

J.P. Mills also writes: "A Naga who takes a head certainly wished to bring home tangible proof of his valour; but he also wishes to add to the soul-force of his village by bringing home the head, in which it resides".[2]

The magic of fertility, which resides in human heads, is firmly established with the Nagas. Bringing enemy hands, legs, ears and teeth is sometimes considered perfect and adequate in fertility contact but sans head, it proved to be less fertile. Sometimes, when a man failed to collect human head, mock raid is conducted to bring a monkey head but it produces no fertility. Human head was symbolically interwoven with fertility cult to crops, cattle and human beings embryo. This ritual indicates that when a man is killed, his soul is released and fertilize the soil, while the bones or skulls which are deposited in the granary act as an additional inducement in the soul-matter to resolve itself into grain.[3]

To induce the fertility, a tall wooden log is carved with pear-shaped face and long vertical noses, square shoulders and long arms, dressed to warrior's costume. This wooden effigy is erected in the name of particular successful warrior after his death over the grave. Although, the effigy is not obviously a representation of the actual likeness of the deceased, but it identified and represented the deceased warrior. It is carved out not merely as a monument but to evoke fertility of its deceased members, whenever the village has gone through a period of misfortune. When calamity befall upon the village men, the village men subscribed rice-bear and pigs, a member of the warrior's family cuts and carves a tree and the village youths drag the effigy onto its site. In some Naga villages, stone effigies are erected near the warrior's grave, indicating the number of heads taken by the deceased. The erection of some sort, edifice of stone and wood carving effigies near the corpse, seems to be common among the Nagas, though there is much variation, but it links with fertility cult. Naga woodcarving of human figure is depicted that sheds some light on the relationship between the soul and the fertility in culture. In literary context, these stone or wooden effigies of warriors referred to various statements of soul-force in fertility, interpreted to our modern concept. Natural calamities, such as famine, epidemic, fire incident, thunder strike, cyclones, hail-storms etc., were believed to be attributed to a decrease in soul-force which is found only in human head. Human heads acted as supernatural power to treat all the social malaise that confronted the people.[4]

Human beings are incapable to contact with supernatural power directly, therefore, the soul-matter which lies in human heads was acted as go-between them. The concept of the Nagas with regard to the idea of soul-force which lies in human heads, hands and feet, Major Butler writes: "......of cutting off the heads, hands and feet of anyone they can meet with, without provocation or per-existing enmity, merely to stick them up in their fields and so ensure a good crop of grain".[5]

The other speculative motive of the head taking was the development of anxiety and refusal among the Naga women to marry with the men who have not taken a single head is culminated with the idea of fertility cult, in the belief that the family would likely to suffer from infertility in child bearing, resulted to barrenness throughout her life for non-possession of head.

Provocation into Raid

The Nagas are belligerent in nature but they did not undertake any war without provocation. Nagas are not easily provoked but when things go away, he can never give up revenge. He must avenge the death of a relative in some way or other, either by stealth ambuscade, kill one or two in return and carry off their heads, staked the paths with a sharp bamboo spikes after their retreat to prevent their enemies' pursue. The Nagas do not allow his enemy to go scot-free but avenged him death on the first chance. Every Naga identified his enemy and avenged at his own dictate. There were many pretty good reasons on which wars were often declared upon the perpetrators. They were:

1. refusal to pay agreed bride price,
2. shelter to a culprit,
3. insult to a village,
4. acceptance of challenge,
5. inter-village land dispute.
6. abduction of women,
7. imbalance of head between the two warring villages,
8. capture of enemy's cattle,
9. attack and counter-attack,
10. shelter to a prisoner of war,
11. refusal to pay tribute,
12. refusal to pay agreed fine.[6]

Provocations alone were not the only motivation, which goaded the Nagas into the warpath. According to the tradition and custom of the Nagas, a man who has taken a head is entitled to wear costly dresses and attires. These ceremonial dresses and attires were not entitled by the commoner and such obligations compelled the young men to follow into the fold of raids. Head takers were also entitled to decorate his house with a carve posts and walls, depicting human skulls, mithun head etc., to represent enemy heads and prowess in war. The desire to wear the gorgeous dresses, ornaments and to live in adorned houses, promotes competitive emulation of status enhancing exploits through the raids.[7]

The Northern Naga tribes, such as Aos, Konyaks, Phoms, Changs, Sangrams etc. developed passionate desire to embellish his body tattooed to indicate his warrior status, and the right to adorn his body, a man is obliged to take an in-road. Exuberant satisfaction of wearing on costly dresses, ornaments and adornment of body and houses urged the young men to venture out for raids or laid in ambush upon the undoubtable enemies. The houses, dresses and ornaments of the Nagas reflected the warrior status of individual's identity as it exists at any particular moment which acts as a means to indicate the status and encourage every individual to strive for higher position among the society. A young man is elevated to the higher status at the cost of enemy's head. Thus through the manifestation of the human heads, a man earned warrior status and enjoyed all the social grading in his lifetime.[8]

Another motive of taking a head is the belief of securing a slave ghost in the next World of the Dead. According to this ritual belief, a slained soul would serve the slayer in the Land of the Dead, after the slayer died. This ritual is designed to fulfil the warrior's spiritual and physical satisfaction during his lifetime and in the Land of the Dead. The other motive was the desire to decorate his grave with a wooden carve of human skull after his death. All the successful warriors were entitled to decorate graves with a carve of human head, widely displayed over the grave to indicate the deceased's prowess in warfare, and such certification induced the men to take human head. Moreover, head hunters often occupied high position among the society. The young man who had a desire to display his bravery, manhood and prowess in warfare before his lady love, sometimes, provoked him to fight for a head.[9]

Weapons

Dao

A Dao was one of the chief offensive weapons of the Nagas. Dao was a close companion of the Naga. A man hardly goes out without holding a Dao in his right hand. It is also carried with the help of dao-box, tied with a string on his back. The length of Naga Dao can be anything from one to three feet and the width of a blade is from two to five inches. Generally Naga Dao has a wider edge towards the head, fitted with a wooden handle and at the end of a helve, it is ornated with goat's trim hair, dyed in red colour. This Dao is involved in all forms of cutting, peeling and chopping the enemy's head. It is also used for agricultural operations and handicraft works. When a man undertakes a raid, a Dao was the chief weapon to chop-off the enemy's head.

Spear

A Spear is another chief offensive weapon, made of strong wooden shaft and at both the ends, sharp pointed blade is fitted on the head and an iron butt spike is fitted at the bottom. The head of a spear is sharpened with a whet-stone till it obtains shining and sharpness. A spear is handled on the middle of a shaft, decorated with goat's trim hair and dyed with red colour on the helve. The length of a spear is always one or two feet above the height of a user. The spear is capable to kill the enemy, at a distance of thirty yards away, smeared with a poison sap. The spear is never leaned against the wall, lest it would spoil the shape and lost the balance when it is hurled at an enemy.

Bow and Arrow

Bow and Arrow were the other chief weapons of the Nagas,

made of hard bamboo split and string. An arrow is a strong bamboo split, fitted with an iron head and smeared with a poison. Arrow was a lethal weapon that a person might be killed at a long distance after a few minutes of the arrow punctured into the body. Some Nagas did not use bow and arrow to kill an enemy, and the use of this weapon was considered as taboo.

Shield

The Shield was the chief defensive weapon of the Nagas. Shields are made of bamboo or cane with a horizontal handle in the centre of the inner side for handling it. Shields can be made in rectangular, concave or bent at the centre axis of slopping roof. This weapon is used to defend the body from enemy's spear and other objects.

Helmet

Helmets are made out of cane peelings, re-inforced with bamboo or cane strips. Coloured dyed hairs of animals, tusks of bears, beaks of birds, horns and feathers are used to awe-inspiring appearance of these conical head-dress. The use of helmet is to protect from enemy's *dao* blow and spear throw. It also protects from enemy's pelting of stone, rain and heat.

Panjis

Panjis is a sharp pointed bamboo spikes, fixed on the head of bamboo splits of about five to six inches in length and three to four feet in breadth were fixed into the ground on a strategic narrow paths, where the enemies are likely to tread, so as to impede the advance movement of the enemies. These spikes were usually embedded into the ground when the warriors are retreated from successful raids, and to prevent the enemies chasing after them. This weapon is also applied for both offensive and defensive game plan. When a village is put under threat, the village surrounding is ensured by staking *panjis* to thwart the enemies movement in and around the village. The village also sank pits in the jungles 6 or 7 feet deep, staked with bamboo spikes vertically inside the pit and camouflage them with dry grasses and earth, while the new earth taken out of the pit is conveyed to a certain distance to prevent from seeing the new earth and avoid the pit. A person who fell into this trap is not expected to escape from body punctured. The enemy who falls alive in such trap might lame for life.[10]

Mode of Warfare

When the Nagas had undertaken a raid, firstly, they collected the information of enemy's defense, disposition, population, obstacles, distance and the route leading to the village. They studied the texture and structure of enemy's village landscape and fortification for escape after their operation. If the village is undertaken a predatory in-road or to take revenge of any village, the warriors and the village elders assembled together and decided on which village to be attacked, and the Chief appointed to command. The Nagas never ventured out for expeditions without taking a good omen in the shape of their dreams and entrails from animals and fowls. Consultation of omen from sorcerers or priestess of the village has become necessary to ascertain whether a hostile incursion on an enemy village would be successful. To obtain the omen, they cut a soft reed into flat pieces, if the slices fall on one side or one upon the other, success is certain, and if on the reverse quarter or scattered, it is ominous in proportion to the number of pieces that have fallen. It also pretends to discover future events by the flight of a cock, if he flies strong and far, it is an auspicious omen. On the contrary, should the flight be for a short distance and weakly, ill luck would inevitably attend any hostile expedition.

If a deer likewise crosses their path when starting on an expedition, the warriors return home immediately and postponed the undertaking to a future day. The other omen is taken by blowing on an egg and wish ill luck on enemy village; they then would seek to place it in the enemy village. Sometimes, wooden models of enemies are made and decapitated them as an indication of an enemy's killing and weakened their fighting spirit through the cutting of an effigy. This ritual is practiced as a source of magic in the head taking ceremony. To perform a ritual, the diviner himself with the broken eggs in a bamboo tube in his left hand, normally led the gang with three strong persons immediately behind him, suitably armed and the rest behind. The diviner then inserting a leaf into the bamboo tube containing the broken eggs, took out a little of the mess and thrown it in the air in a magical way towards the village proceeded against, invoking and falsely requesting the Chief and the villagers not to take notice of the advancing party and to spare a few heads of their persons. The final action of the men is depended upon the indication of ritual that if the result gives negative signal, then the raid is put off for another day but if the indication is good, the raid is carried out on the treacherous war path. When a raid is decided, a man who is to take part must sleep apart from their wives on the night before the expeditions. A cock or pig is killed and meat eaten. If a cock squawked when its throat is being cut, it is regarded as a bad omen and the expedition is usually put off. Similarly, a man who hiccup while eating the pork, stayed behind, for if he went, misfortune would befall upon him.[11]

A woman had to remain chaste while her husband was away on raid. Any breach of this rule, it was believed that her husband would be killed by the enemy. She was also forbidden to weave; lest her husband's feet would be entangled with jungle creepers and he should be caught and killed. The woman had to observe taboo till her husband returned from raids. She is tabooed to fetch fire from another house, and in case the fire went out, she had to produce fire-thong by herself. She would always pretend that her husband is at home and talk to him as if he is there. Her strict taboo would decide the fate of her husband's successful raids, but any breach of this taboo would cost her husband's life.[12]

The warriors who decided to launch an attack, conducted intensive military training along with self-restraint, taboo and observation of certain rituals. The entire operation is put under the command of the warrior, whose bravery and prowess in warfare had already been put to test. The man is held responsible to carry out the entire process of operation, which may direct against the common enemy, drawn from several numbers of villages. Sometimes, joint operations were organized from a number of villages, pulled their manpower forces against the common enemy, and all these men acted under one leader, who was responsible for the operation. To challenge the feuding village, a symbolic message, consisting of a splinter of wood, in the form of a small bundle wrapped in cloth is sent to an enemy village. The meaning of such symbolic message is that the enemy would be butchered or cut like a splinter. Sending a symbolic message often treated as an insult to a village, which resulted, to inter-village feud.[13]

The attackers sometimes travelled for several days to avenge the enemy. Generally raids were preferably undertaken after the first cock-crow at night, when enemies were dead to the world. A village is usually enveloped and attacked from all possible directions, subjected to the location of a site. When the raid is directed to avenge an enemy, the entire village could be set on fire, after they killed all the straggler children, old men and women. Most of the occupants were caught unaware by a raging fire, and those who tried to escape were speared or hacked to death with a dao. However, granaries were often spared from arson attacked. Bow and arrow is used to kill an escaping enemy from afar. Captured enemies were taken as prisoners of war and were sold to the rich men, and there had been cases when the slaves were murdered in cold blood to quench the thirst of the skull-hungry masters who are sitting in their palaces and swell their treasure of skulls and enhance their status with the aid of their wealth. Prisoners of war were seldom taken by the attackers and it was a matter of great shame on the part of the Nagas to fall alive into the hands of an enemy. Prisoners were kept at the mercy of his master, and it could be sold and resold but the slaves could not make frantic effort to escape because an escaping slave was put to death.[14]

When the warrior decided to set out on a war expedition, they equipped themselves with spears, daos, shields and a small bamboo basket, carrying the bamboo spikes, boiled rice and meat wrapped it up in banana leaves and set out for the village to be attacked. The warrior lie near to in ambush during the night till the break of day, when they rush in upon it with a great noise and spear the first they meet with, and afterwards cut off the head, hands and feet of their enemies, roll them up in a cloth and return home. The head is taken to each house in the village, pour the rice-beer over it and induce the soul of the skull to call their relatives. Returning from successful raids, the warriors abstained from taking food, cooked by their women and do not cook in their accustomed cooking pots, and neither do the warriors have any communication with their wives during five days, but after fifth day, the heads or the skulls are buried and a great feast is given with pigs and cows. When the ritual is observed, they took bathe and return to their usual avocations.[15]

A Rengma successful warrior is ritually unclean for several days. His hands cannot be washed, he must eat with a special spoon and he cannot sleep in his own house until certain ceremonies of re-integration into normal life have occurred. The head he has taken is mollified, in the hope that the dead man's spirit will be more angered with his co-villagers who failed to protect him then with the men who in fact killed him. A man is separated off from women, before, during and after a raid. When a man returned from a raid, he must sleep apart and eat separately from his wife for ten days. The warrior who had taken enemy heads were required to perform a ritual individually to ward-off the spirits of the victims, lest he would fall into the hands of the victim's relatives. The man who had taken a head must sleep apart from their wives for six nights and were forbidden to eat meat from a tiger's kill. A wounded man should not sleep that night, for his soul would obey the summon call by his slayer and leave him in his sleep and he would die. A man who escaped with a spear through him had to keep on the tray over the fire-grate to dry the spear, so that his wound would dry and recover quickly.[16]

The Nagas hardly go out singly inroads, but in bodies commit predatory onslaught. The incursions of the Nagas were chiefly confined to attacks on small defenceless villages or the feuding villages. Naga warriors generally avoid pitched battle and they usually undertake surreptive attack upon the unwary enemies. They were known for their notorious surprise and deceptive attack when the enemies are least expected. The usual tactic was to lay in ambush behind the bush, tree, stone or mound in an unexpected place. They completely concealed themselves so that their presence was unknown to the defenders. When the defenders discovered that the attackers are too powerful, they fled for safety or should they discovered the infiltration of the enemies into the villages, the defenders overpowered them and killed them. Naga warriors proved themselves superb by having the knowledge of moving agility in the hill terrain and adopted certain methods of guerilla warfare which were inherited from its instinct, and need to be trained in this field. They were capable to travel across all types of rugged mountains, ridges, valleys and plains, moving days together without any sign of fatigue. They are martial race which can be put to test through bravery, energy and prowess in warfare. They fight to the last man in the face of parlous. Naga warriors were known for their swiftness and accuracy in an attack like a leopard, leaving no trace of their escape from their defenders. Pursuing after the warriors they encountered more difficulty and danger from their impediments of bamboo spikes which are staked into the ground on the paths they fled. The defender chasing after them at the heat of fury would have impaled themselves with the spikes. The Naga seldom engaged in pitched battle but there had been cases where one village challenged another village to fight at a particular place. The Nagas themselves distinguished different kinds of fighting, but largely on the ground of tactics. Naga warriors carried out their raids on an enemy village, ambushed on the path, jungle and attacked the solitary worker in the field. Pitch battle takes place only when a village is insulted and challenged to fight on appointed day. Inviting an enemy into the village and butchered treacherously the slayer was not considered as a warrior, and the Nagas tried to avoid such barbarous act meted upon the faithful enemy. Head-taking competition was high among the Nagas, and more alert to any possible insult or slight from a neighbouring village, meant more head-taking ritual. Fatalities were low in pitched battle than in comparison to the typical stealthy raid on unwitting village, in which one party had the advantage of surprise.[17]

When men folk undertake the raids, their womenfolk did not prevent them from head taking. Their womenfolk did not show any sign of fear for them and expected that their husbands would return with heads. If a husband undertakes an expedition, his wife would prepare food and other necessary arrangement. For instance, if the expedition takes more than one day journey, millets are cooked and some crashed pieces of smoked meat are wrapped in the banana leaves which can last for several days without fermentation. Rice-beer is brewed and filled in his gourd-jar. The husband then put on his warrior attires and set out for expedition, while the wife induced him to fight courageously and bring many heads. The husband who returned home without head is humiliated by his wife, while for successful husband, prized *mithun,* pig or cattle is killed to celebrate his heroic deeds. The family is not expected to lead a prosperous life without bringing a head. Naga womenfolk directly encouraged and indirectly participated in head-taking. Women plays a vital role in the head receiving rituals. When her husband brought a head, she boiled the head and removed the skins, feed the skull with rice-beer, which conspicuously indicated that womenfolk constituted and promote head-taking. The wife usually induced the slained head by uttering a few incantations and pour rice-beer onto its skull, inviting the deceased father, mother and relatives to join him in feeding, and they would kill with the same sword. She further spelled in magical way, inducing the enemy the wife would perform head-receiving rituals again. It is also noticeable that women goaded the men to undertake head-taking as a prerequisite to marriage. Head-taking among the Nagas, therefore, had become necessity, which urged the young men to be fully eligible for marriage partners.[18]

Among the Northern Nagas, human head is taken in every installation of a new log-drum which is carved in the vicinity of jungle and brought in the village. They venerated the drum by bringing an enemy head to propitiate the spirit of a drum. Once the drum is installed, it is pacified as a deity, and human or animal blood is smeared the drum. When the drum is in position, a human head must somehow be got, and until a head is offered, the drum must not be beaten. If a stranger happens to pass by the village, he is immediately beheaded. It is, therefore, when a village installed a new log-drum, all the neighbouring villages are on the alert. The village sometimes had to go far a field to get an enemy's head which takes many months. When a head is brought to the village, the young men who are not warriors, touched the head with their *daos,* spears and then they put the head in the hollow groove of a drum and everyone joined in beating the drum. Then the warriors who have shared in the killing gave animals for a village feast and there would be a general dance around the drum. In the evening, the head is removed from the drum and the head taker cuts a pointed sharp bamboo. A hole is then bored in the head by an old man and the head is tied to the top of the bamboo and leant against the head-tree. This is the opportunity for a young man to touch the head with their *daos* and spears. By touching the head, they could earn the status of a warrior, since it was a necessity to have physical contact with an enemy head before a man undertakes the raids[19]

Inter-tribal feud was common among the Nagas but it involved between the two warring tribal villages and it did not necessarily involved by the entire tribe against another tribal villages. No particular tribe appears to have or ever united as a tribe against another tribe. Although, the Lothas observed a taboo on taking other Lotha heads but this does not meant that all Lotha villages were unitedly put in conflict with the other Naga tribes. Even if this were possible, it would be war and not a feud which is by definition a balanced, particular relationship between paired villages. Each Naga village identify their own feuding villages and wage war with such villages along, and not necessarily treated all the villages as their adversary. In some exception, head-taking is carried out between the two *khels* or clans in the village or with the other villages, but it was so happened because the village was a non-functional conglomeration of autonomous clans, each well defended and pursuing its own foreign policy. Taking a head with other villages, often created feuding village which necessarily involved a kind of debt relationship and mutual claims between groups, who often seeks to recover until head is paid off. However, it was not a purely financial kind of debt which cannot be repaid with currency units. Hence, it involved with heads to balance the fulfilment of rituals. Sometimes, the entire village is raided and looted the booty, consisting of weapons, ornaments and shawls, while the cattle, pigs and fowls were killed and eaten up. The hands, feet and ears of the victims were also collected as a war trophy. In case, three or four attackers pounced on a single enemy, the first man who speared at the enemy would own the head, the second man is entitled with the hands, the third man took the feet, while the fourth man claimed the ears, and they proved themselves as successful warriors.[20]

When men attained the age of eight or nine years, they accompany their fathers or brothers on the way to the battle field. They wore a body cloth which their mother's tied on their chest into a knot and filled their bags with a pack of food. The warriors encamped the boys preferably on a hillock of a dense jungle, where they could watch the following day for returning group. These boys began to learn how to lay in ambush and counter with the enemies. The boys also help their warriors in carrying the war trophies and looted objects, returned home proudly with war cries, singing, dancing and yelling. War drums would be beaten in every *khel* to welcome the return of their heroic warriors. The trophies of chase is carried into the village and paraded around the parameter of the village before it is, finally, deposited into the *Morung* or head-tree. According to Konyak tradition, the captured head is deposited in the Chief's house, while the individual is permitted to erect a stone in the common head-yard, outside the Chief's house, to represent the head, and he received full warrior's status in his lifetime.[21]

Amongst the Nagas, it is considered a point of honour to recover the skulls of their friends, who have fallen in an attack made on their villages, and war prisoners were always decapitated, if they refused to accompany or return with the victors to their homes. It is totally incompatible with Naga honour also to forego in taking revenge, and it is incumbent on him to ransom or recover the skull of a relative killed or captured in war, years may elapse but the killing of relative is never forgotten and when a favourable opportunity offers, probably, twice the number of victims are sacrificed. Retaliation against enemy ensures and consequently, there can never be a termination to these exterminating feuds. The idea of reason of indulging in feuding was to prove superiority over a neighbouring villages. The reason of indulging in feuding relations was not so much the desire to inflict a loss on a given section, as to use these victories to enhance individuals and community at large. To take the head of a woman and children was considered acceptable challenge for the loss of a relative. Naga feuds were, therefore, considered ostensibly impersonal without malice. Rather it was a social pride of justice and to prove man's successful warriors in the Naga warfare arena. The tangible result of Naga feuds was based on trophies of war.

Bringing of women's and children's head were considered most highly prized trophies on the following grounds:

(1) It contained soul-force of fertility cult.
(2) The curious long hairs of the women were highly in demand to decorate the weapons, like *dao,* spear and war basket.
(3) Children teethes were used for ornaments and ornated the house.[22]

However, to kill the women and children was not easy task, since special protection was given to these groups by the defenders. To take the heads from these groups, one has to penetrate deep into the enemy's village and killed all the able bodied men with all the concomitant risk. A man might be killed anywhere by a successful raids or ambush, but taking the head of woman and children, it is required greater skill and risks. However, despite strong protection given to these groups, maximum victims belonged to the helpless women and children, who were slained without any contrite and the slayer was held in high esteem. There had been cases where the able bodied men were at work in the rice-fields, raiding party slowly entered the village and killed them, making their good escape before the villagers returned home.

The scene of attacking village was horrific: children, old men and women became the ultimate war trophy of the attackers; while the able bodied men either resisted or fell in fighting. Dogs are barking at and many headless men and women are lying in a pool of blood, while the burnt down houses look like deserted villages. On the other side of the battle, the attackers carried away huge booty and war trophies and they return home triumphantly, leaping, yelling and dancing around the village.[23]

Warrior's Status Symbol

The Naga ceremonial dresses and ornaments were associated with the successful head-taking ritual. A Naga young man exhibited his manhood and wearing of gorgeous dresses through his prowess in warfare. Every Naga head-taker is entitled to wear special designs and highly embroidered ceremonial dresses and ornaments. A man who did not own a single head, he is not entitled to put on the warrior attires and ornaments, and this obligation compelled the young men to follow the war-path. When a man attained at the age of manhood, he puts on ivory anklets or else wooden ones, or red coloured cane round his neck, he suspends with a black thread and the sunk shell, put on brass earrings into his ears, and wears the black kilt, and if a man has killed another in war, he wears three or four rows of cowries round the kilt, and ties up his hair with cotton band. If a man has killed another in war, he is entitled to wear white cotton rosette on his hairs and one hornbill feather over the head-gear. One feather is added for every man he has killed, and these feathers are also fastened to their shields. The warriors also used coloured platted cane leggings to carry the war sword, spear shield and bamboo vessels tube for carrying sharp bamboo or wooden spikes for staking into the ground. When the Nagas undertake a raid, the warrior wears a collar round the neck, reaching to the waist of goat's trim hair, dyed in red is intermixed with long following locks of hairs of the person's he has killed, ornamented with cowrie shells. The shield is attached with two pieces of wood in the shape of buffalo's horn with the locks of hair of human beings killed in action hanging from the centre.[24]

The Angami head-taker wears ear rosette of hair and beetle-wing, a kilt with several rows of cowries and leggings made of cane-rings. The warrior's womenfolk wear cowries-shells waist-wrapper (*mekhela*). No Angami man is entitled to wear the kilt, ornamented with cowrie shells, until he had slained an enemy, and no girl would marry a man unless he has so decorated. The Sema head-taker wears necklet of boar's tusks, and put on *lengta*, embedded with cowries aprons without leggings, and their womenfolk wears highly embroidered shawls and waist-wrapper, made of pure cotton cloth and studded with cowrie shells. Both the Angamis and the Semas used hornbill feathers in their fur head circlet to signify warrior status, and their ivory armlet signify military prowess. The Rengmas, Lothas and Aos warriors wear the classic enemy's teeth ornament. This ornament is a flat piece of wood, usually about one foot long, representing the head of enemy, studded with cowries or job's tears seed for the teeth, red cane for mouth and fringe of red hairs, represent the blood pouring out of the mouth which is worn by a warrior. It is either worn on the chest or on the back horizontally or vertically. One Hornbill feather in Angami head-gear indicated the wearer's had taken one enemy's head, while according to the Aos, it is indicated a man who has participated in the raid. Two hornbill feathers in the Angami head-gears indicated two enemy's heads were taken, but the Aos indicated the man who first spear in killing an enemy. According to the custom of Khiamniungan Nagas, two hornbill feathers in head-dress indicated a warrior status but does not necessarily reflect to be a head-taker. Two feathers in Konyak head-dress indicated warrior status or the daughter of *ang* or Chief is entitled to wear it. One feather in Lotha head-dress indicated that a man had taken a head or touched an enemy corpse. Three feathers in Rengma and Sema head-dress indicated a warrior status that the wearer had taken an enemy's head. The Hornbill feathers were an element of common language and it indicates high or low status of one sort or another. The dresses and ornaments often speak the status of a warrior and ordinary person amongst the Naga society.

The same sort of diversity can be seen also in wearing of ornament, such as boar's tusks, leggings, armlets, earrings, necklace etc., which is always indicating the insignia of a warrior. The wearing of *Drongo*-tails in the ear-lobe too indicate the status of a warrior. Similarly, the use of cowrie-shells studded in the shawls, *lengta*, aprons and waist-wrappers dominantly indicated the warrior status or symbol. Among the Aos an apron made of cowrie-shells, woven in zigzag patterns indicated the warrior of many expeditions, while a shawl embroidered with a cowrie-shells in circles, indicated the daughter or head-taker, who has burnt an enemy village. Four rows of cowries lines in the Angami man's kilt indicated the highest status of a warrior. A trefoil belt of a Sema man indicated a drawn blood of an enemy; an apron embedded with cowrie-shells in circles indicated a man who first speared an enemy corpse, and a circle cowrie-shells embroidered in a cloth indicated a great warrior, in which a circlet cowrie-shells represented the head of an enemy. A Sema women who wears a shawl embroidered with rows of cowrie-and trefoils, represented a daughter of a Chief or a warrior. A Rengma apron and cloth embroidered with a cowrie-shells in circles, represented bravery and prowess in warfare, and their women who wear shawls embroidered with cowrie-shells in the circles and lines, indicated the daughter of a warrior or the killer of a tiger, where the circle represents tiger eyes.

A highly ornamentation of dresses, ornaments and the dwelling houses of the Nagas, symbolized the common language of head taking culture. The warrior wears a spectacular warrior's tail, made of cotton woven, and a long projecting object is worn at the down of the back, made of wood with black hair hanging down from it. The Angamis worn this ornaments as a mark of military prowess, but for the Rengmas it signified completion of head-taking *genna*. When a warrior undertakes a raid, he wears bear's skin caps, decorated with boar tusks and plumes of feathers with *daos*, spears, shields, etc., in fighting position to search a straggler enemy. The use of hornbill feather is restricted to warriors alone. A Lotha man is entitled to put on the ornaments, like hornbill feather in his bearskin wig, boar's tusk necklace, red fringed gauntlets, red *dao*-belt and dark blue *lengta* with red lines, if he either had taken a head or at least touched an enemy's corpse. In every head-taking ceremony, one hornbill feather is worn. Naga warrior worn different types of cloth in addition of two long scarlet tassels of dyed goat's hair worn down from the ears in front, a thread fastening them together running the back of the head over the hair which is worn down the back. The men's ceremonial dress is adorned with wheel of hornbill feathers. This feather is entitled to wear only by a man of warrior, who had taken a head. Every feather in the head-dress represented the enemy's head taken by the wearer. Another head-dress is made of buffalo horn, and the wearer of this head-gear is the man who have led an attack upon the enemy and fought with an enemy hand to hand. The ceremonial dress of the warrior's ears are ornamented with emerald beetle's wing, hanging down to the shoulder. A stripe of white woven cloth is used as a belt with lozenge patterns in coloured hair or wool, and a tail of about a foot long is worn by veteran warriors. This tail is made of human hair or goat's trim hair. The baldrics worn across the breast, signifies that the wearer killed a man, the armlet hairs inform the spectator of the fact that the enemy arms have been taken by the wearer, while the gauntlets signify the head taken and leggings signify the legs taken.

Dresses and ornaments signify the man's position in warrior status, and even to his wife's and family. These insignias were highly desirable because of their achievements that they deserved the right to wear them. For a personal material culture, it was a multiplicity of cloths rather than ornaments which were awarded for feasts of prestige and ornaments, rather cloths for head-hunting. The Rengma warrior, who has taken the enemy's head, wears a prestigious woven shawls known as '*Teri Phiketsu*'. This cloth is woven with a dark blue and with a thin zigzag pattern in a red at the edge and a median band elaborately painted in black sap woven separately and stitch is given at the middle to join the two broad band together at the edge. Patterns are consisted of regular pattern, symbolizing the warrior's standing in a rod. A little spoon is depicted next to each warrior to symbolize the blood of the enemies in hand, and that the warrior is taboo to eat with his hand but he should use a spoon while eating. Apart from this paintings, a small line indicate bows and arrows which were not used as a weapon to kill men but to kill animal and birds are the indication of this figure. Just below the spoon design, a straight line is drawn in each side of the edges is to denote the bridge which a warrior uses to come across into the area of the enemy after the enemy shut the gate and come out over the same bridge with his trophy. The zigzag paintings on the lower side of the median white band is the symbolic representation of the sentry post on which the soldiers keep guard. *Juda-phe* and *Chonyu-phe* were the prestigious shawls worn only by the warriors, who had taken an enemy head through a successful raid. A Rengma warrior who has got first spear at an enemy killing has three small circlets of cowries on the black cloth at the top of his apron, and wears an ornament, made of small spirals of brass form with a red tassel dangles in the lobe. A man who had taken a head may wear long scarlet, goat's hair, ear ornaments and boar tusk. The Sema's body cloth which tie the top corner of one end is again drawn from behind over the left shoulder and the bottom corner of the same end is brought under the right arm, and these two corners are knotted on the chest. The falling end of the cloth is doubled back again towards the tied ends and the two corners are tied round the waist, the corner opposite the one under the right arm, coming round the left side and the corner opposite the one which goes over the left shoulder, coming round the right shoulder and the left side towards the front is worn by a warrior on the war-path, where the heads are carried inside the two folded cloths. *Asukuda-phi* was a warrior's shawl, worn only by the head-taker. *Tsungkotepsu* was the most prestigious shawl of the Aos warrior, woven with a white band in the centre and on the either side, a horizontal bands of contrasting black, red and white. The median band is painted with a pattern in black, depicting the figures of elephant and tiger which represents the bravery and the prowess in warfare, while the figures of *dao*, spear and cock represented the valour and wisdom of a warrior. This shawl was exclusively worn by the head-taker and the commoners were not entitled to wear nor touch it. Every Naga head-taker or the man who touch an enemy corpse were entitled to put on the ceremonial dresses and ornaments, such as hornbill feathers in his bearskin wig, boar's tusk neckles, red fringed gauntlet, red *dao* belt and dark blue kilt with red-lines. The Chang Naga head-taker's mugs bear significant decorations to mark his prowess in warfare.[25]

Another status symbol associated with the warriors was the practice of tattooing to represent the head-taker. Tattooing was a painful job, hammering the skin with a thorn implement and a black sap mixed with rice-beer is applied into the cut mark. Naga warriors might be tattooed on the face, shoulders, stomach, chest, arm, wrist, calf and on the back to indicate the warriors status. Tattooing was practiced so that the variations among the Naga tribes in the pattern, convey different messages about the wearer. Men tattoos tend to be more representational, and concerned with signifying achieved head-taking status. The Chang head-taker tattoos were also given in their house-posts, drinking mugs, smoking pipes and weapon handles in zigzag patterns. Men monopolize this tattooing symbol as a part of their achievement of status in head-taking. The attainment of the tattoo was a kind of rite of passage. Tattoos were considered as ornaments to embellish the body as well as to indicate the warrior status. The head-taker's ornaments may thus be seen as the symbols of the ultimate transformation. Among the Chang tribe, the women whose blood relation with the head-taker male side may cook the head with chillies to get the flesh off and then assume the male tattoo the double hornbill feather tattoo, were worn by head taker. This custom suggests that the head-taking tattoo was a symbol of natural transformation in which the women by cooking the head is also contributing to the transformation and thus earns the right to wear the same tattoo as the man. A successful head-taker is entitled to get his body tattooed to indicate his warriorship. The tattoos on their chest, consist of geometric patterns combined with small figures of men which represent the enemies killed in war. The Ao warrior who had taken a head, had circle tattooed on their back, while some tattooed on each side of the back near the shoulder blades. Tattooing was thus practiced as a distinguishing mark on the body which speaks of the bearer's status through successful raids. Tattoo mark was given to the warrior in recognititon of his prowess in the warfare and he enjoyed special privilege in the society.[26]

According to the Naga context, there is nothing more glorious than bravery and success in battle; the bringing of an enemy's head to the village was a heroic deed, which would be sung. A deeper lying motive seems to have been the fertility contact and greed of social position, which entirely depended on his success in war. The largest number of head-taker in the village occupies the highest position in social esteem among the society.

The entire underlying concept was the fertility cult and the prestige issue in front of the society. A young man who attended the village feast without adornment on his body was scornfully laughed at by the womenfolk because it conspicuously distinguish himself from the successful warrior and this urged the young men to undertake head-taking ritual as a prerequisite avocation.

NOTES

1. This information is based on oral traditions of the Nagas, compiled during the fieldwork. The Nagas passionately developed the idea that fertility of mankind, domestic animals and agricultural products lies in human skulls, and the prosperity of the people is the direct contact with human heads.
2. Julian Jacobs, *The Nagas (Hills Peoples of North East India),* (London: Thames and Hudson, 1990), p.124.
3. The village elders of Tseminyu, Kuthur, Noklak, Tuensang, Chui etc. told to the scholar. Fertility which lies in human heads was one of the mystic belief of the Nagas and this concept goaded the Nagas into the raids.
4. Based on Interview at Leshemi, Chizami, Kikruma villages. It was the tradition of the Chakhesangs that a stone or wooden effigy is carved and erected near the warrior's grave to indicate the number of enemy's head taken by the deceased.
5. J.H. Hutton, *The Angami Nagas* (London: Oxford University Press, 1921), p.160.
6. Fieldwork.
7. Fieldwork.
8. This information is given by the village elders of Ungma and Mon villages. Unlike the other Nagas, the Aos and Konyaks tattooed their body to indicate as warrior status.
9. Fieldwork.
10. Fieldwork.
11. Fieldwork.
12. Fieldwork. The Naga have the same tradition on this Taboo.
13. Fieldwork.
14. Fieldwork.
15. Fieldwork.

16. Fieldwork. Village elders belonging to Rengma Nagas, told to the scholar.
17. Fieldwork.
18. Fieldwork.
19. This information is based on fieldwork, compiled from the village elders of Ungma, Sakshi, Phir-Ahir, Tuensang, Kuthur, Noklak and Mon villages.
20. Fieldwork.
21. Fieldwork.
22. Fieldwork.
23. Fieldwork.
24. Fieldwork.
25. Fieldwork.
26. Fieldwork.

4

Ahom Tactics of War
The Espionage System

Jahnabi Gogoi Nath

"Know the enemy and know yourself; in a hundred battles you will never be in peril". This is what Sun Tzu, the 4th century BC Chinese philosopher, opines about the tactics of war of his age.[1] Indeed, espionage system is an indispensable adjunct of the conduct of war as of all governments everywhere throughout the ages. The Ahom rulers who ruled Assam from the early 13th century AD till the first quarter of the 19th century, too was not an exception in this regard. It may be argued that this long history of Ahom rule in Assam was largely due to their efficient intelligence system in the warfare, which they had to engage with almost the entire tribal states of the north east, the Bengal Sultans and the great Mughals. This chapter attempts at analyzing the system of espionage and the role of the different classes of spies in Assam in the Ahom administration.

The espionage system formed an important part of the organization of the armed forces of the Ahoms. They are variously known as *chor, chorangchowa, chorbacha, sajati* (group of trusted persons), *ghorachows, batarijoganiya* or *kataki.* The spies travelled in disguise and collected informations from both in and outside the state. The chronicles mention a group of Assamese spies in guise of beggars travelling in the Kachari kingdom during the rule of the king Suhungmung *alias* Dihingiya Raja (1497-1539), seeking shelter there.[2]

The most well-known and trained group of spies were the *Chors* or *Chorbachas*. It was in the 17th century when the Ahoms had to defend their state against recurring Mughal invasions, that they organized their wing of spies into an efficient and selected group of devoted workers to whom life was not much important than their country. Recruited from among the most intelligent of the young people, they were properly trained in the art of spying by the state including training in language of the enemies and their ways of living habits and customs. The *Deodhai Asam Buranji*[3], one of the early Assamese chronicles, records the incident of a group of spies who visited the Mughal camps in disguise in the year 1636 AD, and brought very important information about the distribution of the Mughal army and creation of garrisons between Hajo and Sualkuchi which part of the territory soon after was occupied by the Ahom forces on being reported by the spies.[4] On the basis of the reports of the spies posted for the same duties, who reported that the Mughal army remained vigilant during the first part of the night and relaxed in the second part, next year also the Ahoms won another battle under Lanmakharu Barphukan.[5] Thus, on the basis of this report, the Ahom army led a late night surprised attack on the Mughal fleet at Srighat.[6] Earlier to that in 1616 AD the Ahom reconnaissance parties intruded into the Mughal camp in disguise at Hajo and stayed there for four five days before they were finally detected.[7]

The efficiency of the *chorbachas* has been conclusively testified by a unique incident during the battle of Agiyathuti in 1636-37. The skeptical Chetiya Rajkhowa Phukan wanted to confirm the information supplied by his spy whom he deputed to collect information about the preparation of the Mughals. The spy reported that the Mughals remained vigilant during the first part of the night and relaxed in the last part and without arms (*puwati nisha bina yatane thake*). The Phukan, still sceptic, asked him if his information was confirmed. The *chorbacha* then left for the

Mughal camp to do something more and genuine to prove his innocence and ability, and there at the stable he left a cow and lifted a horse and brought it to the Phukan. The guard of the Mughal camp remarked that the horse developed horns (*ghorar sing gajil*). The Nawab, finding that there was a cow instead of a horse, had the guard executed. Still the Phukan wanted to get the tobacco-server (*dhowa khowa*) of Islam Khan to finally certify the excellent service of his spy. The *chorbacha* there upon entered the servant's quarter and when everyone there was asleep towards the end of the night, brought the tobacco server to the Phukan.[8] The Phukan, however, believed the story only when it was confirmed by his son Abhaypuriya who was the overseer of the spy.[9]

The Ahom kings from the very beginning used to appoint a class of officers called *katakis* to other states in order to cement good neighbourly relations as well as to dispatch secret information to their king about the affairs of the capital which they visited. Assamese chronicles mention that even king Sukapha sent a *kataki* to the Nara kingdom in upper Burma possibly to obtain information about if the Nara king was still planning to invade his territory upto which the Nara king chased Sukapha and his men.[10] Envoys to the Nara kingdom were sent by almost all early rulers of the Ahom kingdom till at least the 15th century in order be confirmed about the design of the Nara king. Similarly, king Sukhrangpha (1281-1332) sent his *kataki* to the Kamata kingdom in order to make friendly relations with him and married princess Rajani as a symbol of friendship and good neighbourly relations.[11] King Sudangpha also (1397-1407) sent secret letters to the Nara king inside a bamboo piece.[12] The *Katakis* as a set of trustworthy intelligence officers was first organized during the early 17th century when the Ahoms had to come into constant conflict with the Koch-Mughal powers in the west. It is worth-mentioning that the *katakis* were largely responsible to collect not only the exact informations of an enemical king's design, but they were also responsible to negate, as far as possible, the possibility of war between the Ahom king and the Koch or the Mughal kings. This was why, very intelligent and shrewed persons were selected to the posts of the *kataki*. The chronicles mention that once a *kataki* who failed to report smartly about the Koch king's court before king Pratap Singha (1603-1641), was forthright removed from his office by the king.[13] It is interesting that this laxity on part of the envoy was considered as a kind of racial inferiority, and therefore, king Pratap Singha since then made it a policy to appoint *katakis* from the more smart and intelligent Brahmans to depute to the Koch or the Mughal and other states in other parts of contemporary India,[14] although *katakis* to the hill tribes such as Nagas and others were appointed from among the Ahoms themselves.[15]

The *katakis* were responsible for protection of all kings of interests of the state when presenting themselves at the foreign court. It is recorded that the Ahom *katakis* misreported to the Mughal General Ahlair Khan (*barnabab*) who came to invade Assam in 1638 and in order to make a pretext for that who asked for elephants, agar wood and pepper.[16] It is reported that when his demand was made known then they, in order to take time for war preparation, told then that they could give those things only after getting permission of the king. Thus they took enough time and informed the king for preparation, and when this was done they returned to the general and reported that the king would not offer even the sand of the river, not to speak of the gold; or elephant or agar wood.[17] Thus deceived, the Mughal General ordered for persecution of the envoys by throwing them into the river when they bribed the police with whatever gold they had with them and escaped.[18] Thus the Ahom *katakis,* in order to defend their state and avoid war or make necessary preparations for war, readily lied and deceived the opponents. Assamese chronicles recorded that Momai Tamuli Barbarua, the shrewed diplomat-cum-chief executive officer of the state during king Pratap Singha, while giving intelligence to this class of officers told them not to divulge important information to the foreigners or tell about serious matters relating to the state.[19]

Similar to the *katakis* was a class of spies called *baragi* or *langta baragi,* which class of visitors to the foreign countries in disguise was created by king Pratap Singha.[20] The duties of this class of spies were to visit Mughal India in guise of mendicants, sometimes singing and dancing, but always observing and collecting carefully information about all sorts of activities that attracted them. At the same time, they were also to inform their king about any development that they could notice in those states also to inform their king about any development that they could notice in those states, which may go against the interest of their state.[21] This class of spies was systematically organized by king Rudra Singha (1696-1714) who created out of it five distinct clans, e.g. *kakati, kataki, doloi, khound* and *baragi*.[22] Although the primary duty of this class of spies apparently seemed to be observance of the cultural activities outside Assam, the period of its creation during Pratap Singha point to their association with intelligence activities too which was normally in connection with warfare.

Before entering a new country the Ahom army used to collect information about the preparation and other activities of the enemy. During such campaigns a chain of garrisons called *koth* were built at regular intervals where newspersons on horse were received. The Assamese chronicle called *Kachari Buranji* records such arrangements during Rudra Singha's campaign against the Kachari territory.[23] Gait has stated that in order "to maintain communications and facilitate the transmission supplies, forts were constructed and garrisoned at regular intervals along the line or march".[24] It is to be noted that so far offensive was concerned, the Ahom invaded the territories of the Kacharis, the Jayantiyas only besides taking offensive within their defensive battles against the Mughals. In such cases of emergency when news from the enemy camp or battle fields were to be supplied to the king at the capital or to the controlling officer at the base camp, informations were supplied by the *ghorachowas* who used horse for speedy delivery of news or reports that they collected. Assamese chronicles have not recorded much about the duties of the *ghorachowas;* but from what has been recorded in the chronicle it can be presumed that a section of the *ghorachowas* was also recruited to collect information from the battlefield including secret news about the enemy and supply them to the responsible officers at the helm of affairs. In contemporary Mughal India, however, the news men on foot and on horse were part of both postal and espionage systems.[25] It appears that Gadadhar Singha during whose reign the *ghorachowas* were recorded to have put in work, might have imported this system from the Mughals for quick delivery of information and news.

It needs to be referred here that according to Kautilya, there should be a regular department of secret service in which services of prostitutes, artisans, actors and singers were to be hired.[26] Early Assamese records, however, have not mentioned recruitment of women in the services of the state as spies. But we obtain a very interesting record left by a foreigner, a Dutch soldier, who accompanied Mir Jumla in his campaign against Assam in 1662, about women moving amidst the enemy soldiers.[27] He records that one day their boat sank in the Brahmaputra due to a strong tempest and all his fellow colleagues drowned. There was no body coming forward to help them. "Here were boats enough", he says, "to help us, had custom permitted it; but in like accidents, the Moors help nobody, nor their kindred, or intimate friends. Yet by good help, there was a lusty well-shaped woman, who on seeing five Hollanders upon the point of drowning, rowed upto them, and maugre two men that withstood her, received them into her boat".[28] The description of the woman and the context in which she has been referred to, makes it almost clear that the woman besides being a courtesan, was acting as a spy.

Spies were equally expert in warfare as the regular armies. Chronicles mention how the Assamese spies went to the camp of the Mughal army at night during the wars before the battle of Saraighat of 1671 and poured water on the mouth of the Mughal guns and cannons arranged and fitted on the ramparts facing the Assamese army.[29] The result was that when war started next day, those cannons and guns did not explode and the Assamese army had easy victory.[30] It is further recorded that Lachit Barphukan and Atan Buragohain Dangariya, the two great generals of the Saraighat war, had made their preparations on the basis of the reports supplied by the Assamese spies.[31] The same chronicle records how tactics applied by the Mughal generals failed to deceit the Assamese Generals because they could realize the Mughal tactics well ahead of time.[32] All this resulted in the final victory of the Assamese under Lachit Barphukan and the great Atan Buragohain over the Mughals in the Battle of Saraighat.

From what is recorded in the chronicles it becomes clear that the situation before any war in Assam in the period during the Ahoms, particularly in the 17th century, when the Assamese had to fight the Mughals to the last bit of their strength, was one of emergency, and everywhere spies frequented and carried reports to the king. It is said that nothing, big or small, could escape the notice of the spies who moved unnoticed everywhere. The Assamese proverbs— *Oote marile tipa Gargaon palegoi sipa or Elagiye bhangile katara Gargaon palegoi batara* truly reflect the intensity of spying in such a situation. As pointed rightly by a scholar,

> "Spies peeped with sharp eyes and pinched everybody's mind, and supplied reports containing information about material and moral capacities of the enemy. The killing of so many officers and persons in the post-war

> reconstruction period on the ground of deceit and treason by king Jayadhavaj Singha was decided largely on the basis of reports supplied by the spies. It, however, appears that the Assamese spies failed to do much during Mir Jumla's campaign in comparison to that which they did after a decade during Ram Singha's war at Saraighat. The fact that in spite of the enemies being at their worst counting days for the day of their return, due to shortage of food, problem of drinking water and epidemics, Assamese spies failed to report it to the royalty who had to accept a humiliating treaty by consenting to pay huge indemnities and tribute to the invaders, shows their utter failure."[35]

Discussion about the espionage system in Assam during the Ahoms lead us to arrive at certain conclusions: (a) although the system of espionage was brought to Assam by the Ahoms along with other aspects of their political culture at the time of their coming to the land, it developed gradually and matured in the 17th century when the Ahom power had to contend the mighty Mughal invaders from the west; (b) the rules and regulations governing the espionage system in Assam was no different than what was prescribed in the early scriptures in India and China; and for that matter it was probably not different from those in any other parts of the medieval world; (c) in context of time the efficiency of the system was beyond question, and it was due to this fact that the Ahom power could rule for long six hundred years, although their efficiency declined along with the decline and fall of the Mughal power; and this was affecting the fortune of the state towards the later part of the 18th century when the great Moamariya revolt had shaken the kingdom and finally led to its fall.

NOTES

1. Sun Tzu, a Chinese by birth, was the first writer of military classic (entitled *The Art of War*). His work was translated into English by S.B. Griffith (Oxford, 1963).
2. S.K. Bhuyan, (ed) *Satsari Asam Buranji,* (ed), 2nd edn., Guwahati, 1964. (henceforth SAB).
3. *Ibid.*
4. S.K. Bhuyan, (ed) *Deodhai Asam Buranji,* 2nd edn., Guwahati, 1964, p.73.
5. *Ibid.*
6. *Ibid.*
7. *Ibid.,* p.65.
8. S.K. Bhuyan, (ed) *Purani Asam Buranji,* 2nd edn., Guwahati, 1977, p.79.
9. *Ibid.*
10. SAB, p.48.
11. *Ibid.,* p.50.
12. SAB, p.53.
13. *Ibid.*
14. PAB, p.54; SAB, p.75.
15. *Ibid.*
16. S.K. Bhuyan, (ed), *Asam Buranji by Harakanta Barua,* 2nd edn., 1962, pp.40f (henceforth ABHB).
17. SAB, p.85.
18. *Ibid.,* p.86.
19. *Ibid.*
20. *Ibid.,* p.87.
21. ABHB, p.39.
22. *Ibid.,* p.65.
23. *Ibid.,* pp.65f.
24. S.K. Bhuyan, (ed) *Kachari Buranji,* 2nd edn., Guwahati, 1964, p.94.
25. E.A. Gait, *A History of Assam,* 2nd edn., Guwahati, 1981, p.172.
26. J.N. Sarkar, *Art of War in Medieval India,* New Delhi, 1984, p.176.
27. *Ibid.,* p.177.
28. *A Relation of an Unfortunate Voyage to the Kingdom of Bangala,* London, 1682, (English translation reprint in 1899), p.16.
29. *Ibid.*

30. SAB, p.170.
31. *Ibid.*
32. *Ibid.*, p.97.
33. *Ibid.*

5

Koch-Ahom Tactics of War
The Guerilla Fighting

D. Nath

An open war is conceived between two powers when both are equal or equivalent in both manpower and resources. Indian history is, however, full of records of warfare between unequal powers beginning with the fight of the Purus with Alexander in 323 B.C. Despite multitudes of rules, regulations and ethics developed in ancient times to govern warfare, therefore, 'there is no method that is considered wrong in warfare', particularly when the invader or the conqueror was superior in terms of resources and manpower. This was exactly the case with the Koch-Ahom powers in Assam in the 16th and 17th centuries when they separately or in combination had to fight the sultanate power of Bengal and later on with the great Mughals. This was the circumstance in which the Koch-Ahom powers developed partisan or guerilla warfare in middle ages.

The north-eastern region with its peculiar geographical characters did not allow cavalry forces to be well organized into a formidable unit of army; and this was the reason why the naval and infantry forces were always in the majority. Shihabuddin Talish, the official chronicler of emperor Aurangzeb, who accompanied Mir Jumla to Assam in his campaign of 1662, has aptly recorded as follows:

> Asses, camels and horses are rare and difficult to procure in this country... They are greatly frightened by horses, and if they catch one, they hamstring it. If a single trooper charges a hundred well armed Assamese, they all throw their arms down and run away, and if they cannot *flee*, they put their hands up to be chained as prisoners. But if one of them encounters ten Musalman infantrymen, they fearlessly tries to slay them and succeed in defeating them. (cf E.A. Gait, *A History of Assam,* Reprint to the 2nd revised edn., Guwahati, 1981, p.148).

So, until urgently urged upon, they avoided open warfare, and went to *daga yuddha* or guerilla method of warfare. On such cases the Assamese used to withdraw to the hills evacuating the plains to be occupied by the invaders and in course of time descended therefrom on the advent of the rainy season, blocked all roads and intercepted supplies and surprised the army with sudden and night attacks, and then immediately withdraw. Jagadishnarayan Sarkar has compared the habit of the Assamese with that of the Russians who fought in this manner with the forces of Napolean during what may be called 'Russian Winter' *(Fredom Struggles in Medieval Assam,* Dibrugarh University, 1989, p.146). It was during the invasion of Kamrup by Muhammad-Ibn-Bakhtiyar Khalji in 1206 that the Kamrupee soldiers left all the road and the bridge open to allow the enemy enter freely into the country, but when the invaders got sufficiently inside the territory, the Kamrupee soldiers had broken down the only bridge over the river Begamati and put the invaders in distress. This invasion resulted in complete annihilation of the Bengal army. (*Tabaqat-I-Nasiri* by Minhaj-ud-din Siraj, Vol. I, Reprint, Delhi, 1970, pp.56 ff). The Assamese chronicles mention that Turbaq, the Bengal general, who invaded Assam in the year 1532, was killed by the Assamese army by way of guerilla form of warfare. (*Purani Asam Buranji,* 2nd edn., Guwahati, 1977, p.47).

The Koch-Ahom powers applied the guerilla warfare not for declaration of independence as assumed in modern sense; this was necessary for them primarily to defend their independence against the invading foreign powers. An early Assamese chronicle, the *Kamrupar Buranji,* mentions how king Nilambar (1481-1498) of Kamata, having lost his throne to Ala-ud-din Hussain Shah (1493-1519), the Sultan of Bengal, withdrew to the hills where he built up dykes and made temporary reservoirs of water to release during the rainy season to put the occupants in trouble. Ralph Fitch, the English traveller, who visited Koch Behar, the Koch capital in the year 1585, has recorded as follows:

> "All the country is set with bamboos or canes made sharp at both ends and driven into the earth, and they can let in the water and drawn the ground above knee-deep, so that men nor horses can pass. They poison all the waters if the wars be". (J.H. Ryley, *Early Travels in India,* London, 1899, p.112).

The invasion of Mir Jumla, the general of Aurangzeb, in the year 1661-62, epitomized the guerilla warfares in Assam undertaken both by the Ahoms and the Koches at Koch Behar. Shihabuddin Talish records that the Mughal forces at Gargaon and Mathurapur were put to great straits by the Assamese army during the rainy season by way of night attacks and other kinds of disturbances. He says:

> With the progress of rains, Mir Jumla found it more and more difficult to maintain his outposts and they were withdrawn to Gargaon and Mathurapur. These places alone remained in his hands. All the rest of the country was reoccupied by the Ahoms, and Jayadhvaj Singha returned to Namrup to Solaguri, only four stages

> distant from Gargaon. Even Gargaon and Mathurapur were so closely invested that, if a man ventured to leave the camp, he was certain to be shot. (cf. Gait, *op. cit.*, p.136).

It is further recorded by Talish that being hard-pressed from all directions due to unfavourable natural conditions and pressure exerted by the Ahom soldiers, when Mir Jumla withdrew to Gargaon, the Ahoms who by now were almost prepared to negotiate, withheld the process, and began a series of night attacks upon the Mughals. In the process they burnt down their houses and entered their forts during night and reoccupied almost half of the capital. The Mughal soldiers were now put to great straits and were exposed to constant attacks in both day and night. During this time the only food available to the Mughal soldiers was coarse rice and limes. Salt was sold at Gargaon thirty rupees per seer, and opium at sixteen rupees a *tola.* (cf. *Ibid*). Glanius, the Dutch sailor, who accompanied Mir Jumla to Assam, has in the same strain, recorded that those who escaped into the woods, came at night to the Mughal army, which was in great distress, and attacked them. (*A Relation of An Unfortunate Voyage to the Kingdom of Bangala,* London, 1682, reproduced in 1852, p.20). He further records as follows:

> "We choose in this pleasant country, a proper place to intrench ourselves, and cut down, to prevent suprisals, all the trees around us. We sent scouts everyday to observe the enemy's motions. Those that fell into the hands of our party, were cruelly scourged, and then had their heads cut off..... If these punishments were cruel, those of the enemy were no less, for they made their prisoners languish so long in their torments, as would have moved the most obdurate to pity. Having made *em expire* by their cruel usage, they fastened them, standing bolt upright, to stakes, upon flat bottom boats,

> and sent them thus down the river, either towards the Army, or the Fleet; where they became such a sad spectacle, that they could be upheld without dread or horror". (*Ibid.,* p.21).

While this was the situation during Mir Jumla's invasion of Assam, situation was not different even during the Saraighat war of 1667-1671 when emperor Aurangzeb sent Ram Singha to assert Mughal occupation of Assam. During this war the Assamese army frequently took the method of night attacks and ambushcades and made surprised attacks upon the enemies and then retreating to the hills where their great generals were encamping. Assamese chronicles bear ample testimony to this fact. The Ahoms during this time tried their best to avoid pitched battles with the army of Ram Singha. It is recorded that once Lachit Barphukan, the general of the Ahoms, attacked the Mughal army in the sandy field of Alaboi on being hardpressed by king Chakradhwaj Singha (1663-1669) when about ten thousand of his best foot soldiers were killed (*Asam Buranji* obtained from the family of Sukumar Mahanta, 2nd edn., Guwahati, 1964, p.97). This sad experience made Lachit and his men to avoid frontal battle with the Mughals as far as possible in the subsequent times. As a part of their defensive programme the Ahoms, therefore, supplemented their open engagements with harassing guerilla tactics, which sorely tried the patience of the invaders. "Swooping unawares on the latter from secret hide-outs in jungles and on hill tops or from their forts at mid-nights, the guerillas would invest the Mughals and if repulsed, hurriedly retreat. On the north bank Premier Atan Buragohain organized from his base at Lathiya hill a harassing campaign with his daring commandos or eaves dropping spies who sneaked into the Mughal camp at night after the commanders had drugged themselves to sleep by smoking *bhang* and *dhatura* through pipes of the *hookas* (hubble-bubble) and purloined treasure, money bags and even the silver *hookahs*. Such activities resembled 'hit and run' tactics on modern guerillas. The Rajput general condemned such night activities as cowardly and dishonourable thieve's affairs, which lowered the dignity of warfare. But the Assamese justified these by saying that lions fought only during the night". (cf. J.N. Sarkar, *Freedom Struggle in Medieval Assam,* op. cit., p.147).

Assamese chronicles mention that not only with the Mughals or the Sultans of Bengal that the Assamese fought guerilla warfare, but they also practiced the same while fighting with some of the north-eastern tribes. An example of this has been found in the Assamese chronicle entitled *Deadhai Asam Buranji* which has mentioned that the Kacharis fought with the Ahoms with guerilla tactics when king Pratap Singha invaded their territory (p.57). This shows that the practice of guerilla tactics of warfare was long prevalent in the north east among the ethnic inhabitants; and they used to practice it as and when they felt it necessary to defend their independence and protect their community.

From the above, it can be safely concluded that the geographical and topographical conditions of the entire north eastern region had formed the background for the development of the guerilla tactics of warfare adopted by its rulers in the middle ages as was practiced by its early rulers. Lack of a strong cavalry due mainly to its geographical condition encouraged the people to adopt guerilla systems against their enemies when they are found to be too strong to be defeated. This was why the Sultans of Bengal, and particularly the Mughals had always to face this form of warfare in Assam and elsewhere in this part of the country. Technological inferiority of the tribal states of the north eastern states in comparison to those of the Mughals and in the field of manpower and resources was another best reason to this historical development. The guerilla tactics were, however, not always determining the results of any contest. In most cases this was a method of slowing down the progress of the enemies or discouraging their advance. All evidences, however, point to the popularity of this form of warfare in this part of the country since long past as it was in many parts of the east and south east Asian countries.

6

War Mechanisms

The Defence and Warfare of the Adis

Tai Nyori

During the long period of their movements and settlements at different places, the Adis faced not only physical hardship but also engaged themselves in hostilities among themselves as well as against their outside enemies. Although the different groups of the Adis are related to each other, the connection between them was very loose in the past due to the lack of common leadership, communication and the remoteness of villages from one another. Besides, each village acted independently in accordance with the dictate of its Kebang and thus there was no common authority of the tribe to enforce common discipline to its different groups. As a result, there were numerous inter-clan and inter-group feuds in the society, which embittered their relations and compelled them to remain prepared for warfare. They also faced external enemies, occasionally from the Tibetans and Membas in the North and from the Mishmis in the East. The British hostility towards the tribe from south was the greatest problem of their defence in the late nineteenth and early twentieth centuries. So the Adis had to organize a common resistance against the British till 1912, in which year they ultimately submitted to the English.

Feuds and their Causes

Political

Feuds between clans and villages arose mainly for violating the traditional boundary of one clan or village by another. In the past, the Adi villages were founded on clan basis. Later on, when the boundary of a village sought to be extended, it came into clash with other villages.

Although some of them had feuds amongst themselves, the Adis in general united against their common enemies. Later on, they resisted every effort of the Britishers to penetrate their territory and they also resented the British interference in their sphere of influence in the foothill areas which ultimately led to the hostility with the British authorities from 1848 to 1912.

Social

Earlier days, when a village contained a single clan, its boys and girls who could not marry among themselves, had to seek their life-partners from other clans of other villages. During those days of hostility, normally such engagements for marriages was not easy. As a result, if a girl had an understanding with a boy of the other village, she could elope (*nyime-jugnam*) with him. But sometimes such elopement was not possible and in such case, the boy kidnapped the girl (*nyime-senam*). Such kidnapping of girls of one clan by a boy of another clan (who had a bad term with the former) for marriage was one of the causes of the feuds and fightings. Capturing of men or women for slaves (*nyime-lanam*) also led to fighting between two clans or villages. Sometimes lifting of cattles (*sole-lanam*) of one clan by another led to feuds.

Murder of or infliction of bodily injuries on a person belonged to other clan, which was not adequately compensated often led to clan feuds in the past and the aggrieved party retaliated by killing a person or inflicting injury on the body of the offender or one of the members of his clan.

Sometimes the activities of the mischievous persons in the society were responsible for some feuds and fightings among the tribes. Thus, the activities of Pasu Chuchik of Karko and Kepsi Simat of Sitang were the immediate causes of two fightings amongst the Adis. The activities of Kepsi Simat of the Sitang village of the Minyongs led to a war amongst the Padams, Minyongs, Panggis, etc. which lasted for many years. Thus, Pasu Chuchik was responsible for the Shimong-Tangam War and Kepsi Simat was for the Padam-Panggi and Minyong War.

Economic

In the early days, for the possession of the good and fertile land the Adis fought against their neighbours and different clans. Trespassing into the territory of another village for the purpose of trade without paying the middle man's fees also led to feuds. For collection of booty and slaves some Adis in the past, used to carry out raids on their neighbouring communities.

Besides political, there were also economic grievances that led to the hostilities between the Adis and the English. Before the British rule, the Adis used to get some conciliatory offerings (*posa*) and trading facilities from the Miris and Beheahs who lived in the Adi foothills. But with the policy and protection of the British authorities, those people moved away from the control of the Adis and refused payment of offerings. This situation ultimately led to the long-drawn hostilities between the Adis and the English.

Adi Weapons or War Implements

The traditional weapons of the Adis consisted of swords, *daos*, knives, bows and arrows and spears. The sword, which is called by the Adis as *yoksa* is about three to four feet long, straight and one-edged. Its handle is plainted with cane strips and is carried in wooden or bamboo sheath. A kind of sword made of strong bamboo called *chokpe* is also used.

The *dao* is a handy weapon, used for all domestic works as well as for hunting and fighting. One type of *dao* is about two feet long with a handle, straight and pointed and the other type is broad and short.

The Adi knife (*yokshik*) is short, about a half-feet long, pointed, one-side edged with a thin blade. Its handle is made of wood or bamboo, plainted with strips of cane and iron tube and is carried in a case by a sling. Their knives are useful for self-defence.

Bows are made of bamboo and are of various sizes. Usually in warfare and in hunting bows of big size are used and it is generally about four feet long. Its string is made of cane or fibre of a creeper called *ogik*. Arrows are of three types—iron-tipped arrow (called *omo* by Galos), arrow without iron-tip (*upuk* or *pukjir*) and *nagger* (ordinary arrow). Arrows are made of bamboo. It is shaven and have one end pointed and hardened over the fire. A concave notch at the butt end of the arrow is made for filling it on the bowstring. This end is splitted a little to feather it with strips of thinca cane leaves. These leaves are inserted into that splitted and diagonally opposite to one another. In order to keep the feather and the concave notch end in position, this portion of the arrow end is again tied. The ordinary (*nagger*) arrow is not feathered with cane-leaves but at the butt end a little portion is shaven out as its feather. Iron-head is inserted to the arrow head and is tied round with a fine fibre string. Such arrow with iron-head is called *mora* by the Galo Adis. An arrow is poisoned by plastering poison over the cane or fibre tied round the place of insertion of the arrow-head. Such poisoned arrow is called *mopum* by the Galo Adis.

This weapon retains its deadly character for a considerable period. When an animal is hit with this arrow, its poison acts on its blood and its affect is almost immediate and in most cases it leads to its death. About its action A. Hamilton says, "The action of the poison, too, is very rapid—sometimes less than one hour, and rarely more than six hours. Violent convulsions are set up, and tetanus supervenes".

Arrows are kept in quiver or bamboo tube of which one end is open and this open end is provided with a lid or cover. About 15 to 20 arrows can be kept in a quiver. Sometimes a *tarek* (a sort of palm ring) is used by the arrow-shooter in his palm to pull the bow string with force. Such Adi bows and arrows can hit an object at about a distance of one hundred yards. This is the only-range weapon of the tribe.

Their spear, called *nebu* is about four to five feet long and is consisted of three parts—the head, the shaft and the butt. The Adis use the spear as both defensive and offensive weapon. They do not throw this weapon, they thrust their enemies with this. They learned the use of gun during the British rule.

In fighting the Adis used the shield (*sotam*) made of mithun hide, and stitched with a frame and handle in the middle, rectangular in shape, and about three by two feet (.914m×.6096m) in size. Some shields are also made of bamboo, or cane strips inter-laced. It is held by the left hand while the sword or *dao* in the right hand. The right hand from wrist to the elbow is covered by a covering made of dried mithun hide known as *Taka Lakbu*. A waist coat called *taker* made of the thick mithun skin was worn to protect the chest and back against attack of arrows and swords.

Of the several types of helmets, called *rai-bolup* used to protect the head, one is made of cane coiled fastened with cane strings. Cane strips are fixed on the upper side of the helmet to strengthen it. Some of these are decorated with wild boar tusks. Another type, round in shape but without projection, is made of cane strip woven. It is decorated in front with two boar tusks placed crosswise, while the top is occasionally decorated with bear-skin or a taft of the Tibetan yak-hair. They are fastened by slings of cane or leather. In the warfare they also wore war-coats made of coarse cotton and wool.

The Role of the Tribal Council (*The Kebang)*

As soon as information is received about the impending attack on a village, or whenever enemy makes any advance towards a village, the villagers immediately convene an emergency meeting of *Kebang*. The *Kebang* makes careful assessment on all the defensive measures like the construction of stone chutes, stockades, making and fixing of panjis, etc. If necessary women and children are also evacuated to safer places. Information is also sent to allied or friendly villages for help. Besides, they prepare for action and train all the able-bodied men, particularly young men of the village for attacking on the enemy's flank. By this time the village *Mosup* plays the vital role for the defence of the village, the *Mosup Kas* (boys of the dormitory) have to keep watch on the village and have to take active part for the attack on the enemies.

Defence of the Village or Defensive Organization

In olden time the Adi villages were built on the hill spurs with only one approach to each village protected by stockades and stone chutes. Access to a village, other than the usual path was extremely difficult as the other sides of the hill involved very steep climb where the enemy could be ambushed easily. The village stood on an open ground but immediately behind it was a patch of forest for safe retreat, in case of danger.

A little away from the village were constructed stonewalls and stockades *rumgo* by putting stones, big logs and wooden posts. Permanent trees were also planted on either side. During the British period, in order to protect themselves from guns, plantains and big trees were felled and their trunks were used for re-inforcing the stone walls. Outside the walls trees were also felled and were thrown in disorderly way all over the foot tracks leading to the stockade and the village to impede the advance of the attackers. Sometimes ditches were also dug around the village. The length and height of the stockades depended on the situation.

The stone-chutes, called *linking,* built of strong bamboo poles arranged horizontally to serve as a platform over which were piled up a large number of boulders, were placed on the hill-slopes and above the approach to a village. One end of the platform rested on the ground and the other end was suspended by bamboo or cane ropes which could easily be cut to release the mass of boulders down the hill side on the advancing enemy. The chutes were kept concealed and were placed in such a way that the enemy while advancing often unknowingly released the ropes. All possible approaches to the villages were thus protected with stone chutes. During the Abor War of 1911-12, the 'Ledum Column' of the expeditionary force had to face a number of such chutes placed by the Adis at Dosing. Col. Shakespear writes, "The advance guard came under a heavy fire of arrows and a few musket shots, while ten rock shoots, were let down above the left flank, sweeping two British Officers, and several men down the hill side."

As defensive measure a number of bows and arrows (which is called *koma* by the Adis) were fixed near the path followed by the enemy. Poisoned arrows fixed on bows were placed ties by means of bamboo or cane rope, the end of which were so laced in the foot-track that a slight touch would immediately release the arrows and hit the desired object. Sometimes these were fixed in hundreds at different angles.

The panji, called *oor* by the Adis, were made from pieces of bamboo, sharpended like spikes, and their points hardened over fire, and sometimes these points were smeared with poison. These were stuck into ground firmly in an inclined position, and concealed skilfully on the bushes or path leading to a village. The unobservant, bare-footed or soft-booted enemies got hurt from these spikes. The panjis had been effectively used against the British expeditionary forces.

Offensive Organization

In case of a retaliatory attack, the initiative for organizing of the clan or village and launching the attack was formally taken by the kinsmen of those who suffered or died at the hands of the enemies. In order to maintain the solidarity of the clan, the loss of men had to be avenged and preparations were made by collecting poison for arrow heads, gathering and sharpening of weapons, making war-helmets, waist-coats, shields, etc. Women of the village wove rough cotton and woollen coats for their male members. Before the raid was launched, their priests conducted a divination with the help of eggs or chicken liver if it would be a successful encounter. Before actually starting the attack, certain ceremonies like *Erap-Tenam, Kame-Panam,* etc. were also performed.

Attackers generally set out for their destination with all their weapons and provisions on dark nights. The leadership was usually taken by those who were known for their fighting quality, hunting skills and doing such arduous jobs. They made surprise attack on the enemy village, killing whoever they found and setting fire to the houses. Then they took away cattle of the enemies and looted beads, bowls, clothes and other valuable articles, captured men and women and returned to their village. The attack was so surprise at the dead of night that the enemy village had no opportunity to organize a resistance against it. If the enemy village by chance received the news of impending raid, the raiders were often tricked and were attacked within the stockade and thus the raiders themselves suffered loss in the encounter. This type of raid on a village by an enemy is called *dolu paanamn* in the Adi. Sometimes raiders attacked the enemies at the common cultivated sites at day time. This type of raid of the village fields is called *rikme-palennam*. Very often raiders unaware of the panjis ran over them and get hurt in their bare feet rendering them helpless. The enemy would then come out of the stockade and fell upon the attackers, killing them and driving others out of the village boundary. This type of battle was known as *migang-mimag* in the Adi. Sometimes, the stone chutes released the mass of boulders crashing down the hillside, hampered the enemy's advance to the village. This method is called the *linking-mimang.*

In another type of attack, the attackers moved in two batches with their weapons and enough food for a few days, and concealed themselves on the path frequented by their enemies, one batch in the upper side, the other in the lower side. When the enemy approached, the batch in the upper side allowed them to proceed, but when they came close to other batch it suddenly fell on them. As enemy started to run back, they were confronted by the other batch. This method of the battle by ambushing is called *magbi* by the Adis. The patrolling or spying the enemy area is known as *magro-ronam.*

Returning from the raid, all the captives of the raid were kept in stocks, which are called *lepa* by the Adis, to ensure that they did not run away and the booty was distributed among the participants. As the spilling of human blood or killing of a man is considered unusual, the killer observed some taboos for a few days after returning from the raid and he performed certain rites in his village.

The Treaty or Agreement *(Dapo)*

Whenever a party desired the cessation of hostility, it engaged a go-between or sent a message to the other party seeking treaty. It was the custom of the Shimong Adis that when one of the warring groups wanted peace they placed broken pieces of an arrow and a broken sword at a place, which the opposite party was likely to frequent. If the opposite party satisfied with this signal, it sent a messenger to convey the acceptance and agreed to meet at the boundary of the village or at any place, mid-way between the two villages or in a third neutral village. If both the parties agreed, after the agreement they arranged a common feast by offering mithuns, pigs and *apong.* Both the parties together with the third village (if it was the venue) joined the feast. To mark the day they engraved signs on the trunks of the trees or erected peace stones as in the case of Boris, Bokars, Ramos and Pailibos.

7

War Weapons in Medieval Assam

Punyadhar Gogoi

Weapons play prominent role in expansion of empire and help to consolidate its authority over the enemies. The medieval period was a period of constant warfare among the political powers within Assam. The various external invasions also threatened the sovereignty of Assam. To repulse internal and external threatening the Ahom king used weapons of various kinds. In this chapter an attempt has been made to write about different types of weapons during the medieval period of Assam.

The weapon of the Ahom period can be divided into two categories: defensive and offensive.

The defensive weapons were of various types. These included a cap (*tupi*) for the head; a thick skin-made jacket (*gati*) for the trunk; two kinds of revolving shields—one was small, called *dhal* and other was bigger known as *baru* made of buffalo, rhino and deer skins. All these were used for the general protection of the body. But these accessories did not cover the whole body for which another kind of shield known as *phar* was used to cover the entire body.[1] Towards the close quarter of the Ahom rule an improved type of defensive dress was introduced by Prime Minister Purnananda Buragohain. These dresses were coats, pants (*kun min kunkha*) and girdle (*komar bandha*) and certain other equipments, e.g. *deomani, dambaru* (small drum), *dhal* and *thenga* (heavy stick).[2]

The offensive weapons were of various types. In the initial periods, the Ahom soldiers, used bows and arrows, spears (*barchah*), swords, *baru* (big shield), flat spear (*yathi*), dagger (*da*) and *hengdang*. *Hengdang* was a special kind of sword and only selected ones like commander and sub-commander used it. Several types of daggers were in use in the battlegrounds. Some had long handle and some had short handle. Daggers were known by different names such as *mit da*, *nakoi da*, *kopi da* and *mesi da*. Axe (*kuthar*) was also used as weapons.[3] Tallish mentions that the Assamese used swords, lances, bows and arrows. The bows were of bamboo and the arrows were pointed with iron.[4] Bows and arrows were more effective. Bows had different types. Apart from the general types of bows; there were special kinds of bows used by the Assamese soldiers. These were *bardhenu, chutiadhenu, karpai dhenu*. As the name indicates, the *chutiadhenu* was acquired by the Ahom from the Chutias. The *bardhenu* was acquired from the Bhuyans.[5]

The arrows were of different shapes and pointed with iron. Some arrows were poisoned in the tip. The sharpest arrow was the *Singimuri Kar*.[6]

Simultaneously with the above mentioned weapons, they began to use the firearms from the time of Suhungmung. Firearms were far more effective as weapons and helped the Ahom to subjugate the other people in Assam. The different types of firearms were cannons and matchlocks. The exact date of introduction of firearms in Assam is not known. Whether they brought this improved type of weapon to Assam is also definitely not known. The Tai, however, used matchlocks since the early time.[7] J.B. Travener mentions, "it is believed that it is the same people who in ancient time first discovered gun and gunpowder, which passed from Assam to Pegu and from Pegu to China. This is the reason why the discovery is generally ascribed to the Chinese."[8] Wade also has written it is said and written in other chronicles that firearms were made in Assam.[9] Traditions pushes about the use of firearms as far back as the reign of Sudangpha (1397-1407). According to the Ahom Buranji the Assamese used firearms during the invasion of Turbak in 1532.[10] John P. Wade also dates the manufacture of firearms in Assam after Turbak's invasion.[11] According to Gait, "the use of firearms by the Ahom dates from the close of this war (Turbak's invasion)."[12] Hitewar Barbarua in his *Ahomar Din* mentions that the Ahom learnt the use of cannon after the defeat of the Chutias by Ahom king Suhungmung. This king acquired a particular type of cannon called *Mithaholong top* from the Chutias and introduced it in Ahom territories.[13] This indicates the Chutias acquired the techonology of making gunpowder and cannon. From the outcome of battle between the Chutias and Ahom, it may also be guessed that the Ahom might have used cannon in the battle. Otherwise it was impossible to fight with the Chutias using less effective bows and arrows. The process of manufacture of heavy cannon started under Suhungmung and reached its apex under Rudra Singha both in numbers and in size.[14]

While writing about the general condition of the people of Assam, Shihabuddin Talish mentions "they cast excellent matchlocks and *bachadar* artillery, and show great skill in this craft. They make first-rate gunpowder, of which they procure materials from the Imperial dominion.......The weapons of war are matchlocks, cannon...."[15] A picture about the manufacture of firearm can be had from the amount of ammunitions taken by Mir Jumla. After the defeat of the Assamese, Mir Jumla seized 370 mds of gunpowder, 1960 chests of powder each weighing about 2 or 2½ mds. The Mughal captured guns of which there was a large iron gun. The cannon ball of the gun was of 3 mds weight. Besides they took away 343 Jumur, 1200 Ramchangi matchlocks, 6570 Pathorkolai and 1828 iron shields. About saltpetre, sulphur and lead there was as measure. Captain Welsh took away 4000 *upor top* from Assam.[16]

The light artillery (*hillai* or *muskets*) of the Ahom period were, namely of eleven types: (i) *Gathia* (ii) *Jambur Hillai* (iii) *Pohulorgi* (iv) *Ramchangi* (v) *Saru Hatnalia* (vi) *Kamayan* (vii) *Jamur* (viii) *Kachai* (ix) *Tow* (x) *Khoka Hillai* (xi) *Bachadari.*

Among the artillery the principal type numbered five (i) *Biagom* (ii) *Hatimuria* (iii) *Baghura* (iv) *Tubuki* (v) *Mithalolong.*[17] Some other varieties of cannon were *Dumukhiya, Tinichari mukhia, Juriamara, Saraimara, Singha mukhia, Lajuathaka.*[18]

All these cannons were manufactured in certain smithy and were made of iron and brass.[19] These smithies were:

Smithy	*Matchlocks*	*Produced in month*
1	Saru Hatnalia Hillai	4 pieces
1	Ramchangi	2 pieces
1	Pohulongi	2 pieces
1	Gathia Jambur	1 piece
1	Mitha Holong Top	1 piece
2	Bagmora	1 piece
4	Tubuki Bartop	1 piece
20	Hatimuria Bartop	1 piece
50	Biagom	1 piece

Apart from the firearms produced in Assam, the Assamese kings brought foreign made matchlocks. Some of the cannons were captured during battles. During the invasion of 1532 AD, the Assamese acquired several cannons from the Muslims. The Assamese soldiers captured some iron and brass cannons in 1627 AD. In 1658 AD, [20] *Kamayun Hillai* and 300 *Tubuki Hillai* were captured. King Rudra Singha (1696-1714) captured 700 matchlocks from the Bongalhat market. These happened in the later part of their rule.[21] Improved type of guns and pistols were also manufactured in the close quarter of their rule.[22]

The Assamese blacksmiths manufactured matchlocks and cannons. One such cannon was known as *Ripunjoy* made by Gandhela Garia of North Guwahati in 1693 on the order of Gargaya Handiqoi Borphukan. Banamali Saikia was another expert in making cannon. He was an inhabitant of Teok.[23] Silakuti Khanikars manufactured cannon balls. Hard stones were used to produce the cannon balls. Cannon balls were produced at Bhajani at Sibsagar.[24]

The Ahoms manufactured first-rate gunpowder. There was a department to look after the activities of workers engaged in production of firearms. The responsible officers were known as *Khargharia Phukan.* A store of gunpowder was built at Kharghuli in Guwahati.[25] Saltpetre is known as *Jabakhar* in Assamese. A *Khel* controlled by Jakhariya Barua produced *Jakhar*. Hiteswar Borborua mentions an indigenous process of manufacturing saltpetre. According to him saltpetre was produced from cow urine. Cows were tied constantly for six months in the same cowshed and compelled them to discharge their urine. After six months cows were brought out from the shed. The cowshed was kept close for a year. Then a white particle came out, from which the saltpetre was manufactured.[26] The technology of manufacturing of saltpetre is not known.

Gunpowder was produced in royal factories under two officers known as Khargharia Phukan and Khargharia Barua. Both were in charge of the *Khel* that produced gunpowder.[27]

Gunnery and cannonry were not open to all. It was restricted to professional known as *Hillaidharias.* King Khora Raja (1552-1603) created another special unit of foot musketeers consisting of princes (*Konwars*). There were two divisions according to age: (i) the older, the Bajua Hillaidhari konwars under Hillaidhari Phukan, and (ii) the younger, Bhitrual Hillaidhari-konwar. A third unit was specially formed with the Nara Hillaidharis.[28]

Coming to the Koch kingdom, the most important offensive weapons were guns and cannons. The first Koch king Biswa Singha appointed his son Mecha in charge of guns and cannons. Muskets, swords, sepals, and bamboo bows resembling those of the Ahoms were also in use. Shihabuddin Talish writes that the Koch armies used matchlocks and arrows with poisonous head.[29]

Buranjis were silent about the devices how the big cannons were transported during the time of battles to the spot. As there was no carriage or vehicles during the Ahom period to carry the ammunition, it can be guessed that people on the shoulders carried all these. Contemporary Mughals transported the cannons by several elephants and cattle.[30]

NOTES

1. H.K. Barpujari, (ed), *The Comprehensive History of Assam,* Vol. III, Guwahati, 1994, p.72.
2. S.K. Bhuyan, (ed) *Satsari Asam Buranji,* 3rd edition, Guwahati, 1999, p.132.
3. L. Gogoi, *Tai-Sanskritik Ruprekha*, Kolkata, 1985, p.264.
4. B.C. Handique, *Puroni Asomar Silpa,* Guwahati, 1959, p.23.
5. Gogoi, *op.cit.*
6. *Ibid.*
7. *Ibid.*
8. Handique, *op. cit.*

9. J.P. Wade, *An Account of Assam,* (ed) by Benudhar Sarma, Sibsagar, 1927, p.96.
10. Barpujari, *op. cit.*, p.73.
11. Wade, *op. cit.*
12. E.A. Gait, *A History of Assam,* Kolkata, 1967, p.67.
13. H. Barbarua, *Ahomar Din,* Guwahati, 1997, p.450.
14. *Ibid.*
15. Gait, *op. cit.,* p.151; Handique, *op.cit.*, pp.25-26.
16. Barpujari, *op. cit.,* p.74.
17. *Ibid.,* p.73.
18. *Ibid.*
19. Barbarua, *op. cit.*
20. *Ibid.*, p.452.
21. S.K. Bhuyan, (ed); *Tung Khungia Buranji,* Guwahati, 1968, p.131.
22. Handique, *op. cit.*
23. Gogoi, *op. cit.*, p.264.
24. *Ibid.*
25. *Ibid.*
26. Barbarua, op. cit., p.473.
27. *Ibid.*, p.553.
28. Barpujari, *op. cit.*, p.74; Gogoi, *op. cit.*, p.285.
29. D. Nath, *History of the Koch Kingdom,* 1515-1615, Delhi, 1989, p.120.
30. S.R. Sharma, *Mughal Empire in India,* Agra, p.172.

8

Defence Strategy of Later-Medieval Assam

P.C. Sarma

To a Mughal or any other westerner of late-medieval India, soldier meant a paid person having requisite training in fighting with the enemy. He would carry arms and accoutrements fit not only for attack or counter attack, but also for defending his own body and soul. Probably, this definition cannot be applied to most of the warriors of late-medieval Assam.

So is the case with defensive planning. The fortresses of any other part of late-medieval India were provided with high, massive masonry walls superimposed with battlements and slits for fitting cannons. In the battlefield, the soldier faces the enemy directly with arms and artillery in a spirit of do or die. Thus, usually more the military power, more chances of victory. This was not the case with Assam.

The warfares of Assam possessed a different scenario from many considerations. Heavy rainfall, swampy terrain, waterlogged areas, steep hills, dense forests, damp climate, pestilential air etc. make military affairs here entirely different.

When the infantry of the entire country widely used gun-powder including swords and shields, bows and arrows remained dominant in Assam.[1] When the soldiers of the rest part of Indian subcontinent wore a tight dress often with armour fit for battle-field, the soldiers here wore a dress which did not differ much from a common man save for a *Tangali* (waist girdle made of cloth). There was no hard and fast regular training for the soldiers in general; most of them were in fact commoners known as Pikes engaged in cultivation: However, this does not meant that all of them were ignorant in using swords and artillery, rather there were troops who, though limited were trained in using all such equipments. When called upon, they faced the enemy more with his innate courage and patriotic zeal than with fixed military norms. Usually, they were not paid a salary but may enjoy revenue free land for farming. Thus, compared to the contemporary West, this region followed an entirely different discipline in battles.

The planners of battle strategy in Assam always maintained a balanced relation with the nature and took full advantage of what nature offered to them in organizing the battle-field.[2] This fact can be best explained by a remark given by Ralph Fitch, the first ever European who visited India during the reign of the Mughal Badshah Jahangir. Visiting Koch Bihar before going to Hughli for his onward journey to the "Spices Inland", i.e., Southeast Asian archipelago, he commented, "All the country is set with bamboos or canes made sharps at both ends and driven into the earth and they can let in the water and drown the ground above knee deep so that man nor horses can pass."[3]

The chronicler accounts of the Ahoms, Kacharis, Jaintias etc. are replete with information at the construction of fortresses, ramparts etc. which speak of a different type of battle strategy that appear to be indispensable in those days for waging battles in this region. Though detail accounts are lacking, it is possible that use of guns and cannons were initially less popular here due to their difficulty in manoeuvre because of undulated topography and probably, muddy and sandy nature of soil. But the late medieval invaders from the west gave more importance to cannons and muskets often loaded on gunboats. This naturally needed for the local army elaborate cover from artillery in the form of ramparts and barrages.

The chronicles of Assam have used two very often in connection with battles, namely "*Koth*" and "*Gadh*" which mean a fortress and a rampart respectively. But, in both the cases they were built by raising earth only. The "*Koth*" generally contained a number of inside divisions as also buildings made of impermanent materials obviously to accommodate soldiers according to rank and file. The ramparts were also generally made of earth, which often continued for several kilometres and may stretch across an open area, along a river, from the river to a hill or in between two hills, the top of which was also generally utilized as a road for movement of army including cavalry. Sometimes, the word '*Buruz*' is also used which invariably indicates a high rampart having bastions and also serve as an embankment beside a river or a water body.

The '*Koth*s' and '*Gadh*' built by the Ahom rulers were sometimes very high (20 to 25 metres) and massive (up to 15 metres in width at top) but they, used only earth to raise them. But a tradition from earlier times seems to have prevailed and followed by the Kacharis in which a brick rampart of moderate size (say 3 metres wide and 2.5 metres high) was built over with a huge earthen rampart of trapezoidal section is raised. The reason behind this system may be to ensure the survival of the rampart against water percolation as also to protect them from burrowing animals, which very often menaced the earthen ramparts in this region. Such ramparts are seen at Numaligarh, Guwahati, Maibang, Barpathar etc. It is interesting to note that the Ahoms devised different types of 'Gadhs' to restrain movement of the enemy, a few of which are described below.

Ramparts Flanked by Moats

This type of earthen 'Gadh' was usually built in-between the river Brahmaputra and a hill beyond the bank, which may extend several tens of kilometres in length. Both sides of such ramparts are provided with wide and deep moats, which are linked to the river with needed gradient to ensure perennial flow of water. The beds of such moats are made unaffordable with iron and bamboo spikes. The tops of such ramparts are generally flat and were used for army movement. The top width in some of them is widened at regular intervals in semi-circular projection and provided with brick or boulder walls to accommodate artillery.

Hilltop Ramparts

These types of ramparts were laid along the sides of steep hills having strategic importance. Generally top of the ridge was levelled in the form of a road by erecting brick walls on either side and the pits and depressions on the alignment were filled up with spoil-earth, stones and rubbles. Stone blocks and heavy blocks of segmented trunks of trees of considerable weight were kept on these ramparts. When the enemy tried to scale the hill slope, the stones and tree-trunks were allowed to roll down causing havoc to the enemy.[4]

Kataha Gadh

This type of rampart is basically earthen rampart of moderate size. But on both sides, a special type of bamboo known as *Kataha* having thick thorny branches coming out of every knot is planted so that, when grown fully, the branches entwine themselves to create an impenetrable barricade. Thus, when the defenders conveniently used the top of such ramparts for manoeuvring their arms and armies, the enemy failed not only to penetrate it but also to shoot arrows, spears and even cannon balls across them.[5]

Tree Trunk Barricades

When the enemy attack was eminent, such a type of not very long '*Gadh*' was erected in strategic points. In such constructions, tree trunks of moderate girth were erected in rows, one attached to the other, and several parallel lines of this sort were built without a pace in-between them. Such a barricade was further faced with layers of bamboo palisades to ensure toughness, so that enemy shots, whether it is an arrow or a cannon ball, cannot penetrate.[6]

Bali Gadh

This rampart is made of river sands. Two rows of full bamboo palisades are thrown parallely with several cubits of space in between them and the space is filled up with river sands.[7] Being done particularly in winter season on sandy riverbanks along which the navel of the enemy had passed, they could build with conspicuous speed and used fruitfully. In fact, such ramparts were used during the famous Battle of Saraighat to defend the city of Guwahati which proved invincible against heavy artillery attack of the Mughal gunboats.

Pachala-Gadh

Pachala in Assamese means the trunk of a banana tree. This '*Gadh*' or rampart was built using banana trees. This tree grows in abundance everywhere in this region. To build this type of '*Gadh*', two rows of solid bamboos were erected parallel to each other with a gap of several cubits in-between and the same is filled high with banana trunks. Records show, very lengthy ramparts of this type were built which could resist all weapons including cannon balls.[8]

Pani Gadh or Water Barrage

Though toughest of all the '*Gadhs*' the planners of the battlefields of Assam utilized water as a means of defence for retaliating enemy charges. Stout Sal post are erected on both the banks of river avoiding the shallow portion of the banks and the posts across are joined like the rope of a suspension bridge by very lengthy and stout *Raidongia Bet* (a kind of cane more than hundred metres in length and stronger than the biggest jute or coconut ropes). Then floating timber platforms are constructed and kept in position against current by these arrangements over which towers are made for defending soldiers. As the impact of the high current of rivers like that of the Brahmaputra can be imagined, such floating barracks to arrest the upward movement of the enemy boats indicate skill of the builders.[9] It is said that the Mughals found it a tough time to overcome such barrages put up at strategic points across the Brahmaputra.

Boka Gadh

In this type a strategic area such as lying in the midst of two precipitous hills which serves as a pass—is taken and the original earth from the passage is removed to a reasonable depth by excavation. Then it is filled up with *Kumar-màti* (potter's soil), which is too sticky and slippery. Sharp wooden and bamboo spikes are planted below the surface of this filling which obstruct movement of both infantry and cavalry.[10]

Kebora Gadh

A type of earthen rampart was constructed in a zigzag alignment probably to confuse the approaching forces of the enemy. They are not very high and hardly 3 to 4 metres above ground level. It is possible that such ramparts were done intervening a length of a lengthy rampart or in a flat terrain covered with thicket. Two of such types are seen near Jamuguri in Nagoan and Chapakhowa in Dibrugarh districts of Assam.

Mazes and Labyrinths

Though not properly described in any chronicle, huge mazes were probably constructed in selective places of Assam, both in battlefields as well as around fortresses to distract the enemies. However, none of these constructions could stand to the test of time due to a number of causes such as, heavy rain, flood-waters, change of river courses, heavy growth of vegetation, and also to some extent due to human agencies who destroyed them to clear land for agriculture and pisciculture. A good number of such mazes of different geometric shapes, such as square, rectangular, round, apsidal, triangular etc. can be seen inscribed on rocks at Biswanath, Bhomoraguri, Dhalpur, etc.

Harassing the enemy applying different tactics was a normal method of battle in Assam. Being dressed with heavy armours and acoutrements, and being accustomed in carrying heavy artillery, the Mughals faced a lot of trouble in their army manoeuvre in this region. The local soldiers not only harassed them with skirmishes and distracted them very often, but also isolated into small groups by inundating the battlefields.

NOTES

1. "The use of firearms by the Ahoms dates from the close of this war (i.e. AD 1532). Up to this time their weapons had consisted of swords, spears, and bows and arrows". *A History of Assam;* Gait, E. Thacker Spink & Co., Calcutta, AD, 1967, p.94.
2. Gait has inserted the following passage from the Mughal historian Shihabuddhin Talish's records on the occupation of the Ahom Capital of Garhgaon in AD 1662-63 by the Mughal general Mir Jumlah: "A similar case had never happened before in the history of Delhi. There were 12000 horses and numerous infantry locked in for six months, prevented by the rains from continuing operations. Yet screcely attacked by enemies that surrounded them". *A History of Assam;* p. 139.
3. *Ralph Fitch,* Ryley. J. Horton, published by T. Fisher Unwin, London, 1899, pp. 111-112.
4. *Satsari Asom Buranji;* Edt. Bhuyan S.K.; Guwahati University Publication, AD 1974, pp. 14, 599.
5. *Ibid.,* pp. 132-33.
6. *Tai Sanskritik Ruprekha;* Gogoi Lila, Calcutta, AD, 1971, p. 132.
7. *Ibid.,* pp. 132-33.
8. *Satsari Asom Buranji;* 1974, p.13.
9. King Udayaditya under whose regime the famous battle of Saraighat caused Bamgadhs (i.e. rampart in shallow water) and Panigadh (i.e.Water rampart) to be built at Guwahati. It is recorded that the king proclaimed rules to the following in fixing Sal posts in shallow waters as also bridging deep water by using the tough *Raidang* cane which was to be kept in positions against current by the help of iron strips and stone blocks using machines.
10. "They make their forts of mud", *A History of Assam,* Gait, E.P. 132. Quoting the Mughal Chronicle Raithiyah - I - Ibriyah, Gait inserts the following passage in regard to the Ahom fort of Jogighopa, "It is a large and high fort on the Brahmaputra. Near it the enemy had dug many holes for the horses to fall into, and pointed pieces of bamboo *(panjis)* had been stuck in the holes. Behind the holes, for about a shot's distance, on even ground, they had made a ditch and behind this ditch, near the fort, another one three yards deep. The latter was also full of pointed bamboos", *A History of Assam,* p.132.

9

The Martial Tradition of the Nyishis
An Overview

N.T. Rikam

Introduction

History is full of infighting and warfare consequent upon which there is destruction, damages and at times complete annihilation of some races or communities. But the tribal warfare is still identical and different from the rest of the communities. It is attributed to their custom, tradition, culture and practices. Thus, their warfare is now treated as monumental or an archaic legacy of the past. Nonetheless, there is quite variations even among the tribal communities depending on their socio-economic condition and, of course, the topographical settings.

The Nyishis who inhabit in the central districts of Arunachal Pradesh is one of the prominent tribal communities in India. They have been recorded as the most turbulent tribal group in the north east who used to disturb peace in the plain area throughout the Ahom as well as British periods in Assam. Their martial tradition can be traced back from the days of *Mahabharata.* It is said that the king of Kamarupa who joined the *Mahabharata* wars in favour of Kaurobos, took the help of the Kiratas and Cinas—their northern neighbours. The Nyishis are believed to be the members among this group. Their martial superiority had been acclaimed by many administrators and rulers in Assam. For instance, the Prime

Minister of Raja Udayaditya Singha while cautioning the king, remarked, "Dafla miscreants can be captured only if an elephant can enter into a rat hole".[1] Similarly, Muhammad Kazim, during the Mughal invasion in Assam, said, "The Dupleus are entirely independent of the Ahom Raja, and plunder the country contiguous to their mountains".[2] Shihabuddhin Talish who accompanied Mir Jumla when he invaded Assam in 1662 AD recorded that the Daflas did not place its feet in the skirt of obedience to the Ahom Raja, but occasionally encroached on his kingdom.[3] Throughout the British period in Assam the Nyishis have been attributed as most naughty and disloyal community in the region. They are recorded as highest raiders in the plain and thereby create lawlessness along the borders.[4] In this way they have jealously defended their territory from the influence or direct control of outsiders.

Till the advent of modern democratic set up particularly after independence, there was no existence of political entity and political system among the Nyishis. They evolved heterogeneous clan system and diverse group who still lived in a primitive stage spreading over large areas but having negligible contact with each other. Each village was practically an entity in itself. In absence of strong and effective political structure, lawlessness prevails in the society. This sometimes led to the occurrence of feuds and even warfare among the people. In fact these are the harsh reality of the past, which every human race had encountered and came across as they were devoid of modernity and modern system of governance.

But unfortunately even today the Nyishis carry this legacy of disrepute status of barbarous and turbulent tribe. Their martial qualities and warfare techniques have been attributed as a negative quality and it was not seen on positive line. With this perception they have been known to the outsiders with a dubious and harsh connotation—Daflas, which means having negative qualities like wild, aggressive, barberry, individualistic, unclean or dirty and so on and so forth.[5] In fact, all good and ideal qualities have been dubbed by their mere act of vengeance along the border areas.[6] Stray incidences of raids or plunder perpetuated by a few Nyishis cannot be taken as yardstick to assess the behavioural pattern of entire Nyishi community. The overwhelming Nyishi population was still in the hilly regions far away from the plain land. The socio-cultural, custom, usages, practices and for that matter the lifestyles of the Nyishis have not been known to the outsider. However, the Nyishis do have a legacy of martial tradition which is depicted in their folklore, myths and legends even today.

II

There are numerous folk items, which depicts the struggle among different creatures of the universe. Fights start from the days of evolution of the universe itself. The earliest possible recalled warfare was between the light and the dark. Fighting took long time but none of them got either victor or vanquish. Their fight became standstill and this is why the Nyishis believe that till today the power of light and dark is equal and so also its importance. Similarly, there was a war between fire and water, the result of which was like that of the light and the dark. There were continuous and protracted infighting between Abo Tani[7] and Weyis.[8] Many a time, Abo Tani proved to be at upper hand as he was blessed by almighty, i.e. Ayu Donyi.[9] The warfare took place even between Abo Tani and Sebi (the monkey). The monkeys were so cunning and disturbing that, Abo Tani decided to finish them all. He induced the Sebis to enter inside a big wooden cage and they were burnt alive. But only one could be able to escape through a small hole. It is believed that the monkeys now belong to that only survived one.[10] It is interesting to know that the fight also took place between the two brothers—Abo Tani and Robu Pacha. Abo Tani, being cunning and powerful, could always defeat his brother—Robu Pacha who was quite innocent and dull by nature. The legacy of warfare was carried forward by the descendents of Abo Tani and their martial traditions are acclaimed even today.

III

Needless to say, that the war mechanism of the Nyishi is identical and quite different, it is basically because the Nyishis as such did not experience a tradition of ruler and ruled or king and queen. In other words, they were neither conquered nor ruled by others. Everyone enjoys freedom and independence. In such a society, naturally the wars are fought not for conquering any territory and subduing the people, rather these are conducted for certain issues and purposes. There are two types of warfare, i.e. the raids and the wars. And these are fought among the villages as well as among the clans or families. However, warfare was not engaged arbitrarily and at random. A war is warranted if all attempts of possible peaceful means of settling the dispute fail. The causes of the warfare are usually related to a dispute over marriage, mithun theft, epidemic, sheltering of enemy or culprit, breach of agreement etc. The war mechanism including the mobilization of forces is quite irregular and there is no uniformity in its strategy or action too. In absence of strong political organization, they do not have regular or standing forces. Forces are generally mobilized amongst the close-relatives temporarily for certain specific purposes. It is derived through a lineage, kinsmen and relatives especially the matrimonial ties.

The preparations for any warfare are always carried in a secret and confidential manner. Initially, there will be close-door consultation amongst the closed relatives. If there is consensus on the proposal of waging war, eventually the plans are mooted and there will be a short listing of the probable participants. Before declaring the actual war, intelligence services or spies are engaged who would report the factual information of the enemy like, their movement and activities, weaknesses and strength etc. It is very interesting that sometimes these spies are caught and the entire warfare plans are foiled. This is why an utmost care is taken while selecting the spies because the fate of any warfare entirely depends on the authentic report or input of the spies. However, for simple raids, even the women and children are engaged for the collection of information but without giving clue to the enemy. After getting clear and factual information, the day and time is fixed and accordingly all concerned are briefed. The mode of attack is akin to guerilla warfare and ambush the enemy at right time. Thus, bring the enemy to a surprise, which will ensure their victory. Generally, the wars are striked during the night hours and at the noon, because these are the ideal times where the enemy can be safely beaten. The targeted village or house is cordoned from all angles and the forward party will attack the village while the remaining members will check the possible retaliation from the enemy. The war weapons are quite simple which can be easily operated and used. Bow and arrow, sword, spear are the principle arms while, shell of animal skin, hat, waist cover, etc. are used as armous.[11] These are used for both offensive as well as defensive purposes.

IV

It is worth mentioning that, in all warfares, the performance of ritual and sacrifice is inevitable. A particular ritual known as *Piriya Pinam*,[12] is performed to make the enemy dull and inactive. By performing another ritual *Sotung-Tamu,* the spiritual skill and the power invoked as so to ensure victory in the warfare. The former is performed by sacrificing fouls or eggs while the latter is done through sacrifice of pet dogs. Moral code of conduct is to be observed by the warriors as such they are not supposed to touch or harm others who are not party to the enemy. If there is indulgence even by mistake also, the party has to compensate the losses, lest they will carry the risk of facing revenge in future. After the accomplishment of the war, the warriors carry the palm of a slain person as a trophy of victory, which will be tied on the trunk of big tree and bows are pierced on it. Before reaching home, they perform war dance (victory dance) called *Busar Sonam.*[13] By performing this ritual it is believed that the god of chase or warfare is propitiated. This dance is performed by all the members of the troop with their war armours, arms and ammunition. They took off their swords and spears, sprinkling above while jumping around the altar. This will be followed by a grand feast by killing mithun, pig, goat etc. In fact, it turns to be a celebration among the victors.

However, there will be a constant fear psychosis about the possible retaliation of the enemy, as such some people were engaged for collection of information from the enemy side. In such situation, a *Bungriang-Bungte*[14] (middlemen or intermediary) plays a vital role. The intermediaries are working from both sides and their efforts will put deterrent to the concerned party. They play a restraining force, which will help in creating congenial environment for entering dialogue between the two parties. Accordingly, a big meeting is arranged for amicable settlement of the dispute under the aegis of elderly people whom we may call the members of modern village council. In local term such meeting is called *Nyele Donam*[15], and again it can be specified as *Yalung Barek* (Meram) whose main purpose is to settle the disputes of violent nature like warfare. Though, the Nyishis do not have institutionalized politico-judicial system, the cases ranging from petty issue to even heinous crime like murder or warfare is solved by means of *Nyele*. In the meeting, the concerned parties are given ample time and opportunity to place their points and grievances. The strength of the decision will depend on how far the parties could raise points with facts and figure. Here the art of oratory also make difference, as the good orator will be scoring more points in their favour. With the amicable settlement of a dispute, Singph-Dapo Dingnam[16] (Pledged or undertaking) ceremony is performed which will bind the parties to honour agreement.

V

It is amply illustrated that the Nyishi warfare including its strategy and method are very simple and the weapons are easy to operate and quite available. Since the warfare was not a regular feature there is no need of having standing forces. The individual plays a vital role with total sense of vigour, skill, commitment, courage, bravery and most importantly the pride of being victor. These are the time-tested qualities, which helped the Nyishis to be recognized as one of the strongest tribal groups in terms of warfare. There are many instances where the strength and martial qualities of the Nyishi had been exhibited. Many references have been made about their martial tradition since the epic age right up to the British period. There are numerous folk traditions, which aptly depict their martial quality and strength. Today the Nyishis boast themselves of having a distinct tradition of a martial race and martial potential. This is why there is a demand for creation of *Nyishi Regiment* in consonance to those of Gurkha Regiment, Sikh Regiment, Assam Rifles, etc.

One way or other their martial quality has also helped them in maintaining independence as nowhere in the history they were subdued or controlled by the outsiders. Their action and behaviour has been viewed by the outsiders with an aberration, but we could see the vitality of their potentials in warfare. In the modern civilized society, we cannot imagine of perpetuating the tribal feuds and for that matter tribal warfare but their skill, courage, sense of commitment, dedication and pride can be imbibed in our modern method of policing and defence system. In the present context where there is lack of work-culture due to rampant corruption and politicization in all aspects, we ought to recollect those ideals and ethos, which had once governed us even in the field of warfare.

NOTES

1. Quoted in V. Elwin, *A Philosophy for NEFA,* Directorate of Research, Government of Arunachal Pradesh, Itanagar, 1988 (First published in 1957), p. 2.
2. *Asiatic Society,* Vol. II (Journal), quoted by A. Mackenzie, *History of the Relations of the Government with the Hill Tribes of the North East Frontier of Bengal,* Calcutta, 1988, p. 27.
3. V. Elwin, *A Philosophy for NEFA, op. cit.*, p.2.
4. (See, Appendix), L.N. Chakravarty, *Glimpses of the Early History of Arunachal,* Directorate of Research, Government of Arunachal Pradesh, Itanagar, 1989.
5. See, F. Hamilton, *An Account of Assam,* edited by S.K. Bhuyan (1940), p.74, cited in Verrier Elwin, (edited), *India's North East Frontier in the Nineteenth Century,* Oxford University Press, Delhi, 1959, p.168. Also see, B.K. Shukla, *Daflas of Subansiri Region,* NEFA, Shillong, 1965, p.1.

6. *Ibid.*
7. Forefathers of the Tani Tribes, which include—Adi, Apatani, Tagin, Miri, Mishing and Nyishi.
8. Spirits—both benevolent and malevolent.
9. Interview with Mr. Nabam Saba, Nirjuli, 20th October, 2003.
10. Narrated by Mr. Nabam Tagum, interviewed at Itanagar, 15th August, 2003.
11. *Ibid.*
12. Ritual that hypnotize a person.
13. War dance generally performed after a successful raids and wars.
14. Intermediary; mediating the parties for amicable settlement especially after arm conflict.
15. Village Council, consisting of elderly people who sit together to settle the disputes.
16. Pledge taken in the name of Almighty which are ritualistically performed after the settlement of a dispute.

10

Tai-Ahom Martial Traditions in Medieval Assam (1228-1682)

Romesh Buragohain

Introduction

Before saying something about the martial traditions of the Ahom people of medieval North East India, it is pertinent to answer as to who were the Ahom people. Many in the north east would believe that they came from Thailand because of the *tai* affixtion before their generic name 'Ahom'. But the fact is otherwise. They belonged to the Mao-Shan branch of the Tai race of Southeast Asia. Their original homeland was in Mung-Mao, in the Kunming province of south western China. Now the Chinese have named it as 'Ruili', located in Dehong Dai Autonomous Prefecture.[1]

Chao-Lung Siu-Ka-Pha, the prince of Mung-Mao, made an adventurous journey through the hills and vales of Upper Myanmar with some nine thousand followers towards the east in search of a new homeland.[2] Crossing the Patkai hill ranges, he entered eastern Assam in 1228 A.D. and founded a small principality at Tipam at the bank of the Buridihing river. On way, he had to fight with the ferocious hill tribes. In the plains, he encountered the opposition of the local autochthonous groups of the Morans and the Borahis who found the martial capability of the Ahoms as superb, invincible and unequal (*na-sama*) in military prowess and so named them as 'Ahom'.

Some Salient Features

It goes without saying that without some basic martial qualities, the Ahoms would not have been able to carve out a kingdom elsewhere far away from their motherland. Wars and warfares, thus, were an inalienable legacy of the Ahom monarchs in medieval Assam. In an unknown land, amongst unknown people and under the new circumstances, some particular traits are discernible in the martial traditions of the Ahom up to the last war they fought against the Mughals in 1682. Herein we will deal with some very specific ones.

Terror Tactics

To overwhelm the turbulent opponents, the Ahom militia resorted to abominable means with ghastly atrocities in order to destroy them morally and mentally. Thus Siu-Ka-Pha while on his way through the Patkai hill ranges had to fight against the undaunted Nagas. The terror inflicted on them is recorded in the Ahom language chronicles runs thus:

> The flesh of the undaunted ones was cut and cooked given to their own brothers to eat.[3]

Again,

> *A great number of Nagas were killed and many were made captives. Some Nagas were cut to pieces and their fleshes cooked. Then the king made a younger brother eat the cooked flesh of his elder brother and a father of his sons.*[4]

This was not an isolated phenomenon in the Ahom military history. Similar situations were also found when those of the Moran, Borahi peoples refused to submit, Siu-Ka-Pha invited their headmen to a feast. They were got intoxicated and were killed. Such terror tactics were used to cause total submission of the turbulent and defiant opponents.[5]

Such terrorism was also inflicted in case of internal opponents. Tipam chiefs were unwilling to co-operate with the king Siu-Dang-Pha *alias* Bamuni Konwar (1397-1407) and conspired against him. The king invited them to an elephant catching celebration and when the festivities were in full swing and all suspicion had been allayed, the conspirators were suddenly overpowered and killed.[6] Siu-Pat-Pha *alias* Gadadhar Singha (1681-1696) also resorted to such abominable terror tactics when the Bhatdhara Phukan incited the Muslims to invade Assam. He was captured along with his son who was killed and the Bhatdhara Phukan was forced to eat the flesh of his son and then was put to death.[7]

Terrorism was a weapon used by the medieval rulers. It was not a new thing for the Ahoms. Neither they had any moral scruples for this and it largely depended upon the exigency of the situation in the interest of the state.

Pyke Militia

The Ahoms had the unique system of organizing the militia. They had no standing army as such. But the *pyke* system happened to be the lever of the Ahom army. All able-bodied persons between the age group of 15-50 were to render compulsory state service divided into *gots* (units) and *khels* (productive guilds) commanded by a gradation of officers. Therefore, a large army could be brought out within a very short notice. Its unique feature was that both military and productive functions were combined in them. The *jai jawan jai kishan* concept was writ large in them. In addition to this, the *pyke* had the unique privilege to change their commanders like the *Bora* (over twenty *pykes*), the *Saikia* (over one hundred) and the *Hazarika* (over one thousand) if they were found to be exploiters and oppressors.[8] Otherwise also, the Ahom state was a sort of military democracy when the three great Gohains (the council of ministers) could change the sovereign if they were found to be inefficient and oppressors.

11

Military System in Early Mizo Society

Sangkima

Like all other hill tribes of the North-East in the past, Mizos lived in a village units of administration headed by a chief whose word was law within the limits of his administration. The political system under the chief was closely related to absolute monarchy because he was the supreme authority in his village by vesting all powers in his hands.

Mizo were war-liked people and therefore, even petty indiscretions could cause hostilities leading to raids and wars. Inter-clan or village feuds and wars were inherent in them and the chief belonging to a particular clan waged war against another chief belonging to other clan. Hence, they lived in a world, as Charles Darwin propounded, where only the fittest ones survived and the unfit ones were eliminated. No one knew when the raiders would attack the village and hence all the young unmarried men of the village would sleep in a house called *Zawlbuk* (bachelors' house or dormitory) where they received various trainings etc.

In olden days, life in a village was so simple and the people lived in the village hardly for more than four years or so.[1] The chief would move out looking for a new field for cultivation. The search for more productive land thus made them not only migratory in nature but also caused tensions leading to wars between the two chiefs. Sometimes, a rising chief could spread his dominion so as to embarrass a lesser chief who would then be compelled to further a field so as to have cultivation without any risks.

Thus, from the statement made above, it may be assumed that the military system was practically lacking under the rule of the chief but a careful study proves otherwise. Therefore, an attempt is made in this paper to bring to light the true nature of military aspects of the administration under the Mizo chief.

Nature of Military Organization

An examination of the administration of the chief during the period under study vividly reveals that there was a good system of military administration in the early Mizo society and their socio-economic and political life was also greatly determined by it. Thus, in order to understand the true picture of the military aspect of the whole system of administration let us now examine the system of administration under the following heads:

The Chief

As already pointed out before, the chief was theoretically the supreme authority in his village and enjoyed extensive political as well as military power. In matters relating to defence, he was the supreme commander [2] and every village was his cantonment and some powerful chiefs had separate cantonments in which a number of dependent villages attached to them. He did not maintain a standing armed-force but every male of age in the village was a member who received a proper training in every aspect of life. Being a sovereign, it was his prerogative to invite and form an alliance with other chiefs in waging war against a particular chief with whom he had enmity. Thus, Hunter has rightly described the duties and responsibilities of the chief as Commander-in-Chief as follows:

> "He shall direct in war, he is the last in the advance and rear-most in the retreat. The messages and errands of a Lal are done by his favourite slaves, they are his ambassadors in war. To collect his people or in fact, to authenticate any order, the chief's spear is sent by a messenger from village to village. Should the message be a hostile one, the message carries a fighting *dao* (kill knife) to which a piece of red cloth is attached".[3]

T.H. Lewin also explained the position of the chief in the following words:

> "Hence there is a fiction that all chiefs are blood-relatives, and it is consequently forbidden to kill a chief, or, as he is called, Lal, save in the heat of battle. The Lal directs in war; he is the last in the advance, and the rearmost in retreat".[4]

In the same way, N. Chatterji has compared the functions of the chief as supreme commander with that of the functions of the President of India who is the Supreme Commander of the Armed Forces in India as follows:

> "...the later (chief) only thought it fit to exercise a remote control leaving the details of functions to be worked out through the self-government of the Zawlbuk group, except, of course, during periods of emergency, very much in the same was the President of India assumes supreme power and issues orders on occasions of national emergency overriding to the states as unit of the Union".[5]

The chief was assisted by a Council of Advisers called *Upa.* The *Upa-Min* or Prime Minister was the most influential man in the Council. In making plans for war or in time of war the *Upa* acted as a War-Council in which the Valupa or the Deputy Commander-in-Chief was also invited. The Valupa, chosen by the Zawlbuk inmates, was appointed by the chief to command the Zawlbuk dwellers even in time of peace as well.

The Regular Army or Militia

One of the important characteristics of chieftainship in a tribal society was the absence or a paid soldier or militia whose main duty was to oversee the safety of the people and the state—the village as well. Therefore, under the Mizo chief there was obviously no paid soldier or regular army but every male of age in the village was member of the Zawlbuk where only young unmarried men, the in-village slept. All those who slept in the Zawlbuk irrespective of unmarried or married men were automatically enlisted as soldiers of the chief and they received regular training in all kinds of welfare and warfare activities under competent men in the village.[6] Here lies the peculiarity of the village administration under the chief.

The Zawlbuk group who acted as a regular army or militia of the chief was directly commanded by a leader called the *Valupa* who, as noted before, was chosen by the group for his undisputed leadership quality. He was the second-in-command next to the chief who was the commander-in-chief. The Zawlbuk group thus acted collectively as the chief's army.[7] He was solely responsible for organizing the group to take up definite responsibilities in looking after the welfare of the general mass and exercising all round vigilance over the protection and security of the village.[8] To assist him, the *Valupa* appointed a number of monitors or lieutenants whose duties were, besides the day-to-day vigilance over the Zawlbuk business, to patrol on the roads at night and signal for collective support whenever the same might become necessary to face any emergency.[9] The non-Zawlbuk dwellers or the common men in the village formed another group. In matters relating to wars or emergency, they had to render the same service as the Zawlbuk group did. In all matters of common issues the groups discussed and took unanimous decision by majority voice. The common men or the third group may be compared with the reservists of modern military system. They should be ready when their services were needed.

The Zawlbuk group who formed the chief's regular army were recruited and enlisted carefully and strictly. They had to pass a queer test. Only an adult was admitted into the Zawlbuk. The test was conducted only amongst the suppliers of firewoods to Zawlbuk called *thingnawifawm*. Generally, the boys who had not yet attained puberty had to supply Zawlbuk with firewood. The one who wanted to become a member of the Zawlbuk had to undergo the test to be verified by the Valupa or any of his lieutenants or assistants. The test was conducted in public by pulling out the longest hair from his public region and that hair should be long enough to circle round the established size of a bamboo pipe *Vaibel*. If the boy was found qualified for the test then he was formally admitted as member of the Zawlbuk group by the *Valupa* by making announcement in the presence of all members of the Zawlbuk.

The discipline and control thus exercised upon the different groups including the junior group were so strict and rigorous. No one in the village was bold enough to challenge the commands and orders issued from the Zawlbuk. In fact, Zawlbuk was the source of strength for maintaining a healthy discipline in the society.

Zawlbuk as Barracks

The Zawlbuk, bachelors' house or dormitory, was the centre where youths were trained and shaped into responsible adult members of the society. Thus, Parry accredited its importance and said, "I ascribe much of the indicipline among the Lakhers to the fact that they have no bachelor's house or equivalent to the Lushai Zawlbuk.

Today, soldiers sleep in barracks. Similarly, unmarried males of the Mizo in the past slept in the Zawlbuk which was not only a sleeping place but also a place where they underwent rigorous training. Strategically, the Zawlbuk was invariably situated at the central place very near to the chief's house because all the able-bodied young persons should easily be available at the beck and call of the chief for any collective work in times of necessity and emergency.[10] In times of danger caused by the attacks of the enemy, the Zawlbuk group provided the much-needed services to the public readily.

The Zawlbuk was like a fort and from a distance it looked like a standing elephant. The way it was designed and built was so strategic that its walls were built of arrow-proof materials. The vacant space between the walls and floor popularly known as *awkpaka* made access to it very difficult. In the same way, a big log, popularly known as *bawhbel,* with a diameter of about two feet placed on the platform thus made the dwellers to scramble over it to find themselves into the Zawlbuk. In short, the entire structure was designed to provide safety to the inmates from the enemies. Thus, Suhas Chatterjee is right when he says, "Fall of the *Jawlbuk* in most cases indicated the fall of the chief".[11] Therefore, from military point of view, the Zawlbuk of the Mizo served the purpose as the military barracks serve today.

Village Fortifications

Every village was generally built and perched high on the top of spurs and ridges. The people select the most inaccessible hilltop to build the village.[12] The hilltop combined with impregnable stronghold was the favourite site mainly for two reasons: for the sake of health and for the purpose of defence.[13]

Having found a suitable site for settlement, the village was planned with a sense of orderly designs. The houses were laid out in streets radiating from a Central Square in which stood the chief's house and the house of the unmarried men of the village.[14] Houses were as far as practicable arranged in two rows and the houses of *Upa* were clustered together near the chief's house. The village was fortified by putting up one or more lines of heavy timber stockade around the whole village supported by rows of bamboo spikes outside and each entrance was protected by a sort of block-house or sentry-tower manned by the local youth day and night on rotation basis.[15] For security reason, generally the village contained not less than 400 houses. As a rule, village had 400 to over 1,000 houses.

Methods of Warfare

Before the advent of the British every village was independent. When feuds arose between the two or more villages thereby leading to war, the whole community did not take part. Instead, both the villages chose one each to fight on their behalf. After selecting the site for encounter, then they made a grave upon which a beam was put. The warriors of both sides then met at the middle of the bridge and started to attack by assaulting themselves with *daos* in their hands. The one who fell first was the loser and the one who knocked him down was the winner. This war was known as *Leilawn Malzawha Indo.*[16] According to B. Lalthangliana the fight between the Kawlni and Siakeng sub-clans of Ralte clan was perhaps the last of this sort.[17]

Another method of warfare practiced by the Mizo was *Vawklu vuakthlaka Indo.*[18] The war was common chiefly amongst the Lusei clans.[19] In this type of war, the attacking party aimed at pulling down the skulls of pigs displayed in the courtyard of the enemy and it was the duty and responsibility of the opposing group to defend them with any kinds of weapons they possessed. If the attacking party could bring down the skulls then they won the war.

As time went on, the system of warfare also developed among the people. Raids and plunders caused by blood feuds originated in a quarrel over the price of a *mithun*, a wife and the quarrel over the land, the division of heritance etc. became the common forms of warfare. Raids were undertaken by a tribe, or a clan, by a village or by a handful of young men in the pretext of revenge. Generally, raids and wars were undertaken only after performing a superstitious rites and if the augery was in their favour the attack took place either at night or daybreak which was continued till the sun was fairly up.[20] Raids were generally committed in two forms: in a party consisting of as many number as the attacking party needed and in a family when a head was needed for a family purpose.[21] Raids were planned with due care and consideration. Having selected the village to be attacked, then fixed the date and strength of the party. Before the attack took place spies were sent to collect information about the fortifications of the village. The spies tried to get information in the best possible way by visiting the village either as a trader or traveller or by sneaking round the village at night.

Meanwhile raids and plunders as the tactics of warfare among the people got changed. About half a century before the advent of the British, open battle or war became a common form of attack amongst the chiefs. As a result, the war of the east and west, of the south and north and so many other famous wars were waged among the chiefs. Such serious encounters amongst the chiefs came to an end only when the British subjugated them and occupied the hills in 1890.

Weapons

Before the introduction of guns, Mizo used only primitive types of weapons like spears of two kinds, bows and arrows, *daos* of three kinds, sword and axe. They also used shield of two kinds made of mithun, buffalo and rhinocero's hide and they were used for self-defence purposes mainly in time of wars. Besides these, a helmet made of brass or copper locally called *darlukhum* was also in use. The helmet was probably obtained from the people of Burma.[22] They were very useful in time of war. A bag called *sahmim* made of cotton covered with a bear's skin was also used to keep rice and other food supply when they went out for war. A woven cloth with specific design of stripes popularly known as *tawlhlohpuan* should accompany the warrior. The cloth denotes that the wearer should not retreat when attacked by the enemy. It was also conveniently used as a night-bedding when outing for a war.

One of the effective weapons used in those days was bamboo spikes as booby-trap. Today, soldiers lay mines so that the enemies may be booby-trapped. Likewise, in those days, a retreating attackers, expecting an attack by the attacked, rendered the path almost impassable to a bare-footed enemy. The spikes were of two kinds: one used round the village and the other, carried in a neat little cane-work quiver and stuck in the path when returning from a raid to delay pursuit.[23] The former were spikes of various lengths while the latter were carefully smoothed bamboo spikes about six inches long and not thicker than a knitting needle. It was designed so as to easily break off after entering the flesh. They were, like mines, concealed and they formed a very serious obstacle to bare footed foe. Even the invading British troops suffered heavily from them.[24] They were poisonous.[25]

When the British first advanced into the hills, the people fought them in the open and from behind stockades. But they soon learnt that they could not stand the quick-firing rifles of British troops. Then they adopted a booby-trap locally known as *sahbuak*.[26] To overwhelm an enemy the method was found very effective and caused a number of casualties to the British troops.

Guns became an important weapon of war of the Mizo only in the later part of the eighteenth century. Parry is of the view that Kukies had no gun before 1777 and guns began to trickle out among the tribes only after the end of the Napoleonic wars in Europe.[27] Having acquired firearms from Burma, the Mizo became better armed than most other north eastern tribes.[28] The guns they used were all muzzle loading as breech-loading guns reached them only after British occupied the hills in 1890.

Dress in War Time

It is not known the Mizo warriors had any kind of uniform in the past as the army has today. But J. Shakespear is of the opinion that the Mizo warriors had garments which looked like a uniform and what said is quoted below:

> "When the Lushais were fighting us in 1892, I was much struck by the whiteness of their garments. The men who ran away from the stockades as we rushed them were always dressed in nice clean coats and cloths and crowds of similar attired warriors used to assemble every morning just out of range and challenge us to come and fight. I was told that it was considered the correct thing to come properly dressed when there was fighting on hand, but a raiding party. I once came across was dressed for more suitably. A single cloth wrapped tightly round the waist, a haversack protected by a bear or tiger skin guard over one shoulder, and a fighting *dao* or *dah* over the other, and a gun in his hand completed each warrior's equipments".[29]

Concluding Remarks

As a matter of fact, in early Mizo society under the chief a modern military system was obviously absent but a primitive form complete in itself was practiced. Every village was a military cantonment of the chief in which the chief himself was the supreme commander. The role of Zawlbuk in the military setup of the society was so strategic that all its inmates were enlisted soldiers who received proper training in all forms of guerrilla warfare. The fortified village was like a fort and this clearly demonstrates that the people were a military genius and advanced in the act of defence. The employment of the intelligent services in the form of spy also indicates that the people were advanced in the field of intelligence activities.

Though the weapons the people used in those days were in deed primitive yet, the manner by which the primitive weapons were used war by no means inferior. The way by which they put up a *booby*-trap with a poisonous bamboo spikes and a sahbuak to overwhelm the enemies shows that the people had already acquired a highly developed form of war-tactics.

After all, taking all the points already highlighted in the preceding paragraphs of this paper into consideration, the Mizo had all forms of military system but of primitive way during the period under review. The improvement upon the primitive form of combating is, however, a different thing.

NOTES

1. A.G. McCall; *Lushai Chryasalis,* Tribal Research Institute (TRI), Aizawl (Reprint) 1977, p. 166.
2. *Sangkima; Mizos: Society and Social Change,* Spectrum Publications, Delhi, 1992, p. 38.
3. W.W. Hunter; *A Statistical Account of Bengal,* Vol. VI, p. 60.
4. T.H. Lewin; *Wild Races of South-Eastern India,* TRI, Aizawl (Reprint), 1978.
5. (Mrs) N. Chatterji; *Zawlbuk as a Social Institution in the Mizo Society,* TRI, Aizawl (Reprint), 1975, p. 17. The bracketed work 'chief' is mine.
6. Suhas Chatterjee; *Mizoram Under the British Rule,* Mittal Publications, Delhi, 1985, p. 4.
7. Sangkima; "Zawlbuk and its Abolition: A significant Event in The History of The Mizos", *Essays on the History of the Mizos,* Spectrum Publication, Delhi, 2004, p. 131.
8. (Mrs) N. Chatterji; *op. cit.*, p. 18.
9. *Ibid.*
10. N.E. Parry; *The Lakhers,* TRI, Aizawl (Reprint), 1997, p. 28.
11. (Mrs) N. Chatterji; *op. cit.*, p. 6.
12. Suhas Chatterjee; *op. cit.*, p. 6.
13. John Macrare; "Accounts of the Kookies or Lunotas" in *Asiatic Researches,* Vol. II, Cosmo Publications, New Delhi, (Reprint), 1979.
14. L.W. Shakespear; *The Assam Rifles,* TRI, Aizwal (Reprint), 1977, p.73.
15. B.C. Allen, E.A. Gait et al.; *Gazetteer of Bengal and North East,* Mittal Publications, New Delhi (Reprint), 2001, p. 462.
16. V.L. Siama; *Mizo History,* Lalrinliana & Sons, Aizawl, 1978, p. 25.
17. Rev. Liangkhaia; *Mizo Awmdan Hlui,* Thakthing Bazar Press, Aizawl, 1984, p. 26.

18. B. Lalthangliana; *Mizo Chanchin,* RMT Press, Aizawl, 2001, p. 172.
19. Rev. Liangkhaia; *Mizo Chanchi,* Academy of Letters, Aizawl (Reprint) 1976, p. 28.
20. Sangkima; *loc. cit.*, p. 45.
21. C.A. Soppitt; *A Short Account of the Kuki-Lushai Tribes,* TRI, Aizawl, (Reprint) 1976, p. 228.
22. Bertram S. Carey and H.N. Tuck; *The Chin Hills,* Vol. I, TRI, Aizawl (Reprint), 1976, p. 228.
23. Lianhmingthanga; *Material Culture of the Mizo,* TRI, Aizawl, 1998, p.49.
24. J. Shakespear; *The Lushai-Kuki Clans,* TRI, Aizawl (Reprint), 1975, p. 15.
25. *Ibid.*
26. Suhas Chatterjee; *op. cit.*, p. 6.
27. Sahbuak was an avalanche of rocks and stones used in hill warfare for overshelling an enemy. Rocks and stones were stockpiled over the path and when enemies came near the place the stockpiling of rocks and stones were let loose and avalanche of rocks and stones took place. It was an effective weapon. It became a practice only after the British came.
28. N.E. Parry; *The Lakhers, op. cit.*, p. 45.
29. L.W. Shakespear; *op. cit.*, p. 77.
30. J. Shakespear; *op. cit.*, p. 10.

12

Aspects of Military Organisation in Early Medieval Assam

Byomakesh Tripathy

Earlier known as Pragjyotisha and Kamarupa,[1] the North-Eastern state of Assam, occupies a prominent place in the history and culture of India. Throughout the historical period the land successfully withstood onslaughts and challenges from within and outside, which could be possible due to peculiar topography of the region, powerful kings at the helm of affairs, expertise of army in various modes of warfare and a sense of patriotism among the people. In fact it is no exaggeration to mention that military organization of early Assam played a very important role in this regard. The expertise of the army of Assam was proved beyond doubt from the fact that during Varmana, Salastambha and Pala rule of early medieval Assam, the army did not even lose a single war or battle, amply revealing the martial traditions of the land.

Warlike Qualities of the Kings

The epigraphs of the period refers to the warlike qualities of the early medieval kings of Kamarupa time without numbers. In fact war was the sports of the king and success in war and valour in battle was the ruler's highest ambition. The early kings of Kamarupa were not only powerful but also blessed with qualities, which made them heroes in the battle field. The *Mahabharata* provides in certain terms the heroic exploits of the historical kings of Assam like Bhagadatta and Vajradatta.[2] About Bhagadatta, the Mahabharata says that he was a friend of Indra and fought on Duryodhana's side in the Kurukshetra war. He was said to have provided one *akshauni* of soldiers including Chinas and Kiratas to the Kaurava king. In this aspect the Nidhanpur copper plate grant of Bhaskaravarman is noteworthy. The epigraph mentions how Bhagadatta was equal to Indra and challenged in battle even the famous conqueror Arjuna.[3] King Vajradatta, the younger brother of Bhagadatta, is eulogized as one who was as fast as lightning and even had the capacity to satisfy Indra in war by his valour.[4] He was credited with a performance of a horse sacrifice and said to be proficient in the art of training and breeding of elephants and equitation. The Varmana rulers like Mahendravarman (c 470-494 AD), Narayana Varmana (c 494-518 AD), Bhutivarman (c 518-542 AD), and Bhaskaravarman (604-650 AD) were said to be expert in warfare. On the basis of the Nalanda clay seals, it is believed that Mahendravarman performed two horse sacrifices, but some scholars assign these two sacrifices to the period of Narayanavarman.[5] The Barganga Rock inscription of Bhutivarman speaks him as Maharajadhiraja, who was credited to have performed an *asvamedha* sacrifice.[6] The Dubi plate, on the other hand, refer Bhaskaravarman as *Rajadhiraja* whose arm was said to be as ostensibly tough as the trunk of the guardian elephant, besides mentioning him as an expert in the science of taming the elephants.[7] The Nidhanpur grant throws light on the accomplishment of the king in all the sixty-four arts, including the art of warfare and further mentions that Bhaskara equaled the prowess of the whole circle of his feudatories by the strength of his own arm. Interestingly, one copper bell inscription of Srikumara, an ancient king of Kamarupa, of whom we know little, compares the king with Indra, and who was credited to be the killer of elephants of the kings of gods and demons.[8] The warlike qualities of the Salastambha ruler Harjara is reflected in the Tezpur[9] and Hayngthal grants.[10] That Harjara was the annihilator of the enemies is revealed from the Nowgong plates of Balavarman.[11] These grants while describing qualities of the ruler, compare him with Bhima and Arjuna for prowess. Such qualities in king Vanamala are reflected in the Tezpur grant, equating the different facets of his personality with the epic heroes Yudhisthira, Karna and Bhima. The king is eulogized as the sun who dispelled the extensive mass of darkness in the shape of the arrays of tuskers of the formidable enemies in the battlefield. King Balavarman was said to be steady in battle and ferocious towards enemies is known from one Howraghat copper plate.[12] The epigraphs of Pala king Brahmapala, mentions him as the abode of state craft and one who was accomplished in all fields[13], while king Ratnapala was said to be Skanda in valour, Arjuna in fame, Bhimasena in war, and Kritanta in wrath.[14] The Guakuchi grant of king Indrapala provides as many as thirty names and title of his exalted majesty and among them the title like Samgramastambha, Vipaksabalabhit, Narasimha Vikrama, Udhatabhubrda Sanipata, Dhanurdharaikapartha, Sahasaikasahaya, Turangaresvanta speaks him as an expert in different aspects of warfare.[15] Gopaplavarmadeva is referred as a good warrior, who was fierceful to the enemy,[16] while the epigraph of Dharmapala [17] refers the king as a great warrior, conqueror of the host of enemy heroes, who could single handedly won victory over his enemies. The Gauhati grant of Indrapala,[18] observes that Purandarapala gave more than one extraordinary proof of warfare by the way in which he captured hostile king like tigers, in netting of arrows, improvised for the occasion, while on the other hand king Vallabhavadeva was credited to have mastered the science of archery.[19]

Composition of the Army

The military organization of the early medieval kings was strong and efficient, as the army was regarded as an important service to be organized and maintained in a condition of efficiency. It is often referred to as Vijayasri (the victorious army). The Nidhanpur grant mentions them as *patti*. However, the Indian concept of four divisions of army (*chaturangabalam*) was probably not followed in this part of the country, as the Nidhanpur grant clearly mentions elephants, horses, foot soldiers and navy (*maha-nau-hastyasvapatti*) leaving chariot as an indispensable unit of the army. The Tezpur grant of Vanamala in certain term refers, to the infantry along with other units of the army, occupying all sides of the capital city Haruppesvara[20]; while that of Ratnapala's foot soldiers were mentioned as those hankering after the plunder of the enemies' camp.[21] The literature of the period makes us to understand that there was a standing army to defend the country as well as to conquer for expansion. The personnel of the army belonged to all classes and consisted of plain as well as hill people of the region. The *Mahabharata* refers to the recruitment of the people of boardering Mongoloid tribes for the army of ancient Assam and that is why, we are informed that Bhagadatta's army consisted of Kiratas, Cinas and many other soldiers dwelling on the marshy region near the sea.[22] It is natural that the adjoining hill people, expert in guriella mode of warfare, were a great asset to the army. The Subhankarapataka and the Kamuali grants, interestingly observe that even the Brahmanas were experts in warfare. One Brahman Himanka was said to have earned royal patronage for skill in archery, and he was considered as expert in reading the omens implied in the movement and fall of other people's arrows, besides being well proficient in various methods of attack and defence.[23]

The elephant squadrons (*gajabala*) formed an important division of Kamarupa army.[24] The *Rigveda*, the *Mahabharata*, the *Visnupurana*, the *Arthasastra*, writings of Strabo refers in growing terms about the elephant corps and best variety of elephants that were found in ancient Assam. Kalidasa provides an idea of catching of wild elephants in the jungles of Assam[25], while Yuan Chwang referred to the supply of elephants in good numbers for war purposes in Assam.[26] The text *Hastyayurveda* of Gupta period, medieval Assamese and Muhammadan literature provides a number of references to war elephants of Assam and about various methods of catching them. No dount, elephants were considered as an inevitable part of the army, as they were not only engaged in clearing jungles and new paths, but also to intimidate the opposition army, by creating terror and confusion during the war. The Bargaon grant[27] gives a specific information in this regard when it states that the chiefs of the neighbouring hill tribes used to supply the Kamarupa monarch with elephants, while the grant of Ratnapala mentions the presentation of war elephants to the king by hundred of kings conquered by the power of the army. Epigraphy bears testimony to the fact that most of the rulers fought with the help of elephants. The epigraph mentions the term like Mahapilupati in charge of the elephant force and *hastibandhake* (a petty officials, having charge with the fastening of elephants).

The cavalry, perhaps, did not seem to have occupied a prominent role in the army, probably due to non-availability of good horses in the region. The *Mahabharata* and *Visnupurana*, however, mention fine variety of horses of ancient Assam. The Vallabhadeva's plate,[28] however, mentions of imported horses from Kamboja (North-Western frontier), while the later Tibetan chronicle, mentions that large number of horses were brought to Assam from a certain town, Karbattan in Tibet during medieval period.[29]

From early time, the people of Assam are said to be expert in navigation in river as well as sea. The classical writer Nonnos refers to the Kiratas.[30] Who have been rightly identified as the indigenous people of western Assam and South East Bengal.[31] The Chinese traveller, Yuan Chwang speaks highly of the naval branch of Kamarupa army by stating that Bhaskaravarman had a flotilla of 30,000 ships. [32] Naval fights between Kamarupa and neighbouring states are known from a number of epigraphs like the Apshad inscription,[33] Nidhanpur grant, and the grant of king Indrapala, Vaidyadeva and others. That the king of Assam successfully withstood the naval fights of the king of neighbouring Bengal region, speaks about their naval achievement. The rock inscription of Harjavarman[34] refers to an eyewitness account of the naval fleet of the king during the incumbency of the commander in chief Mahasamanta Suchitta. Though we do not get any idea about the naval officials in epigraphs, petty officials such as Naubandhaka incharge of fastening of boats and Naurajjuka, incharge of dragging of boats with the help of ropes are sometimes mentioned.[35]

Warfare and War Implements

Literary sources mention three kinds of warfare: Prakasa (open fight between equals), and *tusnim yuddha* (to win over leaders of the enemy by intrigues or other means). Besides, *khanda yuddha, askasa yuddha,* and siege warfare are also part and parcel of ancient Indian warfare.[36] Regarding siege-craft, the *Tabaquat-I-Nasairi* provides an interesting account of the methods of warfare of the Assamese people by stating that when Muhammad-I-Bakhatyar was returning to Kamarupa after his Tibetan campaign, everything in the way were burnt and destroyed by the people and communication was cut off and finally, the Kamarupa King succeeded in annihilating the whole force.[37] One can believe that wars were generally undertaken after sacrifices, consultation of omens and a meeting of the council in early Assam as observed during the wars and battles among the tribes of the Northeastern frontier. Most probably the surprise attack or lying in ambush and then suddenly falling upon the enemy, was the chief strategy of the soldiers. The Doobi grant[38] provides an idea of nature of actual open fighting by stating that when the Gauda army arrived at the frontier, Bhaskaravarman and his brother with a handful soldiers could successfully pierce through the huge troops of mighty elephants of the Gauda army with sharp arrows and various types of deadly weapons, they in turn were attacked by a large number of elephants. Examples are not lacking in medieval period by which enemies were harassed to the extent of starving them to death.

Scanty references indicate to the types of war implements used in actual warfare. Kautilya has listed various types of war implements like *sakti, sula, tomara, bhindivala, gada*, swords, bows and arrows in addition to armour of iron and skin.[39] Most of these were used in Assam. Verse of the Dubi copper plate lists the weapons of war like arrows, *saktis*, wheels, *parsas,* swords, javelin etc. The chief weapons of war were *ash* (sword), *Parasu* (axe), *Khatvanga* (spear), *Gada* (mace) as well as the bow and arrow. The bow was the special weapon of heroes and *Dhanurdhara* was a title of much distinction. Records say that the people of Assam were expert archers using poison on arrow tips. The plates of Vallabhadeva refer to the use of *churika* (dagger) as a weapon of war. Words like *kavaca* and *varman* occur in the sense of war like protections for the body of warriors. The Bargaon grant aptly mentions "the cloth which protects the king's broad chest." Even *dhavaja* (flag) and *Pataka* (banners) were used in the battlefield. Names of instrument of war music are not provided in the epigraph, although there is one expression '*Pancha Mahasabda*'[40] which according to some denotes five different musical sounds. Iron implements were used during the period, though we do not find explicit mention to the existence of iron in the epigraph. Writing in 17th century, Tavernier had an interesting observation when he remarked that the people of Assam in ancient times first discovered gun powder and gun, which cannot be attested in our present state of knowledge[41]. The use of the war drum, though it does not find mention in epigraphs, is mentioned in literature, which refers to various types of drum such as *bheri, danka, dandubhi, jayadhaka, ramabheri* and others.[42] In fact, many war implements can be noticed, as attributes of Brahmanical gods and goddesses of early medieval Assam, though all those might not be used in actual warfare.

Foreign Policy and Diplomacy

The espionage system was in vogue in Assam and spies were employed to inform internal trouble, impending external invasion and on the resources of an enemy is state. The kings used to have good diplomatic relations with neighbouring states and feudatories, as one can glean from the Doobi grant, Hayun and the Gauhati grant. In fact war and diplomacy formed an important element of the state policy. Epigraphs refer to Mahasamantas, and Samantas, who as feudatories helped the king with military contingents. *Raja, Rajaputra, Ranaka, Rajnayaka, Rajavallabha,* and others were the chieftains who ruled feudatory states as the king's subordinates and used to help the king during the time of war.[43] By both peaceful means and wars, the rulers of Assam tried to bring the feudatories under their control. The *Harshacharita, Rajatarangini,*[44] literary sources and epigraphs of the period do refer to the matrimonial alliances of the royal family of

Kamarupa with those of other parts of the country. The ambassadors used to play an important role in the foreign policy of the king. The undying alliance between Bhaskara and Harsha of Kanauj could be cemented, it is told, due to Hamsavaga, the messenger of Bhaskara, to the court of Harsha.[45]

Ethics of War

Though organisation of the military machine was efficient, it did not mean that wars were undertaken at all times. The conquering kings tried to avoid war as far as possible. The *Kalikapurana* lays emphasis on the four fold policy to be followed by a ruler in his relations with other rulers—*Samadanca, Bhedanca Dandasceti Catustayan* that is war to be taken when all pacific means fail.[46] Defeated kings or princes were not treated unkindly as we have instances that feudatories were appointed even to posts in the centre, as in the case of the Mahasamanta Divakara, who was appointed to the post of the *Bhandagarika.* Vanquished kings were given a honourable place in the state affairs and used to attend even the coronation ceremony and audience hall of the king.[47] In Indrapala's audience hall, they sat near entry bowing before the king.[48] Though the rulers in ancient India were guided by a moral standard in actual fighting, no clear cut evidence in this regard is noticed in early medieval Assam.

Defence Mechanism

The mountainous character of the land helped in the construction of forts, which along with natural barrier played an important part against external invasions. The kings of Assam realized the importance of construction of forts from early times. The *Kalikapurana* classifies the forts into water (*audaka*), mountain (*parvata*), desert (*dhanvana*), forest (*vana*), earth (*bhumi*), Tree (*Vriksha*) forts and lays down rules for their construction by stating that they should be either triangular, semi-circular, circular or square.[49] The cities of early medieval Assam were well fortified, both by natural barriers and forts. The big cities like Pragjyotisha, Sonitapur, Haruppesvara and Durjaya were well fortified, both by natural barriers and forts. The ancient capital city, Pragjyotishapura was well protected by a *giri durga* of *sarvatobhadra* design that was said to be unassailable even by the Gods. The *Mahabharata*, the *Bhagavatapurana*, the *Visnupurana* and the *Kalikapurana* have noted the impregnable features of the city Pragjyotishapura in great details.[50] The Bargaon grant of Ratanapala [51] informs us about a fortress city, named Durjaya, evidently because of the impregnable nature of its defences. It is said to be encompassed by a rampart and flourished further with a strong fence, which defended it like cloth, which protected the kings's broad chest. The *Yogini Tantra* refers to a sacred city called Apunarabava (modern Hajo area), which was said to be surrounded by moats and protected by a fully equipped army.[52] Actual remains of forts are noticed at Gauhati, Visvanath, Ratanpur, Dimapur, Sadiya and other places. Recent excavation at Bhaitbari, has yielded a mud-cum-burnt brick fortification having four gateways and a number of bastions of 10th century in a circular fashion with a very deep moat running all along the outerside of the fortification.[53] A few forts were constructed in the North East frontier of the state and among those, the brick fort at Bhishmaknagar and Rukmininagar, a mud fort near Sadiya and a stone fort at Bhalukpong, datable to 11th -12th century A.D. are noteworthy.

Military Administration

The king was the supreme authority of the army and went to war in person and took a leading part in the organization of the army. The kings were probably helped by a war minister. The *Saciva*, mentioned in the Kamauli grant most probably refers to the minister of war. Vaidyadeva said to have served as a war minister under Kumarapala of Gauda and fought against Tingyadeva.[54] Under the minister, there was a commander in chief. The Nidhanpur grant mentions one Gopala, who happened to be the general of Bhaskaravarman's army. A scrutiny of epigraphs of the period would indicate that organization of army was probably two-fold, namely the fighting force under *Mahasenapati* and organization wing under the *baladhyaksha*. The Hayungthal grant refers to one Sri Gana as *Mahasenapati* the supreme commander to the army under Harjaravarman.[55] The fendal lords or *samantas* also shared such responsibilities. Suchita, the *Mahasamanta* was also the *Senadhyaksha*, while Samanta Chitragharadaksha Bhatta of the Tezpur Rock Inscription of Harjaravarman,[56] was the *baladhyaksha*. There was another *mahasamanta* Divakara, who was appointed as *Bhandagarika* (most probably in charge of supply or the Nayakas of the grants were probably minor chiefs with military duties). Petty officials such as *hastibandhaka, naubandhaka, naurajjaka* and other are also referred in the epigraphs. A scrutiny of epigraphs point out that there was division of responsibilities between the fighting and organizational wings, and the feudal lord shared these responsibilities. At the same time, adequate arrangements were made for supplies of foodstuffs for the army. The military administration was quite efficient and that is why the Kamarupa army won laurels in the wars and battles they undertook during early medieval period.

War Scenes in Assamese Art

Representation of war scenes are very rare in the art of Assam. Two terracotta panels recovered from Bhishmaknagar dateable to 11th-12th century AD, depicts typical soldiers of early medieval Assam.[57] In the first instance a warrior is shown holding a shield and sword, while the other depicts a running soldier. Representation of soldiers of later period can be noticed in the ruins of Jaintiapur temple, of late medieval period. A frieze from Deopahar, of early medieval period illustrates a combat between two warriors. The actual combat is shown in one panel, while in the other, one of the warriors marches off in triumph with the severed head of the other held in his hand, the headless trunk staggering behind.[58] Another frieze recovered from cole park, Tezpur, of 9th to 10th century in having three panels, depicting a duet. From left to right the first one show two men fighting only with their hands, the second one shows them lying on the ground with one overpowering the other and third one represents both lying straight in opposite directions; the right one holding the legs of the other, who seems to have surrendered.[59] Actual war scene is reflected in another panel, found from Deoparvat, where Lord Krishna with his bow, arrow and sword is fighting with demon Vakasura (Krsan-Vakasura Badha Panel).[60] A few late medieval paintings do reflect some incidents of the battle fields. The Lavakusar Yuddha manuscript of Harivar Bipara (1714-44 AD) contains various drawings of elephants in war scenes. One of its scene depicts marching of elephants, while another reveals chariots in fragments, dismembered bodies, giving an idea of the actual battle fields in great details.[61] The Hastividyarnava [62] and Darrang Rajavamsavai[63] manuscript also reveal aspects of war scene with remarkable effect and beauty.

In retrospect, it can be surmised that the army of early medieval Assam reached to a great height due to their valour, warriorship and patriotism. The fighting tradition continued during later Ahom rulers and even the Muslim historians of the period have complimented the fighting force for its efficiency and bravery, which bespeak the glorious warrior traditions of medieval Assam.

NOTES

1. Edward Gait, *A History of Assam,* Guwahati, 1997, (Seventh edition), p. 10.
2. K.L. Barua, *Early History of Kamarupa,* Guwahati 1996 (second edition), pp. 21-23.
3. D. Sarma (ed), *Kamarupa Sasanavali,* Part-III (English translation), Gauhati, 1981, p. 161. Most of the epigraphs referred in the article are published in the book *Kamarupa Sasanavali.*
4. *Ibid.*
5. *Ibid.*, p.151.
6. *Ibid.,* p. 150.
7. *Ibid.*, pp. 157-160.
8. *Ibid.*, p. 167.
9. *Ibid.*, pp., 170-172.
10. *Ibid.*, pp. 168-169.
11. *Ibid.*, p.. 182.
12. *Ibid.*, pp. 187-188.
13. *Ibid.*, pp. 214-216.
14. *Ibid.*, pp. 190-192.
15. *Ibid.*, pp. 204-206.
16. *Ibid.*, pp. 212.
17. *Ibid.*, pp 218-219.
18. *Ibid.*, p. 200.
19. B.K. Barua, *A Cultural History of Assam* (Early Period) Gauhati, 1986 (3rd edition), p. 74.
20. D. Sarma (ed) *op.cit,* pp. 173-176.
21. *Ibid.*, pp. 190-196.
22. *Sabha Parva* XXV, XXXIII, Udyogaparva, XVIII.
23. D. Sarma (ed) p. 220, V. 20.

24. B. Tripathy, Elephant in Medieval Art and Literature of Assam, *Journal of North East Council for Social Science Research*, April, 2002, Shillong, pp. 47-52.
25. Kalidasa's *Raghuvamsa,* canto IV, Verse 83-84.
26. Watters, *on Yuan Chwang's Travels in India,* Vol.-II, London, 1904, p. 185.
27. Bargaon Grant of Ratnapara, Lines 297.
28. Vallabhadeva plates, V. 12.
29. B.K. Barua, *op. cit.,* pp. 70-71.
30. McCrindle, J.W., *Ancient India as Described in Classical Literature,* Westminster, 1901, p. 199.
31. E.B. Taylor, JASB, Calcutta, 1847, pp. 10-11.
32. S. Beal, *Life of Yuan Chawang,* London, 1911, p. 1711.
33. J.F. Fleet, *Corpus Inscrptionum Indicarum* (CII) Vol.-III, Calcutta, 1881, p. 203.
34. D. Sarma (ed), *op. cit.* pp. 171-172.
35. B. Tripathy, *Navigational Activities in Ancient Assam,* INDICA, Vol.-39, No. 1, Bombay, March, 2002, pp. 31-38.
36. *Arthasastra*, VII, 6, 10.
37. Doobi grant, V. 48-58.
38. Raverty, Tabaqat - I Nasiri, pp. 569-571.
39. *Arthasastra,* B.K. II, XVIII.
40. B.K. Barua, *op. cit.*, p. 74.
41. R. MacLagan, *on Early Asiatic Fire Weapons,* JASB, XLV, I, pp. 30-71.
42. *Kalika Purana,* VI, V. 40.
43. See, Nowgong grant; Bargaon Grant, Guakuchi Greant etc.
44. M.A. Stein (ed), *Kalhana's Rajatarangini,* BK-II, 9, London, 890.
45. E.B. Cowell, and P.W. Thomas, *Banabhatta's Harsacharita*, London, 1897, pp. 2117.
46. *Kalikapurana* 84/34-35.
47. Hayunthal Grant, VV, 13-14.
48. Gauhati Grants V. 15.
49. *Kalika Purana,* chap. LXXXIV, VV 1127.
50. P.C. Choudhury, *The History of civilization of the people of Assam to the twelfth century A.D*, Delhi, 1987 (3rd edition), p. 292. H.K. Barpujari (ed). *The Comprehensive History of Assam,* Vol-I, Guwahati, 1990, pp. 424-426.
51. Bargaon Inscription, Line 34-35.
52. *Yogini Tantra,* Chapter-II, IX, 122-3.

53. A.K. Sharma, *Early Culture in North East India,* New Delhi, 1993, pp. 29-35.
54. Kamauli Grant, VV. 10-14.
55. Hayunthal Grant, V. 27.
56. Tezpur Rock Inscription, VV. 6-7.
57. R.D. Choudhury, *Archaeological Remains of the Brahmaputra Valley,* Delhi, 1985 pp. 167-168.
58. ARASI (Annual Report Archaeological Survey of India) pp. 36-37 pt. XVIIIc.
59. N.P. Choudhury, *Historical Archaeology of Central Assam,* Delhi, 1985, p. 192.
60. Manoranjan Dutta, *Sculptures of Medieval Assam,* Delhi, 1990, p. 83.
61. H.C. Goswami, *Descriptive Catalogue of Assamese Manuscript,* Calcutta, 1930, p. 5.
62. P.C. Choudhury (ed), *Hastividyarnava,* Publication Board, Assam, Gauhati, 1976, Introudction, IV-XI.
63. K.L. Barua, *op.cit.*, p. 80.

13

Historical Importance of the Battle of Saraighat 1671
Saga of Medieval Assam

Bharat Kalita

The battle of Saraighat 1671 cannot be considered as an isolated event of sudden and surprise development of Medieval Assam. It was the final outcome of challenge and counter challenge of 400 years of Muslim policy of destroying the Assamese pride and Assamese determination to punish the invaders and to cripple them permanently.

Attempted Invasion of Assam

Attempted Muslim invasion of Assam started in 1205 AD with the Delhi Sultanate and practically ended in 1671 AD with the decline of Mughal Empire after Aurangzeb. This period of about 460 years can be divided into two phases in a cut off line 1529 AD when a treaty agreement was made by the Assamese with Muslim invaders granting some concession of establishing police outpost (Thana) in some selected places in Lower Assam for trade and commercial purpose with Muslim Bengal. With the powerful policy of Emperor Akbar for one India under Mughal rule, Mughal expeditions to Assam started from 1613 AD and this policy was vigorously pursued by Emperor Shahjehan and Aurangzeb. Mir Jumla's occupation of Gargaon in 1663 and Raja Ramsing's engagement in the Battle of Saraighat 1671 AD took place in Aurangzeb's time.

Ahom invasion of Assam from 1228 AD from East synchronized the attempted invasion of Assam by the Muslim from the west. While the Muslim onslaughts remained confined in Lower Assam from river Manaha to Kaliabar, Ahoms conquest remained confined in Upper Assam from Sadia to Kaliabar. The nature and characteristics of Muslim and Ahom invasion differed drastically in that Muslim underestimated the Assamese with their pround feeling of superiority in cultural, religious and military matters whereas Ahoms did not foster any ego against the local population. Soon after their entry into Assam the Ahom considered the land to be their own domain and the process of integration and absorbing with local population was carried out almost spontaneously. To the Ahoms Assam was MUNGDUNSHUNKHAM land full with the gardens of Gold, the name initially given to Assam.

The Ahoms after their all pervading campaign and consolidation in Upper Assam turned their attention to Lower Assam. Though their encounter with the Koch King (1556) of Lower Assam was demoralizing and humiliating yet the maturity of Ahom political thinking and patience adequately helped them to overcome the situation maintaining their glamorous confidence. Subsequently all the eighteen Rajas of frontier states of Lower Assam extended their willing subordination to the Ahoms by the middle of 16th century. However distantly might be, Ahom Swargadeo became the ruler and guiding spirit to the Lower Assam region and hence after the second half of 16th century Lower Assam also felt the presence of Ahom authority at all the time of their distress and despondency.

Attempted Muslim invasion of Assam led to three strategic treaties signed between the Muhamedans and the Assamese, i.e. 1529, 1639 and in 1663. In the treaties of 1529 and 1639 Muhamedans were granted the right to establish their police outpost in selected places of Lower Assam including at Pandu, Hajo, Dhubri and carrying out trade and commerce. The Ghiladharighat Treaty of 1663 (After Mir Jumla's Assam Invasion) was the most humiliating. This treaty had given the Lower Assam to Mughal. A huge amount of annual war indemnity had to be paid. Mughal made Itakhuli in Gauhati their administrative headquarter.

Glory to Ahoms

The period from 1663 to 1671 was the most agonizing one to Ahom Swargodeos. Jayadhawaj Sing, Chakradhwaj Sing and Udayaditya Sing had the most trying, uneasy time under Mughal's conduct. The Swargodeos even could not eat the morsel of food peacefully. Hence all preparations to undo what was done in the Treaty of Ghiladharighat was undertaken with determination and proper puparation leading to the most successful battle of Saraighat in 1671 under the generalship of Lachit Barphukan and with the wise and able guidance of Prime Minister Atan Buragohain, who was placed in Gauhati by Swargodeo for the benefit to Lachit Barphukan. During wartime Atan Buragohain made his headquarter in North Gauhati hill.

The battle of Saraighat was a turning point in the history of Assam. This battle needs an analytical approach from military history point of view. After the determination of the principle of defeating and expelling out the Mughals from Assam, the Swargodoes maintained this aim with hard labour and good thinking. The action-plan undertaken by three Swargodeos Jayadwaj Sing (1648-1663), Chakradwaj Sing (1663-1669) and Udayditya Sing (1669-1673) for making the war preparation against the powerful Mughals needs to be enumerated for its war-wisdom.

War Preparation

Steps taken by Ahom Kings for the preparation of war against the mighty Mughal demonstrated fighting qualities of Assamese people:

1. Production of guns and equipments in ordinance factory under direct control of King inside palace vicinity.
2. Training to the fighting force.
3. Arrangement to stock large scale food grains and other provisions.
4. Reorganisation of Civil and Military Administration.
5. Selection of a right person as General to command anti-Mughal Expedition.
6. Diplomatic correspondence with Mughal to gain time and to mislead of actual Ahom intention.
7. Securing help from subordinate local rulers and neighbouring Kings of Hill areas.
8. Revitalization of Nation in Arms theory.
9. Upgrading morale of the common people.
10. Construction of Forts and Ramparts in strategic Zone/ Repair of old forts.
11. Construction of more than 3000 war boats and training of sailors.
12. Despatch of highly responsible personnel to Namjani (lower Assam) including Atan Burahgohain.
13. Delegation of supreme decision making powers to General Barphukan when the action was on.
14. Counsel from scientific astrologer for appropriate moment for action.
15. Training to persons to make excellent kataki (*Duta*). Now onwards learned and intelligent Brahmins were appointed for the job.

16. Propaganda to mislead enemy even to spread ghost stories and the role of black magic in Assam.
17. Pretended betrayers to mislead enemy camp.
18. Training for Night fighting and guerilla tactics.
19. Direct supervision by King wherever possible.
20. Rehabilitation of people who left home and hearth during Mir Jumla's invasion.
21. Letters of request to the neighbouring Kings of Koch Behar, Jayantia and Kachar to organize confederacy.
22. Training of singing soldiers, dancing girls and progapanda squadrons to extol enemy's fighting morale.
23. Intelligence to assess own loopholes and lapses for elimination of internal weakness.

The Offensive

After gaining full confidence in the war preparation, the Ahom force-marched out from Gargaon on August 1667 suggested to be auspicious by royal astrologer. Customary religious performance was done according to the Hindu rites. Also the king reminded again to the general of his responsibility—"If you prove incompetent in the task of defeating the enemy at Itakhuli, you shall not be let off with impunity". Lachit Barphukan, the General-in-Chief of the campaign with full confidence and high sense of responsibility to the cause of his country led the army marching at the head of the non-compromising force with Atan Burahgohain,—the wisest man of Assam, as his second in command in the battle field.

Encamping at Kaliabar on first week of September 1667, the Ahom army made surprise attack and captured the Mughal garrison at Bhbari on the north bank with two Mughal Commanders and substantial quantity of arms and ammunition. Next was captured the garrisons at Kajali,

Sonapur, Panikhaity and Tatimara between Guwahati and Kapili. Hundreds of Assamese captives were released. After these preliminary tasks the main target Itakhuli was captured on 4th November 1667 by a well-planned surprise night attack, and several Mughal Sardars including Feroz Khan, the Fouzder of Guwahati, along with elephants, horses, guns, food stores and coins.

On hearing this victory the king expressed happiness— "It is now that I can eat my morsel of food with pleasure".

Emperor Aurangzeb sent a powerful force under the command of Mirza Raja Ramsing to reconquer Assam. A well-trained and well-equipped force with infantry, artillery, swordmen, navy and also accompanied by Sikh Guru Teghbahadur and five pirs to neutralize the so believed 'black magic' of Assam, reached Hajo in the year 1669 (April) From 1669 to 1671 Ramsing played diplomacy to persuade Lachit Barphukan to withdraw to Ahom territory by handing over Guwahati to Mughal. This gameplans made by Ramsing to demoralize and destabilise Assamese strength had given additional time to Lachit Barphukan to create a well demarcated fighting zone with his advantage in a triangular location between Kamakhya, Aswakranta and Itakhuli hill on the bed of the river Brahmaputra. A war zone of about 15 miles by 20 miles on the north and south bank of Brahmaputra was prepared fully to meet the enemy. Creation of strong sense of discipline, construction of forts, ramparts and specific responsibilities to 18 other generals decentralizing their area of operation created a picture of victory zone.

Desired battle came and Lachit with his ill health commanded the battle in his expected zone of fighting field. Victory came as expected and the Mughal withdrew. Comparative armed strength of both the sides, as found in various accounts may be listed as under:-

Raja Ramsing	*Lachit Barphukan*
8000 cavalry	1,00,000 soldiers of all varieties
15000 Imperial force	32,000 men in a Naval fleet of 3000 ships.
5000 Swordmen of Turkey	
15000 Infantry from Koch Behar	
Naval Fleet with 50 ships.	

Significance of the Battle

The battle of Saraighat was significant to Assam for various decisive results.

(a) Attempted Muslim invasions of Assam covering a period of about 450 years almost ended with this battle.

(b) This battle also established the consolidation of Ahom rules in Assam solidifying the geopolitical consistency of north-east till it was separated by independent India creating Seven Sisters.

(c) Till 1671 there was social and administrative differences between Upper and Lower Assam. After this battle assimilation between the two parts and cohesion of the people made its beginning.

(d) This battle also helped regaining full confidence and splendour by the Assamese community.

(e) With appreciation of Assamese quality of fighting by the Mughals, the region ceased to be underestimated by outsiders.

(f) As the Bengal Zamindars with all their force of undivided Bengal (with Dhaka as Headquarters of Muslim Governors) accompanied the Assam campaign of the Muslims, the Assamese people adopted the term Bengal, synonymous to foreign invaders or as unwanted element of Assam or a work of despise.

Conclusion

The Battle of Saraighat and its architects are yet to get due attention. Historians and Military Historians may dig into this event for further critical analysis and appeciation.

Bibliography

MSS-O 60 Tr. 0.82; — Account of the Ahom King from the reign of Jayadhawaj Singha to Rudra Singha. Author unknown. Department of Historical Antiquarian.

Fathiya-I-Ibriya — (0. D/72 ASL) by Shihabuddhin Talish who accompanied Mir Jumla in his Koch Behar and Assam campaign.

Barua, G.C. — *Ahom Buranji,* a chronicle in Ahom Language with parallel English Tr. Ist. Edi., 1930.

Borah, Dr.M.I. (Eng. Tra) — Baharistan-I-Ghaybi of Mirza Nathan—A History of conflicts of the Mughals with Assam, Bengal, Bihar, Orissa during the reign of Jehangir and Shahjehan. 2 vols., published by DHAS, 1936.

Bhuayn, S.K. — Lachit Barphukan and His Times, DHAS Edu. 1947.

Bhuayn, S.K. — Atan Burhagohain and his Times, DHAS, Edu. 1947.

Kalita, B.C. — *Military Activities of Medieval Assam,* D.K. Publishing ed. 1988.

14

Participation of Tribal in Some Selected Defence Mechanisms of Princely Tripura

Satyadeo Poddar

Like other Princely States of India, the defence mechanism of Tripura constituted one of the important sectors of state administration and ample references are available in Rajamala, Political Agency Reports, etc. The dynasty which ruled Tripura for centuries claimed descent from a legendry figure 'Durhya' of the Lunar dynasty who was said to have migrated at his royal father's behest to the trans-Gangetic country occupied by the so-called 'Kiratas' and established his first capital in the island of Sagar on the confluence of the Bhagirathi and the sea, around which soon sprung up the nucleus of a prosperous kingdom. As the conquest of Druhya and his successors proceeded eastwards, the seat of Government, according to Rajamal, was removed to the bank of the 'Kapila' (old Brahmaputra) and both capital and kingdom came to be renamed 'Tribeg' after the river trijunction on which the new capital stood. To king Tripur, the 40th in descent from Druhya, is ascribed the change of the name of kingdom to 'Tripura'.[1] The task of consolidation of the growing kingdom involved the rulers of Tripura in active conflict, not only with the neighbouring kings of Kamrup, Cachar, Arakan and Rangamati, but with the rulers of Gour across the Ganges and a remarkable episode of which was the route of the invading forces of Gour in a bloody battle by the defending armies of Tripura, led personally by heroic queen, Tripura

Sundari, in disregard of her husband, King Changthung Pha/ Singhatunga's (*alias* Kiritdhar's) eagerness to sue for peace.[2] This comfiture of Gour, according to popular belief, was partially retrieved in 1279 AD. Tughril Khan, the Pathan 'Malik' of Gour, assisted Rattan Fa, the founder of the subsequent ruling dynasty of Tripura, in establishing the latter's claim to the throne in supersession of his elder brother Raja Fa and bestowed on Rattan Fa in exchange for the friendly present of a rare gem 'Manik', the title of 'Manikya', which the rulers of Tripura inherited upto the last one.[3] During the reign of Pratap Manikya, the son of Rattan Manikya, as the capital of Bengal was transferred to Subarangram, the Muslim rulers of Bengal came into closer touch with Tripura in 1347 AD.

The first regular warfare with the Muslim rulers of Bengal was during the time of Dhanya Manikya[4]. Dhanya Manikya used the title 'Vijayindra' (conquerer) in his coin Saka 1428 (1506 AD) and "Chatigrama" (i.e. conqueror of Chittagong) in his coin of Saka 1435 (i.e. 1513-1514 AD). These two coins were perhaps issued on the occasion of his grand victory over Hussain Shah.[5] The Rajamala (Chronicles of the kings of Tripura) eulogizes the military achievement of Dhanya Manikya. In all the three campaigns the Generals of both Hussain Shah and Dhanya Manikya adopted the intelligent tactical use of terrain causing surprise and havoc on the opponent. Under the generalship of Gour Mallik, Hussain Shah sent a vast army gathered from 1513 AD. The Sultan's army attacked from the south and reached upto 'Meherkul', the fort of the king of Tripura. The Tripura army could not resist the enemy and the Bengal force-marched into the interior instead.[6] Under the General Chaichang Rai of Dhanya Manikya, the soldiers of Tripura then took shelter in the fort of 'Chandigarh' and unreisted Sultan's army advanced towards 'Rangamati', the then capital of Tripura. Meanwhile, the Tripura soldiers dammed up the river Gumti at 'Sonamura', where it debauches into the plains. The Tripura soldiers then cut open the dyke at night as a result of which the Mughal encampment was swept away and most of the soldiers were drowned.[7]

Regarding the selection of the Senapati (Commander-in-Chief), kings of Tripura followed the same pattern where the personal consideration of king and the evaluation of a person is taken into account. Throughout the history of Tripura, the normal practice was to appoint a Senapati amongst the close relatives of the king.[8] Dhanya Manikya (1490-1520 AD), with a view to consolidate his power and place his throne on a firmer footing, reorganized the Army and introduced many reforms. The old generals who aspired to, and practically did, for some time control the affairs of the government were removed and put to death and new posts of different grades were created and filled up by able officers.[9] Since the time of Dhanya Manikya, the kings relied upon the ability of some other persons irrespective of caste and religion. In this connection, it may be said that Senapati Rai Kachhag of Dhanya Manikya belonging to a Reang community (not in kinship with the royal Tripuri tribe) was appointed by the king in special circumstances.[10] The persons appointed as a Senapati were not always loyal to their masters. On quite a few occasions, they, in spite of being close relatives of the king, initiated and encouraged palace intrigues and dissatisfaction among the soldiers against their monarch. In support of it, reference may be made of Daitya Narayan, Senapati of Vijay Manikya (c. 1532-1563 AD), Senapati Gopiprasad Narayan of Ananta Manikya (c. 1564-1566 AD), Ranagan Narayan of Jay Manikya (c. 1573-1577 AD) etc., who tried to dethrone the kings of Tripura in order to capture power.[11]

Sri Rajamala[12] states that the Jamatias were the important fighting tribes of Tripura during the reign of the early kings and formed hard core of royal army. From 'Pancha Manikya'[13], it is known that among the Hill subjects of Tripura, the Jamatias were the fighting caste. They, in the olden days, used to work in the army of the king of Tripura. The army constituted by them was called 'Jamat', and from the word 'Jamat', they later on, came to be known as Jamatias. "The Jamatias were", Kailash Chandra Singha writes, "one of the pure branches of Tripuris. They were in the ancient period, predominant in the army of Tripura".[14] B.A. Allen also calls them the fighting caste of Tripura.[15]

Regarding the term 'Jamatia', which denotes a particular group of people, Omesh Saighal opines, "The Jamat in Urdu means an assembly of persons. The former rulers of Tripura used to recruit his army from a class of tribal people who were not only warriors but also had proved their loyalty to him. A fair portion of his armed forces were drawn from amongst the Jamatias who formed a group in his army, and it was from this fact that they derived their clan name.[16] According to Jamatia, the word 'Jamatia' is derived from the word 'Jama' and 'Twia'. 'Jama' means 'Tax' and 'Twia' means 'not to bear the burden of'. Thus to them, the word 'Jamatia' means a person who does not bear the burden of taxes.[17] In the 1860s of the 19th century there took place an extended series of raids in Tripura. These raids were commonly known as the 'Great Kuki invasion of 1860s. In January 1860 a large body of Kukis after raiding the upper Feni 'burst into the plains of Tipperah at Chagulneyah, burnt or plundered 15 villages, butchered 185 British subjects and carried off about 101 captives'.[17A] The Kukis took away from these villages gold, silver and iron. Troops and police were dispatched immediately to the spot by the Magistrate of District Tipperah, but the Kukis already retired to the hills and jungles after staying one or two days in the plains. Being disgusted by the oppressions of the unparalleled corrupt officials, the Jamatias under the leadership of Parikshit, the then Sardar of the Jamatias, revolted in 1863 against the government. Parikshit was really a man of revolution. A Jamatia hearsay goes: "If two or three men lie down with Parikshit in a line, they become hardly visible for the physique of Parikshit is so big and high. High strength can only be compared with that of a tiger or an elephant".[18] Disputes and intrigues vitiated the politico-administrative conditions of Hill Tipperah. Rajah Birchandra, in his overwhelming situation, entrusted Oakhirai, the Hazari[19], a rapacious and devious official to collect rents from the Jamatias. The imposition of Tyethung by the Oakhirai was regarded as one of the factors of the Jamatia revolt. Having considered the Jamatias to be seditious, the Rajah sent a large number of Darlong-Kukis to the Jamatia villages to subjugate the Jamatias. "As a natural consequence of sending out a number of armed ruffians under no command or discipline whatever, an affray very soon occurred, in which three of the Rajah's men were wounded by spears, and two of the Jamatias shot; the head of these were cut off and are now hanging up in terrarium in Agartala".[20] Birchandra employed Murchhui and Hampui (Kuki sardar) to suppress the Jamatia revolt. 600 Kukis killed 200 Jamatias.[21]

On 14-04-53 T.E. (1943 AD), the King of Tripura came to know that about 1200 Reangs and 7000 Noatias were being organized under the leadership of Ratanmani to put a strong resistance against the administration.[22] The government was, by the same letter, apprised that the Jamatias would not remain neutral. Having heard this information, Rajah issued an order *vide* No. 142 dated 14-04-53 T.E. to capture and punish the armed 'dacoits' in Amarpur, Udaipur, etc. In accordance with the order of the Maharaja, Major Nagendra Debbarma moved towards the disturbed areas along with Bodyguard Jamadars, namely Sri Ramesh Chandra Deb and Prabat Chandra Deb. 30 Bodyguards of other ranks were also sent with them. In addition to that, the officer of the Rajya Rakshi Bahini, a few Reang Sardars and some other officers and police forces from the state administration were dispatched. They were ordered that the captured dacoits be brought to the capital; the soldiers should open fire in case of self-defence and if faced with eventuality from the dacoits; the dacoits' arms and ammunitions be captured and seized. If they are not found at home, their houses must be set ablaze after removing the properties, women, children and elderly persons from houses, and the relatives of dacoits be arrested and brought to the capital, and if necessary, the force commander should mobilize more forces from Amarpur and Udaipur divisional offices.[23]

Frightened at the increasing developments, the administration of Rajah raised security forces from amongst the loyal hill people to crash the revolt. The security forces created history in committing inhuman barbarities, including arson and pillages, rapes and setting ablaze the houses and the villages of the Reangs.[24] The government was apprised by repeated reports from the police and tribal chiefs of Amarpur and Udaipur that the Reangs had turned violent. The Reang rebels looted paddy from the granaries of the rich, specially the Reang Chakdiris. The ordinary Reang people opened Dramagoals[25] to solve food crisis, which arose mainly for the Rajah's heavy contributions to the war fund of the British. The Reangs were reported to have established a 'Council of Ministers', and regarded Ratanmoni as their Rajah.[26] In conflicting situation, information had already been sent to the Jamatia Akras (Sardars) to provide young men. Manu Ranjan Debbarma, a member of the maharaja's personal staff, went to Udaipur area with gunpowder, caps and lead ball for use in matchlock guns and sufficient money. Having obtained this information, the Jamatia Sardars sent five hundred armed Jamatias to march over the villages of the alleged Reang rebels. The said gunpowder, caps, lead balls and money were spent for the newly assembled Jamatia soldiers.[27] The Reang rebels were brutally suppressed and forced to leave their hearth and homes,[28] by the Binindias and soldiers under the Captainship of Nagendra Debbarma. Some Jamatias of Shilghati and Hadra villages, namely Sri Chertwng Jamatia and Sri Kanai Lal Jamatia were reported to have taken part in the monarchial administered anti-rebellion operations.

From the above analysis, it can be inferred that the kings of Tripura, in order to protect and expand their territory, persistently took the help of tribal chiefs in their day-to-day administrative activities and sometimes defence system became solely dependable on the tactical war methods of tribal communities. During modern time, even the British had to rely on the technical style of Kuki raids. The kings of Tripura in late 19th and 20th century, became successful to control the local revolts, only by the unique functioning tribal defence mechanism.

NOTES

1. "Appendix to Analysis of Rajamala by Rev. James Log" in the *Journal of Asiatic Society to Bengal,* 1850, Vol. XIX, Calcutta, see also, N.R. Roychoudhury, *Tripura Throught the Ages,* Agartala, 1977, pp.7-8.
2. Kailash Chandra Singha, *Rajamala,* Part III, Chapter 2, pp.23-24 (New Edition, Vol. I, pp. 62-63) "King Chhengthum Fa or Kirtidhar" to quote A.C. Bhattacharyya, "is the 21st ruler after Jangefa, the most noticeable event during his reign is the annexation of Meherkul by his Queen who inflicted a heavy defeat in 1280 AD on the king of Gour to whose territory it belonged. Chhengthum Fa died after the victorious battle of Meherkul and was followed

by Achang (Raja Surya) Khichung (Mohan) and Dangar Fa (Hari Roy). From this time onwards, the kings of Tripura came into frequent clash with the Mahomedan rulers of Gour, one of whom played the important part of giving shelter to a refugee Tripur Prince named Ratan Fa. (A.C. Bhattacharyya, *op. cit.*, pp.15-16).

3. K.R. Qanungo, *Bengal under the House of Balban,* in Jadunath Sarkar (ed), *The History of Bengal Muslim Period 1200-1757*, Patna, 1973, p.59.
4. B. No.1/S.4/1329 T.E. (1919 AD), File No. F1-1. p.3, Secretariat Archives, Government of Tripura.
5. Suprasanna Bandyopadhyay, *Tripura Itihas* (in Bengali), Kolkata, 1982, p.5.
6. Sushila Mandal, *History of Bengal,* Part I, Calcutta, 1978, p.221.
7. E.F. Sandys, *History of Tripura,* Calcutta, 1915, p.15.
8. Kaliprasanna Sen, *op. cit.*, vol. II, p.119.
9. A.C. Bhattacharyya, *Progressive Tripura,* Calcutta, 1930, p.19.
10. Kailash Chandra Singha, *Rajamala* (in Bengali), Comilla, 1896, Part III, Chapter-3 (see new edition, 1984, Agartala, edited by Mahadev Chakravarti, *et al.*, vol. I, p.73).
11. Kaliprasanna Sen, *op. cit.*, vol. II, pp.141-43.
12. Kaliprasanna Sen, *Sri Rajmala,* vol. II, p.175.
13. *Op. cit., Panch Manikya,* Tripura State Cultural Centre and Museum, Agartala, 1996, p.62.
14. Kailash Chandra Singha (ed), *Sri Rajmala,* vol. II, p.175.
15. B.C. Allen, E.A. Gait and H.F. Howard, *Gazetteer of Bengal and North East India,* Mittal Publication, New Delhi, 1984 (Reprint), p.608.
16. Omesh Saigal, *Tripura: Its History and Culture,* Concept Publishing House, Delhi, 1978, pp.102-103.
17. According to Sri Lalit Mohan Jamatia of Shil Ghati, Udaipur, South Tripura, who is an Ex. Hoda Akra of Jamatia community and interview was conducted with him on 12-4-1997 while doing survey work under personal research project.

17A. Sir Alexander Mackenzie, *Memorandum on the North Eastern Frontier of Bengal,* Calcutta, 1869, p.53.

18. Nagendra Jamatia: *Jamatia Chaba Bakharak Parikshit,* (in Kok Borok), Tripura Tribal Research Insituire, Government of Tripura, Agartala, 1999, p.15.
19. Hazari means, *Bindiroha Bibarten O. Tripura, Tripura Darpan,* 1985, Agartala, p.6.

20. Alexander Mackenzie, *The North East Frontier of India,* p.67.
21. Kailash Chandra Singha, *Rajamala,* p.183.
22. Udaipur Camp, 14-04-53, 1.30 P.M. from J.S. Debbarma to Kumar B.L. Debbarma.
23. No.299/C dated 28-07-43, Ujjanta Palace, Agartala, Kash Series, being quoted in the book of Manimay Debbarma: *Bidrohi Neta Ratanmani: Ekti Bitarkita Charita* (in Bengali, pp.6-7).
24. Jagat Chakraborty, *Sangrami Tripurar Amar Vahini* (in Bengali), *Deshhitoishi*, Autumn issue, 1977, p.119.
25. Dharmagola is a kind of traditional cooperative system of the Reangs. Such type of cooperative system was prevalent among other tribes like Jamatias also. The main purpose of this cooperative was to provide monetary assistance of the villagers in times of necessity and need. Each individual family of a village generally deposit 10 kg. of paddy in the Dharmagola as a first instalment to become its member.
26. Aghore Debbarma, *Reang Krishak Bidroha O Sahid Raanmani in Tripura Katha,* CPI Organ, Special No.1954, Agartala, *op. cit.*, p. 32.
27. Tripura Chandra Sen, *Tripura in Transition,* op. cit., p.17.
28. Jagat Chakraborty, *op. cit.*, p. 17.

15

Technology and Society
In Pre-Colonial and Colonial Perspective of Arunachal Pradesh

Amrendra Kr. Thakur

Technology is basic to human nature and it interacts deeply with human society to produce an impact on the directions and pace of social evolution. In the evolution of human society, many anthropologists believe, language is associated with the early stages. It is sensible to say that Neolithic or Paleolithic tool making technology would be assisted and its continuity ensured by language. It may well be suggested that language has the same evolutionary history as technology. It is plausible to argue that the need for elaborate communication must have preserving, communicating and diffusing technology, thus providing an impetus also to its improvement. Technology may have played a similar reinforcing role in the development of language and the evolution of man. In this evolutionary time scale, science is quite a recent expression of human societal activity. One could thus make the distinction that since science is a recent acquisition while technology is almost contemporary with the presence of man as anthropologists describe him, science is more a product of social evolution and social conditions, unlike technology which appear to be embedded in our biological nature. Indulging in further speculation, one is tempted to seek linkages between language, technology and early human evolution.

Even from the fragmentary evidence it becomes apparent that technological change half a million years ago was certainly slow; our ancestors at that time were quite small-brained. It appears that evolution speeded up in the last hundred thousand years.[1] From Paleolithic times onward, the parallel growth of social and technological progress becomes easier to trace. However, it is not until Neolithic times that we obtain evidence that in a social group or tribe the technologist finds a special niche; he is the medicine man, the potter, the weaver, and the arms maker. His skills and knowledge serve his society. At the same time these skills and knowledge set him apart. He uses them to benefit the tribal chief, the king, the priest, the village elders, and in return, has more power and influence. As long as this extra influence was small and as long as his own skills and knowledge were not extensive enough to unbalance neighbouring societies or his own, the extra influence did not seriously upset the Neolithic or the later Chalcolithic societies. Finally, the pressure of social needs is so apparent in many of the processes of our innovation that the coupling between technology and society cannot be thought of only as the innovator's innate drive, without any social interaction. The anthropological, archaeological and historical evidence of stagnant societies and their lack of technological innovation tend to argue for a closer and more intense interaction between the two. It is in this perspective that we have discussed here the aspects of defence technology of the people of Arunachal Pradesh in pre-colonial and colonial perspective.[2]

I

Technology inquiries in India have virtually remained confined to the macro level of inquiries; the inquiries into the aspects of rural and agrarian technologies, technologies of the periphery and that of the marginal and the tribal are not very popular. Nonetheless, the influence and impact of their approaches, trends and findings are quite useful for the study of tribal technology. In this regard three major shades of opinion can be identified. To the first category belongs to the majority of contemporary European travellers and several subsequent British officials and scholars who find everything in India 'black and bleak'. In sharp contrast, another set of opinion is quite enthusiastic about India's scientific credentials and potentialities in the pre-colonial period. A third set of opinion treats cautiously and offers guarded comments. No single model, formula or explanation can cover all these aspects. Human needs are constantly changing; a particular technology or a set of technologies appropriate to one times and culture may not necessarily be appropriate to another.[3]

The accounts of contemporary European travellers show that the symptoms of change in science and technology had no echo in India. From them came the stories of the 'oriental mind' and Indian resistance to innovation and change, and these were to become the obsession of European scholarship for generation to come. Wallace, Munro, Buchanan and Orlich, for example, condemned Indian agricultural technology as being for a 'very low standard, stagnated since centuries', and dominated by Martin, Fraser, Moorcroft and Dubois as 'most primitive, crude, clumsy, unscientific and stagnated heritage of the oriental nation'. The condemnation may as well be part of the process of hegemonization. Without criticizing Indian science and technology they could not have justified colonization. For European observers there may also have been some genuine difficulties in understanding and an abstruse treatise or in appreciating a simple technical devise, which would appear 'appropriate' only when viewed against the existing socio-economic context. The early colonizers in India realized that they had to treat cautiously. The state they sought to establish had to borrow, and yet be substantially different, from the pre-colonial structure and texts. For this, the condemnation of the immediate past was considered necessary. Indians were declared unscientific, superstitious and resistant to change; India was identified with dirt and disease. Travellers, scholars and officials of both the Orientalist and Anglicist variety subscribed to this view. William Jones, the foremost orientalist, declared that in scientific accomplishments the Asiatics were 'mere children' when compared with the Europeans. Thus was established a paternalistic Raj which would be caring and dismissive at the same time. It was to be based on claims to not only superior musketry, but to a superior knowledge as well. This sense of superiority came from western discourse on rationality and progress, and was promptly used to denounce whatever scientific knowledge (e.g. in astronomy and medicine) the Indians could boast of. Yet this denunciation was not total. Several early colonial scholars showed respect for certain indigenous scientific traditions and techniques. They wanted western knowledge to permeate slowly and cause gradual displacement.

Though critical to their core, these accounts do throw some light on the level of science and technology in pre-colonial India.[4] Astronomy, medicine, and the Indian textile and steel-making processes impressed travellers the most. Most of the travellers recorded that Indians had made remarkable progress in mathematics and astronomy in ancient times, which gradually fell from grace, particularly after the establishment of the Muslim rule. Later several British and Indian historians uncritically accepted this. Thus grew the notion that science flourished only in ancient India and not in medieval India. However, scholars like Rahman, Dharampal, Alvares and Ansari have raised strong objections to this notion. Rahman has compiled a 'Bibliography of Source Materials in Sanskrit, Arabic and Persian'. He argues that throughout the medieval period, scientific and technological activity, as is evident from the number of manuscripts, was both continuous and vigorous. The number of manuscripts listed in this Bibliography is quite large. On the basis of tributes paid to Indian textiles, metal works, construction and ship-building techniques by several early European travellers, Sangwan argues that: "....by the beginning of the eighteenth century India had attained the distinct status of a technologically advanced country. Indian workmen excelled in their profession. They had also adopted some new techniques and technologies, which appeared more useful. There was thus a continuous process of technological change in pre-industrial (pre-colonial?) India".[5]

Thus it was during the 17th and 18th centuries the post-renaissance epoch (that of Descartes and Newton) that Europe began to out distance India in the natural sciences. Dharampal also concedes that it is impossible that the various sciences and technologies were on a decline in India around 1750 and perhaps had been on a similar course for several centuries previously. Irfan Habib does not accept any description of pre-colonial technology as primitive but calls for 'a wider study of the social constrains that prevented either an endogenous development of industrial technology comparable to that of modern Europe or, at least, a rapid absorption of the European technology itself'. He argues that many mechanical principles frequently employed in modern machine were in use in Mughal India, but adds that the range of their application was rather limited. Pre-colonial science and technology was definitely not primitive. A better description perhaps would be 'proto-science and technology', clearly distinguishing it from the post-seventeenth-century modern scientific tradition based on the experimental method.[6]

The above description of the major approaches clearly indicates, that there has never been a serious desire among scholars working on the aspects of science and technology and their role in social evolution to look into the aspects of that of the tribals in India. The studies have been mostly on the main land of India and its dominant issues. Even the studies on the life and condition of tribals in India have ignored the features of technology.[7] The absence of the studies on technology of tribal people is mainly because of the success of the industrial revolution in Europe and the consequent political hegemony that followed. It brought the Europeans face to face with people who being somewhat archaic in terms of technology and remained tied up with distinct ways of life. To European eyes, tribal people were nothing but queer and exotic. The necessity of colonial administration nevertheless made the bureaucrats study the life and culture of such people intensively. However, because of mental pre-occupation the alien subject population, particularly those under colonial subjugation largely, appeared only as savage. Lacking the experiences of heterogeneous realities, the very approach to the study of alien tribes became an exercise on cultural isolates. With the gradual growing accessibility to the interior tribal areas during post-independence period, the nature of contacts with the tribes met with considerable qualitative improvement. This was adequately reflected in the subsequent studies. Nevertheless, the writings were not devoid of the inadequacies of the ethnographic studies conducted mostly exclusively under the influence of the British tradition. We inherited not only concepts, techniques, theories and methods of study but also topics of study. Hence, the study of tribal technology did not receive the deserved attention of the scholars.

The state of study of technology in northeast India is not very different. Though in the *Proceeding Volumes of the North East India History Association,* the first paper on this aspect in northeast India appeared in 1987 the studies on technology could not catch the attention of other scholars of this region till as late as 1994. Even after these two isolated efforts, however, pioneer, the study of technology in this region could not get momentum and only two articles have appeared afterwards.[8] Here it is needless to mention that none of these four articles deals with any aspect of technology in Arunachal Pradesh. Stray references to the village defence technological studies can be found elsewhere.

II

Coming to the aspects of technology and society in Arunachal Pradesh, there are a number of important areas to reconstruct the historical past of the people, such as, building construction, paper making, sericulture, weaving and dying of cloth, indigenous poison, windmills, handlooms and handicrafts etc. Besides, we have analyzed here the defence technology. It is mainly because of the nature of the seminar and the proposed publication of the papers. Traces of earliest human society have been scattered in almost all area of Arunachal Pradesh. There is an important collection of stone tools from Arunachal Pradesh, which have been preserved in the Pitt River Museum, Oxford. J.P. Mills and J.H. Grace collected these during 1933-35. A.H. Dani made the first scientific report of this collection in 1960. In 1966, T.C. Sharma also studied the collection and pointed out that 10 specimens out of 16 are made on varieties of locally available rocks such as, sand stone, basalt, gneiss, schist and talcose. The rest of the implements are made on jadeite, which is not locally available, and thus these implements, according to him, reached Arunachal Pradesh either from north Burma or China. Technologically, these are chipped and edged ground tools. Some implements of jadeite were initially shaped by sawing technique. Typologically, there are two dominant types in this collection, viz. stone axes with lenticular cross-section and quadrangular type with rectangular cross-section. The minor types are hog-backed type of celt and slender chisels of jadeite. Later also, neoliths have been collected and reported from almost all parts of Arunachal Pradesh. As regards period, nothing could be definitely said. Yet, on typological grounds it could be surmised that the Neolithic stage could have started in Arunachal Pradesh by about 2000 B.C.[10] Here it is important to mention about a solitary megalithic site in Arunachal, at Jamiri in the West Kameng District. The area is inhabited by the Akas. Here, the mention of some important pre-historic artifacts found in Arunachal Pradesh will not be out of context.

1. In 1870 E.H. Steel noticed a few neoliths made of jade in the villages of the 'Namsang Nagas', i.e. Noctes of Tirap district.
2. By the end of the 19th century Capt. Gregony found one curvilinear rounded butt axe from Mishmi Hills.
3. By 1917 Healy of Geological Survey of India collected one curvilinear facetted tool made of streaked and mottled jadeite. Through the actual find spot has not been recorded, typologically it appears to have come from the Sadiya Frontier Zone.
4. About 1925-26 R.D. Banerji noticed on adze in Padam Abor (Adi) village.
5. In 1933 J.P. Mills found one curvilinear facetted tool and three rounded butt axe from Ningru, north of Noa Dihing river in Tirap district.
6. In 1935, J.H. Crace collected from Sadiya Frontier Zone three facetted tools, three rounded butt axe and two miscellaneous type long implements, one made of gneiss and another of jadeite. The last one found from Ningru, north of Noa Dihing river.
7. In 1937, J.P. Mills found a rounded butt axe from Tigra (Minyong) Abor (Adi) hills.

8. One more curvilinear facetted tool made of dolerite and a rounded butt axe made of gneiss found from Sadiya Frontier Zone have been preserved in Pitt Rivers Museum, Oxford.
9. Between 1962-64 N. Sarkar noticed two triangular and two shouldered axes in possession of villagers in Singpho and Aka areas. Apart from these he collected three chisels, ten complete axes and four broken pieces of axes from different parts of Arunachal Pradesh.
10. One polished chisel found from Bokar area in Siang by 1960 was in District Museum, Along. It was later transferred to the Central Museum, Shillong.
11. In 1968 M.C. Goswami of Gauhati University collected three Neolithic Celts from Rupa in Kameng district. (Now in the collection of Anthropology Department, Gauhati University).
12. In 1969-70, in the excavation at Bhishmaknagar, Y.A. Raikar found four neoliths but without stratigrphic context. Three were triangular ground axes and one was a bar type polished broken celt. These are now in the Central Museum, Shillong.
13. In 1969-70 B.P. Boparkikar found, in course of an expedition in Daphabum area of Lohit district, the following artifacts: one unifacial and one bifacial choppers from Alubari near Chowkham; a board rectangular flake with one side serrated near Chamba; a few cleavers, ovats and one neolith (Chisel) from Kale; a proto-hand axe, a few cores, flakes and points from around Teehum; one ovate, cleaver, scraper, flakes and neoliths (a shouldered and a triangular played axes) near Glow; stone age tools including a side scraper near Chakho; one unificial chopper and a flake from Tawling near Hayuliang.

14. In 1971 Y. A. Raikar collected chipa of semi-precious stones like chalcedony, jasper etc. from Vijaynagar. (This indicates possibility of getting more microliths in the valley of the Dyun, i.e., Neo Dihing river).
15. In 1979 D.K. Duarah reported three Neolithic Celts found from Damin circle of Subansiri District. Two of these are ground axes and one is a working pat of an axe.

The archaeological remains and the material culture indicate that, after the Neolithic stage there is a long gap in our knowledge of the past. No traces of the early ancient period are found in Arunachal Pradesh so far. The earliest probable date, of which material evidence is available, goes back to the tenth century A.D. Legends of Parasurma, Bana, Vidarbha, Rukmini, Bhishmak and Sisupal associated with historical ruins and other places do exit, but they are all later phenomena of the migration of ideas and their superimposition on historical ruins etc. This only indicates how people and ideas migrated from one end of the country to the other and how sentiments got rooted in new soils.

At the outset of the discussion on the defence technology in Arunachal Pradesh, it is important to mention that we have evidences of planned destruction of centuries old archaeological features of defence technology. The British official planned the destruction because the fortification was regarded as the symbol of resistance to colonialism. Hence for the reconstruction of defence technology we have used literary and archaeological evidences, as far as available, and field studies and consultation with the locals, either to corroborate each other or to fill up the lacuna; to get a really satisfying complete picture in serving the cause of history.

In the geo-political, socio-cultural and economic evolutions of Arunachal Pradesh tribal feuds and aggressions of tribal-peasant militia had a significant impact. Technology as a basic to human nature gave birth to and made to develop the defence as well as offence technology. The defence technology is evident from the making and placing of stockades, panjies, stone chutes (boody traps) as well as selection of sites for establishing village etc. Here, all these have been combined into one term—the defence technology, because of their combined and effective use for the defence of village against any external surprise attack or planned aggression.

The placing of stockades were the principal elements of fortification of a village among almost all the tribes. They were constructed by placing stout tree trunks into the ground and tying them with cane. The end of each post was sharpened to a point and the height of the structure was also sufficiently difficult to be crossed. The bamboo stockades were temporary affairs and were used mainly for field fortification; however, bamboo was also common in use to reinforce the timber. Sometimes big stone pieces (boulders) were also used for the stockades. These stockades usually encircled a village, except where the ground made it unnecessary.

The *panjies* were spikes of bamboo or other hard wood of eight-ten inches, sharpened to a needle-like point and hardened by fire, impregnated with fatal *Be* at one end and while the other used to be inserted in the ground amongst the grass at an angle that just could catch the feet of any unobservant walker. They were laid in thousands in number all around the village or were concealed under leaves about the paths leading to it where it was imperceptible to the eager invader. As the attackers unknown with the position of planting of *panjies* and generally attacked in the depth of night or adopted the method of surprise attack, one by one fell to the ground and met instantaneous death or in this state *panjies* easily penetrated a soft boot or gaiter and were disastrous to a barefooted coolie or tribal-peasant militia. Sometimes, similar pieces of bamboo were placed horizontally some two or three feet from the ground were also employed for the same.

The stone chutes or 'booby traps' was also a part and parcel of the fortification. It is assumed that most of the villages were cordoned of stone chutes formed of boulders which were so placed that they were released by the enemy himself as he advanced along a jungle path through some defile leading to the village. In some cases the stone chutes were so skilfully placed and tied that a single cut in a rope or cane used to release a number of chutes from above on the attackers.

The selection of site for establishing a village was very important aspect of the defence technique. The approaches to the villages were often up through tortuous narrow covered ways or lanes, with high banks on either sides, sometimes through a steep ravine and the bed of an old torrent. It has been rightly stated that they selected, "...very inaccessible places for their villages. Surrounded with bamboo palisades or protected by a stockade of tree trunks, with all approaches carefully 'panjied' and flanked by 'chutes' the village present very formidable position to an attacking party".[11]

After the field studies of the Namsang area of Tirap district, I have come across an added feature to the defence technology practiced earlier. The villages of this area, like other villages of Arunachal Pradesh were as usually stockaded (*zanpan*) but these stockades were further supported by the natural or deep-dug and sufficiently wide *nullah* (*jo* or *jonchha*) from outside. In addition to the use of *panjies* (*waat*) around the stockades, they were also used for personal defence. The shield (*lac*) made up of buffalo hide was also an important component of the personal defence of the Noctes. Besides, the local hand made guns (*wantho*) and the gunpowder (*khaat*) also played significant role in the defence of the villages too. More interesting is the fact that for manufacturing the *khaat* the coal of a particular wood, again locally available, (*baasaa*) was found the most suitable.

Besides field studies, unpublished archival materials as well as diaries, memoirs, reports etc. of the British period are very important source materials for the reconstruction of defence technology. It has been reported that the initial British operations against the Singphos (1824-26) were invariably against fortified villages and entrenched positions.[12] More detailed account of the Singpho technological base of stockades, warfare etc. have also been reported subsequently. It mentions, "The Singphos like to have their villages on bank of a running stream... a number of their villages are stockaded...."[13] Further, F. Jenkins writes in detail to formulate a policy regarding the Singphos. He writes, "The Singpho country is eminently unfavourable to the operation of regular troops,.... I think war should be avoided—the more so that a little experience must teach the Singphos how to take advantage of the natural defences of their country, and recent evidence show that they are improving in this respect."[14]

The Khampti villages were also strongly fortified. Not only during those troubled years but even half a century later. The military report[15] clearly shows that village fortifications were not a thing of past, "All the big villages are stockaded: the stockades are very strong and high 16′ to 20′, the stockades are double and up to a height of 4′ from the ground, the space between area filled with earth and stone; the tops of stockades are pointed; a sharp pointed *panjees* are indigenuously placed to prevent men from scaling up the sides. Within the stockades which surround the village is often an inner one, in which is built the house inhabited by the Raja."

The technological base of the Khamptis is more importantly conveyed in the proposal of 1840. It mentions, "I would beg to recommend that Khampti *Dhaos* (hatchet) be purchased for the whole of the sepoys at an estimated expense of 1350 rupees as proposed by Captain Vetch... that the *Dhaos* should always be kept up complete hereafter and be mustered as a part of the regular equipment of the Regiment..."

"I would also urge the great advantage, may by necessity for adding Khampti *Dhaos to the equipment of the corps. as in the jungle warfare in the Frontier, the men are in a measure helpless without some instrument of the kind, either for cutting into an enemy's stockade, or in erecting one for themselves... and calculate the average price of each at Rupees 2-8 it would require an expenditure of Rupees 1350 to complete the equipment for the whole regiment but as these Dhaos are brought from a great distance it would probably a year or two before enough would be procured if my suggestions be approved."*[16]

About the Khamptis, the findings of Verrier Elwin are also very important to be mentioned here. He writes, "Wood carving and ivory-work have persisted to this day.... The Khamptis still make embossed shields and are fond of masks, mainly of the horror type...." He also quotes specific practices of the Khampti chiefs: "It is customary for the chiefs also to employ themselves in useful and ornamental arts. They work in gold, silver and iron, forge their own weapons and make their wives" jewels. They also manufacture embossed shields of buffalo or rhinoceros hide, gilding and lacquering them with skill and taste.[17]

The control over iron by the Khamptis in their hills and the technology evolved by them for the *Dhaos* and other war weapons and the settled agriculture in the Dihing river valleys must have positively contributed to the formation and expansion of the pre-colonial states of eastern Arunachal Pradesh. The permanent place of Khampti chief in the "Great Council" of Ahoms is also indicative of the power and privileges enjoyed by them. Even the British continued their privilege after the occupation of Assam and were proposing to procure the Khampti *Dhaos* for the British soldiers stationed in the area.[18]

Though among the Adis there did not evolve the chiefdom like the Singphos and the Khamptis, their village defence technology was very elaborate during the pre-colonial period and had some sorts of advancements during the period of British aggressions to the area. The response and necessities made the indigenous techniques more effective. The advancement is in form of rapid strategic changes and in the stockades techniques. The system of double row of stockades with earth and stone in between is a later innovation and was the result of the introduction of firearms by the British. Another technological development is in the placing of the stockades. Earlier it was a "defence perimeter" of village, later on for the safety of the villages, minimum loss of the defenders of the village as well as the villages and making the evacuation of the village more safe and easy, the stockades were even "two miles" away from the village.[19] Further advancement to the defence technology can be seen during the third expedition as the combined use of stockades, stone-shoots and fire from the arrows and muskets. As a consequence the possibility of heavy and tactical casualties on the aggressor became quite real and the defence of the local population became more effective. The defence techniques of the Adis, on the one hand, demonstrate the gradual advancement and on the other it also demonstrates state of defence arrangements according to the status of the village. As reported[20] (during the expedition of 1911-12), "This *brings* us to the next occasion on which the British encountered with the Abors.

To punish the tribes and also to explore and survey this country, for owing to China's move in Tibet and along its south-eastern boarders a real interest was at last being stirred in this long stretch of unknown border lands... From Rohtang reconnoitering parties of Goorkhas and M.P. located very large stockades some 3 miles up to the Dihang Valley at Kakyar Monying... Unlike other such defences, this one could be seen built down to the water's edge, which beyond it was a large Abor encampment, and here it was hoped to inflict a severe blow before the chief village was reached" (Kebabg village).

Like many uncommon traits among various tribes of Arunachal Pradesh, their defence technology is also different. It has rightly been reported that "among the Dafla (Nyishis or Nishings) tribes of Arunachal Pradesh, there was neither any attempt to fortify their village nor were the village sites selected with a view to facilitate defence".[21] The Nyishis tended to migrate, dispersal was its defence and it was impossible for a raiding force to surround the whole village. Their security lay in their number. Besides, the institution of *gingdung* assured the settlement of their own feuds and strong clan affiliation made possible combination against forces. In addition to the strategic analysis of the Nyishis, their indigenous genius has come to light through our discussion during my field studies. They justify their scattered village establishment techniques to cater to demand of defence against sudden attack or planned aggression. In such a case with just sort of a call for emergency preparedness people from all the houses from every direction could come rushing thereby leaving the attackers in confusion and bewilderment, consequently compelling them to flee for their own self-defence.

In the discussion of the defence technology of Arunachal Pradesh the analysis of the remains of the forts/fortress are also important. Here, it is important to mention that after independence much of the energy and resources of the Department of Research, Government of Arunachal Pradesh was channelised in the ethnographic studies of different tribes and on the studies of Itafort and the forts of Bhishmaknagar and Rukmininagar.[22] The remains of forts/fortresses of Bhalukpong and Thembang could not catch the attention of earlier scholars practically. Though, the forts of Arunachal Pradesh cannot be compared with the Muslim, Maratha and Rajput forts of India in their structural technology, the forts of Arunachal Pradesh would have been best suited to the nature of terrain and to the warfare of those days.

The Itafort[23] (built between 1350 and 1450) is within the new capital of Arunachal Pradesh, Itanagar. The fort could be identified with Mayapur, of a local king Ramchandra *alias* Mayamatta and his son Arimatta. The fort is actually a fortified area of an irregular shape enclosed with natural ridges and brick ramparts. There are two brick walls and three gates. The walls cross over uneven terrain and deep nallahs, where remains of culverts, steps etc. exist. The area thus fortified is more than a sq. km., is slopping from south to north and has a number of nallahs and gorges providing ample water as well as escape routes. The bricks are of varied sizes. Even decorative bricks are also available. Most likely, their production was carried at the site itself. The sand stone seems to have been brought from nearby hills. Thus, the entire complex is, indeed, a meticulously planned work. It is a monumental task based on intimate knowledge of the terrain and involving immense resources, human as well as materials.

The forts of Bhishmaknagar and Rukmininagar actually represent the first Aryansied kingdom of the easternmost India that extended in the plains between the Dibang and Lohit river. The tradition of Rukmini, the daughter of Bhishmaka, the king of Vidarbha (Berar) who was kidnapped by Lord Krishna, can be associated with this area. The forts existed as early as in the 10th century and in the 13th century came under the Chutiyas and passed on to the Ahoms in the 16th century. The excavated evidence is clearly indicative of their know-how. Besides, classical fort architecture they also knew—turned pottery, terracotta art and advanced metallurgy. [24]

The fort of Bhishmaknagar, is built on a flat piece of land, jutted out towards the south, from the northern hills. In the mountain wall provides natural defence and three other sides an eastern rampart runs about 5 km. in length, though broken in between. The fort has an elongated semicircle shape, extending over area of about 10 sq. km. After the excavation of the area "...it became quite clear that it was a well planned and well protected city inhabited by the people who reached a high degree of culture and civilization."[25]

Regarding the study of technology of Bhalukpong fort very pathetic scene emerges on account of non-existence of remains today. It is shocking to see that a road (connecting three districts of Arunachal Pradesh with Assam) passes through the fort complex and its bricks were used for construction purposes. And, the entire area was levelled mainly for the construction of the government buildings and also for the private purposes. However, recent archaeological find[26] of 248 silver of mainly two types (small and big) of Muslim ruler of Bengal encourages us to look afresh on the aspects of the fort. As reported,[27] the fort was situated on a hillock 300ft. high at the debouch point of the Kameng or Bhareli river. Three sides were surrounded by a brick-wall and on the fourth the fortifications carried across to an adjoining hillock that sloped gradually to the plain. Hewn stones remains of plinths within the ramparts and a steep pathway paved with stones leading to the eastern face of the hills also existed.

Out of my field studies of the area, I came across the fact that the treasury of the king was in the northwestern side of the complex. A very thick (3 to 4 feet) boundary wall, almost touching the treasury was constructed over a rivulet (50-60 feet deep) perhaps for the protection of the fort in general and treasury in particular. Alternative source of water was obtained in the fort complex by digging two wells—one in the southeast and the other in the southwest part of the complex. The whole complex of about three sq. kms. provides ample scope for archaeological excavations by experts.

The fort (*Durga*) and treasury (*Kosa*), which are the important elements of state described by Kautilya, are also significant in case of Arunachal Pradesh.[28] The forts lie along the foothills, connected with rivers and were constructed actually on strategic spots, intelligently fortified for defence purposes. A position of geographic vantage, water supply, sufficient land to support the population inside, secret routes for escape, the expected direction of enemy's attack, and communication with Brahmaputra Valley have been the major considerations in building the Bhalukpong fort. Similar in most of these features except for its location in the foothills and sufficient land to support the population inside is another important consideration for fort in Arunachal Pradesh, which provides great potentials to be discussed in our studies.

The fortified village Thembang, under the Dirang Circle of West Kameng District, Bomdila, is inhabited by the Buddhist and the villagers have separate identity as "Thembang Monpa".[29] The village was fortified after shifting the village from the plain land to the slope of a hill mainly because of persistent pressure from Rupa, Rurang and Sangti villages of the area. The fortified area about 400 mt east-west and 200 mt north-south of the village surrounded the compact houses of the kings (*Bapus*) and their dependents (*Gilas*). In the eastern and western sides of the village two heavily built gates were constructed of stone pieces of irregular sizes with the provision to close them during night. Though the gates exist, the 8 to 10 feet high boundary wall of the village (as reported by the villagers) is almost non-existing presently.

The fortification was possible mainly with the manual labour of the villagers of Khoina, Boot (now Jirigaon), Khoitiam and Rahung as well as the *Gilas* (tribal/peasant militia). Their services were also utilized for seed sowing (*ungyangben*), plantation of tree (*ungashing cheewn*), carrying goods (*rongbanghen*), construction of houses (*phijangben*) and the most important here is construction of fortification wall (*jangri*), adopting the method of *tchikpen* (putting the stone pieces one above the other) etc. They also served the Bapus as tribal-peasant militia. The villages of Khoitam beheaded the military commander of Rupa village while he was returning from an attack from Thembang. They sent the head of the commander to the Bapus and the body to Rupa (the Shertukpen rajas, *Thongs*). From the incident the people of Rupa area call the villagers of Khoitam the *songa-sha-benkenba* (divider of human flesh). The forts provided the kings of Thembang (better known as the Thebengia Bhutias in the British Records) upper hand in the area and to some extent also upon their neighbouring counterparts. The Tibetan gun/rifle under the possession of the Bapus was another advantage, which the others lacked. These two elements combined with high agricultural production and fairly a large tax base extending up to modern Assam, significantly contributed not only to the establishment of their authority in the area but also successfully resisted the expansion of the Monastic Order in their areas. [30]

III

Conclusion

Forgoing discussion on village defence technology of Arunachal Pradesh reinforces the crude truth that the tools and techniques developed and used here were largely the products of indigenous materials and native genius, used suitably in the varied ecological niches. During the pre-colonial period the pace of development in the village defence system must had been slow, mainly because of the fact that the level of technological advancement among the tribes were almost of the same technological level. Subsequently, the emergence of a distinct trend of imperial expansion *versus* indigenous protection is witnessed in Arunachal Pradesh. Unlike other parts of the country the Britishers with all their modern scientific and technological knowledge to their side had to face very stiff opposition from indigenous village defence technology, which culminated into a distinct administrative policy of the Britishers towards the people of Arunachal Pradesh. In this field of study, the influences of the neighbouring areas of Arunachal Pradesh such as Assam, Bhutan, China/Tibet and Myanmar are also very important which deserve more specialized detailed studies dealing with the exposure and response syndrome, migration of the people and fusion of technology. In this regard, the influences of geographical and allied factors would be another welcome addition. The present study on Arunachal Pradesh makes it amply clear that a single uniform archaeological model on Indian studies will always lead to wrong conclusion about the past. For each region and even tribe one has to search separate models, which are basically necessitated by the growth of regional cultural variants, geographic situation, scientific and technological development and above all politico-economic condition. Any attempt by armed-chair historians and outside scholars to universalize the pattern for Arunachal Pradesh will not only be intellectually hazardous but also grossly misleading. It also poses an important challenge for entering into the temple of Clio for reconstruction of historical past of Arunachal Pradesh if studied objectively on the lines of text-aided archaeology and archaeology aided texts.

NOTES

1. For details see, B.D. Nag Chaudhuri's, *Technology and Society: An Indian View,* Simla, 1979, pp. 1-14.
2. This is possible because the I.C.H.R., New Delhi, has financially sponsored my research project on Archaeology of Arunachal Pradesh. I thankfully acknowledge the grants received.
3. For details of the approaches see, Deepak Kumar's, *Science and the Raj:* 1857-1905, Delhi, 1997 (paper back), pp.18-31 and 229-230; and a brief survey of the historical literature on technology in India can also be seen in my article "*Rural Technology in Arunachal Pradesh: Interface of Defence and Agrarian Technology*" in V.K.Thakur and K.K. Mandal (eds) *Science, Technology and Medicine in Indian History,* Patna, 2000, pp. 253-74.
4. Satpal Sangwan has referred to hundreds of pamphlets, Travelogues and books published mostly during the 18th and 19th centuries in his book, *Science, Technology and Colonisation: An Indian Experience 1757-1857,* Delhi, 1991, pp. 167-87 and Deepak Kumar, *Science and the Raj, op. cit.*, p.6.
5. Satpal Sangwan, *Science, Technology and Colonisation, op. cit.*, p.6.
6. For details of the approach of Irfan Habib, see "*Technological Change and Society,* 13th and 14th Centuries, *(Presidential Address: Section II),* Indian History Congress, Varanasi Session, 1969; idem, '*The Technology and Economy of Mughal India*' Dev Raj Chanana Lectures, (Mimeographed), Delhi, 1970; and idem, '*Changes in Technology in Mughal India*', paper presented at a

Symposium on Technology and Society at the Indian History Congress, Waltair, 1979.

7. For details, see Ajit K. Danda's, *Tribal Ethnography,* New Delhi, 1996. David R. Syiemlieh's *Survey of Research in History of North-East India 1970-1990,* New Delhi 2000 also testifies the neglect of the studies of the technology of the tribals of the North East India.
8. David R. Syiemlieh, 'Khasi Iron Culture and Iron Trade with Sylhet in the late 18th and early 19th centuries', *Proceedings of North East India History Association,* (hereafter PNEIHA), Kohima session, 1987; O.R. Singh, '*Silk Industry in Manipur in the 18th and 19th centuries',* PNEIHA, Doimukh session, 1994 and S.K. Bose, '*A Glimpses of 9th century Minting Technology in Assam',* PNEIHA, Silchar, 1994.
9. For details, see Imdad Hussain, 'Village Fortification in Tribal North East India: A Preliminary Note', in J.P. Singh and Gautam Sengupta (ed) *Archaeology in North East India,* New Delhi, 1991 and A.K.Thakur, 'Defence Mechanism in Arunachal Pradesh: A Study of Fortification and Forts', World Archaeological Congress, New Delhi, 1994 in the theme papers, *State City and Society.*
10. A.A. Ashraf, *Prehistoric Arunachal: A Study on Prehistory and Ethno-archaeology of Kamla Valley,* Itanagar, 1990, pp.3-5.
11. A. Hamilton, *In Abor Jungles of North East India,* (Indian Reprint), Delhi, 1984, p.22.
12. Military Consultations, 16th December, 1828, Nos. 28-29. Even as late as December 1828, Capt. J.B. Neufville was asking for light mountain howitzers and rockets against these fortification. For details of the village fortification in North East India see the article of Imdad Hussain, "Village Fortification in Tribal North East India: A preliminary Note", *op. cit.*
13. Foreign Department Political Br. 12 June, 1837, No.64.
14. Letter from F. Jenkins to H.T. Prinsep, Esq. In Foreign Dept., Political Branch, 18th April, 1838, Nos. 56-57.
15. For details see, C.R. Mac Gregor, *Military Report on Khampti Singpho,* Calcutta, 1887.
16. Foreign Dept. Political Branch, 1 March, 1840, No. 169.
17. Verrier Elwin, *The Art of the North East Frontier of India,* Itanagar, 1988, p.84.
18. For details see, Huhammad Kazim, *Alamgir Nama* (ed) Khadim Husain and Abdul Hai, Calcutta, 1863-73, in Shireen Moosvi's *Man and Nature in Mughal Era,* (Indian History Congress,

Thematic Symposium), Delhi, 1993; for details of the areas of the possessions, military force maintained by the chiefs, populations etc. see Foreign Dept. Political Branch, K.W. File, 7 Jan., 1833, No. 82. This file is not only important for the pre-colonial chiefs of Arunachal Pradesh but also for most other chiefs of north east India; and the Letter from J. Brodie to F. Jenkins, Foreign Dept. Political Branch, 1 March, 1840, Nos. 176-77.

19. For details, see A.K. Thakur, *'Rural Technology in Arunachal Pradesh'*, *op. cit.*
20. L.W. Shakespeare, *op. cit.*, pp.125-26 and 129-30.
21. For details of the Dafla defence see, John F. Michell, *Report on the North East Frontier of India,* Calcutta, 1883 (Dafla section); U.G. Bower, *The Hidden Land,* London, 1953, (the fifth chapter); C.F. Haimendorf, *Highlanders of Arunachal Pradesh,* New Delhi, 1982, pp.30-36 (Passim).
22. For details see, Y.A. Raiker, *Itafort, Itanagar,* 1990 (1976); L.N. Chakravarty, *Glimpses of Early History of Arunachal Pradesh,* Itanagar, 1989, pp.93-121; Y.A. Raiker and S. Chatterjee, *Archaeology in Arunachal Pradesh,* Itanagar, 1980, pp.24-34 and A.K.Thakur, "*Defence Mechanism in Arunchal Pradesh: A Study of Fortification and Forts*", *op. cit.*
23. For details see, Y.A. Raiker, *Itafort, op. cit.;* D.N. Das, "Ruins of Mayapur" *The Journal of the Assam Research Society,* Vol. VIII, No.2, 1941, pp. 43-49 and L.N. Chakravarty, *op. cit.*
24. Y.A. Raiker and S. Chatterjee, *op. cit.*, p.28 and L.N. Chakravarty, *op. cit.*, pp. 119-20.
25. L.N. Chakravarty, *op. cit.*, p.117.
26. The coins were sent to the Director, Department of Research, Government of Arunachal Pradesh, *vide* letter No.BPG/DEV/B/10/98 dated, 24-08-1998. This was unearthed while making a toilet pit for the residential quarters in the fort complex, presently a complex of the G.R.E.F.
27. Though good number of Government records provides information regarding the fort, they are mostly in slipshod manner, for some other details of the fort see, the relevant parts in B.C. Allen, *Assam District Gazetteers,* Vol.V, Darrang, Allahabad, 1905; B.C. Allen *et al., Gazetteer of Bengal and North East India,* Delhi, 1979 (first reprint).
28. For details see, A.K. Thakur, "State Formation in Arunachal Pradesh", *NEHU Journal of Social Science and Humanities,* 1-1, 1998.

29. The Buddhists of Western Arunachal Pradesh are of the two socio-cultural groups *viz.* the Shertukpens, and the Monpas (the Thembang - Namsu Monpa, the Dirang Monpa, the Kalaktang Monpa, the Tawang Monpa etc.).
30. For details, see A.K. Thakur, "Process and Agency of Pre-colonial States in Arunachal Pradesh", *The NEHU Journal* Vol.1, No.1, January 2003, pp.1-25 (New name and serial number).

16

Forts – Indicatory of Martial Tradition
A Case Study of Arunachal Pradesh

Sasikanta Dash and *Ritu Bhatt*

The study of forts constitute an important source for the constitution of local/regional history. Archaeology plays an important role where written materials are at scare. Moreover, Archaeology enriches the study of history where literary sources are in abundance. In Arunachal Pradesh archaeology can play a major role in the construction of the local history due to the scare availability of literary sources. Forts are important ingredients of Archaeological study. In the areas like Arunachal Pradesh, the study of forts is a fascinating one. The study of forts is a step towards understanding Arunachal people and their traditions.

Resource mobilization and resource utilization in the hilly and desert region are most conducive to the growth of Martial tradition. Existence of a strong martial tradition among the Marathas of Sahayadri hills, Rajputs of Aravali hills and Thar Desert are the proven examples in Indian history. Coming to the case of Arunachal Pradesh we find that compatible natural condition and ecological niche have been instrumental in generating martial tradition among the various tribes living in the first range of hills. Further, it seems that their martial tradition have matured during their long and intermittent struggle with the organized state system of the Brahmaputra Valley.

Natural defence mechanism of the tribes matured gradually in shape of forts and fortress. These were so significant that the initial phase Britishers were afraid of leading long lasting expedition to the hill areas since they believed that with little experience they could improvised their defence mechanism to give a match to the British modern system of warfare.

Instead of various limitations, i.e. scanty evidence,[1] natural hazards,[2] destructions already been caused by floods,[3] environmental problems,[4] there are lots of scope for the study of forts in Arunachal Pradesh. This would render invaluable help in reconstructing the history of the local inhabitants, their contact with outside people and martial tradition of the Arunachalees.

In 1965-66, L.N. Chakravarty carried out the first excavation in NEFA with R.G. Pandeya of ASI. Later Dr. Chakravarty excavated Bhishmaknagar in 1966-67 and Malinithan during 1970-72.[5] Y.A. Raikar carried out excavations at Bhishmaknagar during 1968-70, Rukmininagar in 1972-74 and Itafort in 1974-77.[6] Dr. D.K. Bora continued Itafort excavation from 1977 for three Seasons.[7]

Till now we come across with five major forts in Arunachal Pradesh. All these forts are attributed to the period between 10th to 16th century A.D. They are Bhalukpong fort (West Kameng Dist.), Itafort, *Bhishmaknagar* fort, Rukmininagar fort and Mud fort (Lohit Dist.). The Brahmaputra Valley culture had occasionally expanded into the foothills of Arunachal Pradesh and sometimes left permanent marks in form of temples and forts.[8] These forts cannot be called as single unit unlike the Rajput and Maratha forts.[9] But these forts had got its independent identity and importance. We have to see these forts from a different angle. They had strategic value, intelligently fortified for defence purposes. They were best suited for the nature of the terrain and the type of warfare fought in those days. They were basically places of hideouts and invading enemy could not trace the hideouts. The basic features of these forts were adequate water supply, sufficient land for the people residing inside, secret routes for escape and communication with Brahmaputra valley. However, it is important to note that Bhalukpong fort, Itafort, and Rukmininagar fort had no prescribed or regular shape while Bhishmaknagar is of semicircular shape and mud fort is rectangular type. Bhalukpong is hill fort, Itafort is a (Giridurga) hill fort, *Vanadurga*, brick burnt fort.[10]

Regarding Bhalukpong fort we find very pathetic scene on account of non-existence of remains today. We notice that a road which connects three districts of Arunachal Pradesh with Assam passes through the fort complex. According to B.C. Allen[11] the fort was situated on a hillock 300 ft. high at the debouch point of the Kameng or Bhareli river. Three sides were surrounded by a brick wall and on the fourth the fortification were carried across to an adjoining hillock that sloped gradually to the plain.

Historically the fort could be either of the late Salastambha or early Pala period, i.e. 10th-12th C.A.D. Recent archaeological finds of 7248 silver coins of mainly two types (small and big) of Muslim ruler of Bengal encourages us to look afresh on the aspects of the forts. The whole complex of about three sq. kms. provides ample scope for archaeological excavation and studies by research scholars. From Bhalukpong fort we gather the information that the local tribe Akas, a small tribe, had created problem for the British government from 1824-1883/84 A.D. The Ahoms had also given the right (*posa*) to collect tax from foothill peasants. They had developed a defence mechanism which was so strong that its martial act was recognized by the Ahoms and subsequently by the

Britishers. The Akas were known as Hazari Khowas—Master of one thousand families.

Itafort

The fort built between 1350 and 1450 A.D. is within the new capital of Arunachal Pradesh, Itanagar.[13] It is connected by a motorable road to Bandardewa on the north trunk road. Lilabari is the nearest airport and Harmoti is the nearest railway station.[14] The name Ita is modern, derived from *Ita* meaning brick. The local people do not make bricks and hence their abundant existence in the area becomes conspicuous. The ruins of the forts were highlighted by B.C. Allan,[15] D.N. Das,[16] S.K. Chakravarti, B.B. Pandey, Y.A. Raikar and others.

The Ahoms had entered Assam by the beginning of 13th century and soon established themselves at Charaideo. Their conflict with Kamata continued,[17] during this time, a number of Bhuyans arose as petty chiefs exercising authority over small tracts. They had controlled eastern Kamarupa as far as the Subansiri.[18] They were actually feudal lords under the Kamarupa Kings, but began asserting independence when the central authority became weak. Under such uncertain conditions, one of the local chiefs has found it convenient to retreat into the hills and the forts could be identified with Mayapur of a local king Ramachandra *alias* Mayamatta and his son, Arimatta.[19] (*Asamar Buranji* by Gohain Barua used by D.N. Das).

The Nyishis associated the local raja of Itafort in their oral tradition.[20] Perhaps the local raja of Itafort had influence on the Nyishi system of warfare. It is striking that the Nyishis of this area fought several times against the Ahoms and also against the British forces. The fort in ruins is a testimony to a historic struggle for survival. The fort in ruins is a testimony to a historic struggle for survival against the odds, put up by the people in North Eastern India. It is to be properly studied for better understanding of defence mechanism in Arunachal.

Bhishmaknagar and Rukmininagar Forts

These two forts represent the first Aryanised kingdom of the easternmost India, that extended in the plains between the Dibang and the Lohit rivers as early as 10th century A.D. In the 13th century it came under the Chutias and passed on to the Ahoms in the 16th century.[21]

Rukmininagar

The fort exists at the foot of Mishmi hill in the lower Dibang Valley of the Lohit district. Very little is known regarding this fort. But a hill fort extended over the two present Idu villages Chidu and Chimn north of Roing. Brick ruins were located at different places in this hilly area. The bricks and pottery at these sites are identical with those found at Bhishmaknagar.[22]

Bhishmaknagar

The fortress of Bhishmaknagar, 24 km. east of Roing is built on a flat piece of land, jutted out towards the south, from the northern hills. In the north the mountain wall provides natural defence from three sides and earthen rampart (average height 4.5 m and width 6 m) runs for about 5 kms in length, though broken in between. The fort has extended over an area of about 10 km. After the excavation it is presumed and the people reached a high degree of culture and civilization.[23]

The Mud Forts

The fort could be ascribed to the 14th-15th centuries A.D. The fort falls on the Sadiya-Tezu road, 6 km. short of Tezu. It is an enclosure of eastern ramparts 366 m × 350 m.[24] The rampart is 2.44 m high and equally broad at the top. The entire construction was meant for defence. It is a mud fort. It is of modern nature and not a fortified habitation like Bhishmaknagar. The fort was meant for a contingent of a few thousand soldiers to take defensive position in a guerilla type of warfare. The rampart and ditches provide adequate support to the defender. The central mound is obviously a cavalier for looking out. The location is at a strategic point. It falls on the main route from Sadiya and Bhishmaknagar to Parasuremkunda. It also faces the Lohit to keep watch on the enemy from its left bank, present Chowkham area. For that reason, probably the Cavalier is closer to the riverside.[25]

The forts gives reference to different methods of warfare, i.e. stone shoots and war structure like wooden platform, bamboo structure. Sometimes, the aboriginals like Idu Mishmis were recruited as soldiers in Chutiya dynasty. Mishmis also supplied elephants to the Ahoms. We also find a fort fortifying the village, i.e. Thembang under the Dirang circle of West Kameng Dist.[26] Dzongs[27] run by Tawang monastery had definite administrative purpose but its defence utility is yet to be confirmed. Sometimes Gonpas, i.e. Rupa Gonpa also acted as a defensive tool to protect trading business but their military utility for war purposes is yet to be established.

Undoubtedly, the forts acted as protection against the warring tribes and safeguarding the cross-country trade. Comprehensive study of the fort and fortification is the need of the time not only to unravel the defence system of various

Arunachalee tribes but also to reconstruct the political economy of the region since all the forts under study had surface communication link with the plain areas of Assam.

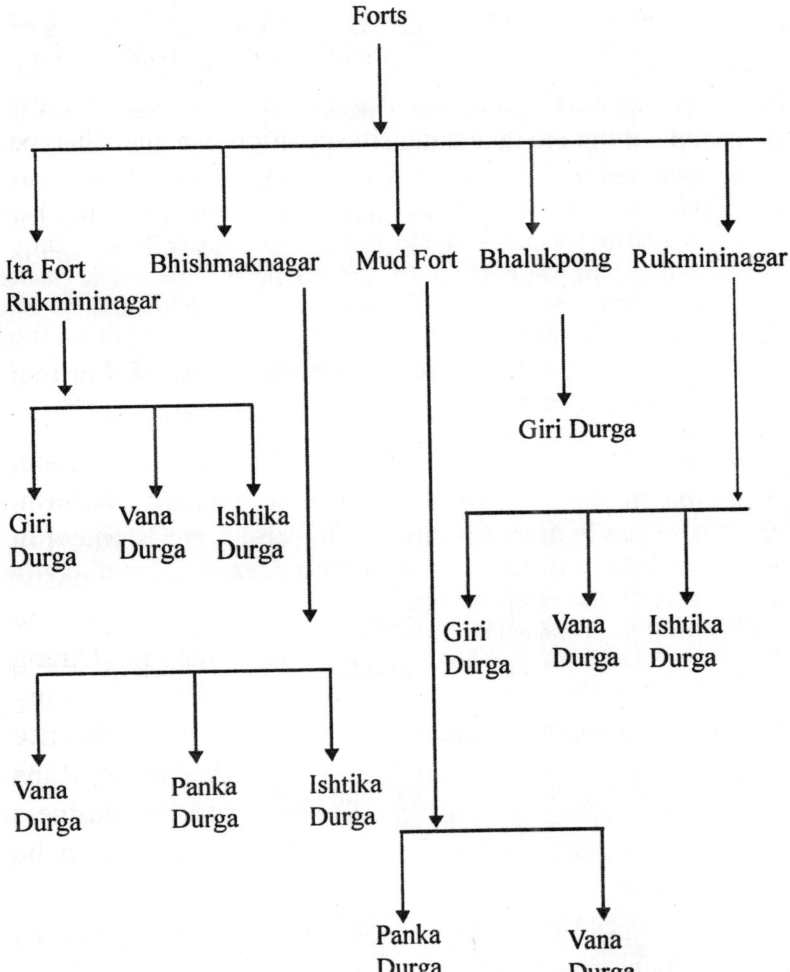

NOTES

1. Due to the physical personality of the area/tract and the life and economy of the various tribes fewer material traces for the archaeologist are left for study.
2. The nature of the soil, frequent landslides, earthquake, heavy rains, floods have kept the face of the land subject to frequent changes. The number of floods and the earthquakes of 1897 and 1950 are two other major events to be noted in this connection. One can hardly expect the archaeological evidence to survive under such conditions.
3. The hill fort Rukmininagar in the hills of north of Roing has been completely lost due to the earthquake of 1950 and floods that followed.
4. Growth of thick vegetation, huge trees and bamboo groves have caused irreparable damage to the brick structures at Bhishmaknagar and Ita Fort. The road construction activity in these remote jungles has also unknowingly contributed to the destruction. Bhalukpong fort is an example.
5. Y.A. Raikar, S. Chatterjee; *Archaeology in Arunachal Pradesh*, Shillong, 1980, p.15.
6. *Ibid.*
7. *Ibid.*
8. *Ibid.*, p.24.
9. The forts in Arunachal Pradesh are spread over a large area and concealed under thick forest could not be easily comprehended as a single unit except on map.
10. All forts lie along the foothills of Arunachal Pradesh.
11. B.C. Allen; *Assam District Gazatteers,* Vol.V, Darrang, Allahabad, 1905, pp.67-68.
12. Y.A. Raikar; *op. cit.*, pp.25-26.
13. *Ibid.*, p.26.
14. Y.A. Raikar; Ita Fort, 1976, Chapter-I.
15. B.C. Allen, *op. cit.*, pp.93-98.
16. D.N. Das; *Journal of the Assam Research Society,* Ghy, Vol. III, No. 1941.
17. The Kingdom of Kamarupa is known as Kamata.
18. Y.A. Raikar; Ita Fort, 1976, Chapter-III.
19. D.N. Das, Ruins of Mayapur, *Journal of the Assam Research Society,* Ghy, 1941, Vol.VIII, No.2.
20. Y.A. Raikar; Ita Fort, 1976, Chapter-III.

21. *Ibid.*
22. Raikar & Chatterjee; *op. cit.*, p.28.
23. *Ibid.*
24. *Ibid.*, pp. 28-29.
25. *Ibid.*, pp.30-31. See Basudev Malik: *History and Archaeology of the Mishmi Hill Region and its Connection with the Brahmaputra Valley Culture, (An Unpublished paper)*, p.6.
26. *Ibid.*
27. It was fortified because of persistent pressure from Rupa, Rurang and Shanli villages.
28. A dzong is something of an administrative centre and each one was run by two senior Monks of the monastery for a term of three years and they were called dzongpen. For details see, N. Sarkar; *Buddhism among the Monpas and Sherdukpens*, Shillong, 1980, p.35.

17

Defence Technique of the Tagins' Traditional Villages

Ashan Riddi

The Tagin is one of the major tribes in Arunachal Pradesh. Demographically, the Tagins inhabit in the upper course of Sinik (Subansiri river) in Upper Subansiri district of Arunachal Pradesh. They have common international border with the Nyeme (Tibet) presently intersected by the McMahon Line. Their territory is bounded by: China (Tibetan Autonomous Region) in the north-east, Siang district of Arunachal Pradesh in the east, Lower Subansiri and Kurung Kumey districts in the west, confluence of Sinik and Sigen rivers in the south-west, and Sinyum river in south-east.

The Tagins were highly individualistic in nature. They lacked any machinery for the application of legal sanction. Their idea of justice and solution entirely relied upon the principle of either reparation or retribution. There was no chief or king to enforce law and regulate the society. The principle of retribution sometimes leads to unending chain of raid and counter raids. Thus, in earlier days, they were frequently engaged in inter-village, intra-tribe and inter-tribe *Yalu* (feud and dispute) and *Nyimak* (raid). The last generation who witnessed the scene of fighting are in their sixties and seventies and have excellent memories of those *yalus* and *Nyimaks*.[1] K.T. Khuma, the Assistant Political Officer, Along, during his first tour to the Tagins territory in 1951 came across a case of capture and treat of retaliation among the Tagins at Bui village, wrote:

> In the evening Dirak Gire, Gam of Yajpog (near Ajor camp) arrived and reported that on the night of 14th November 1951 Yaegi Niakar, one of their village women who slept in the jhum house were captured and taken away by villagers of Digli on the other side of Subansiri. They feared that she might be sold away to a far place unless immediate action be taken by Government as in that case they would be compelled to retaliate.[2]

Khuma also commented that a situation of lawlessness prevailed in the Tagins territory where the life and property were insecure. He wrote that:

> This is the first time the interior Subansiri area where the wild and savagous. Tagins lived in their primitive and barbarous state of life has even been visited by any officer... The whole area beyond Ule which was the last point ever visited by an Officer before, right up to the McMahon Line is occupied by the wild and ferocious Tagins to whom human life is as cheap as that of cow or mythun. They are still in their primitive stage undisturbed by any outside influence. Although there is no chief system, the rich and brave have full control over the rest of other villages... Life though very free there, is insecure. A man may be killed without any inquiry. For instance, a few days before we reached Laplo Mori camp a man was killed by his neighbour with a dagger, only because he happened to go together with the wife of that neighbour on journey and that he might have get illegal intercourse with her.[3]

B.C. Bhuyan comments in his tour diary—

> The Tagins are wild to whom life is very cheap; they are still in primitive stage. The rich and the brave have full control over the rest and the poorer people are always at the mercy of the former.[4]

The Tagins were divided into innumerable independent groups in form of lineage, sub-clan and clan. The household, lineage, sub-clan and clan form the principal political and defence unit. Therefore, each family and lineage had its own network of friendships and alliances for their defence. However, most fundamental traditional defensive organization was village. Because, initially the Tagins started their settlement clan or sub-clan base for security and defence of their own, sub-clan or clan. The village became vital defence unit for particular clan thus defence of village becomes essential for survival and continuity of the particular clan. In this sense, the Tagin villages were analogous to the forts of the feudality lords.

Village Defence Technique

In the Tagin society there were no dormitory or other institutions that would guard the village. In absence of such institution, the Tagins had to adopt certain defensive technique to guard themselves from the attack by the enemy.

Choosing of the site for settlement is also important defence mechanism. The location of the village was so critical, the Tagin village was habitually settled on slope, hilltop, under the shade of hills and on the side of rivers etc. that offers natural defence and protection from attack by the enemies. Therefore, most of the traditional villages were located in isolation and difficult to approach from entrance part.[5]

Tagins choose the site for village and house by way of divination by egg or chicken. If divination foretells future eventuality and misfortune to the family in particular site, they discard the site and look for an alternative site. Because, eventuality and misfortune foretold may be raids or attacks by enemies.[6]

In case their village is threatened to attack or raids, they formed into groups. All able male villagers play collective defensive role. At night, women and children were shifted to safer den or place in the jungle secretly called 'Rachup'.[7] All able male with full aromour formed groups to gaurd the village in replacement way.

The most common defensive technique was that the village was completely fenced round with stick in upright position. Single entrance point was made. In the evening the entrance was closed with door and ropes tied at the fencing were connected to all houses in the village. If intruders attempt to break or cross the fencing, through the sound produced from those ropes villagers become alert of invaders.[8]

Another, technique was when all villagers come back to village, expert warriors secretly plants pointed spike made of bamboo all around the village. The spikes were of three types: first, about a feet long that planted up straight to injure foot. Second, one metre and two metres long planted with 90 degree to cause injuries to knee and chest of the enemy.[9]

House Defence Technique

In the construction of house the Tagins adopted certain defensive technologies. They used to construct thatch house at least two metres above the ground by planting wooden or bamboo posts. All sides of the house walled with bamboo or leaves or wood. Single entrance point was made to put ladder and climb up to house. At night the ladder was taken up on house and leave bamboo or wooden mat was put on to close the climbing point. The space between ground and house was well fenced all around. In case of attack by enemy, the defender climb down to ground from inside the house and take position to shoot at the enemy with bow and arrow. There was also method to escape from the house in case of imminent defeat. Tall wooden or bamboo posts were planted at side of the house. The ropes were tied on top end of the posts and during the night the posts were pulled towards the house and then tied. In case of defeat, defenders hold the post and cut off the tied ropes, and then he would be thrown out into the jungle for run away.[10]

Ritual and Divination Defence Technique

When new site is chosen for settlement and during the construction of the houses on the site, *Namtu-Uyi, Turbu-Uyi and Pekia-Uyi* (spirits of home, protection and strength) are invoked by offering sacrifice for protection of the family and clan. *Namtu-Benam* (ritual chanting by priest) is performed particularly at the time of planting first main post of the houses, so that the chosen site may not bring any misfortune.[11]

Very important technique to determine the imminent raid by enemies was by divinations. Expert warriors in the village secretly conduct divination by egg, chicken and pig to determine whether their village is threatened to raid by enemy or not. If, all divination foretells such raid, then they go for further deviations to decide the form of defence like where to shift children and women at night and how to guard village.[12]

For supernatural protection of the village the Tagins also perform ritual called 'Potor'. During this ritual the priest would chant to invoke all protective and dangerous spirits to guard the village and bestow village warriors power, strength and courage so that raiders shall not overpower them. In this ritual all children and women folk were strictly restricted. After ritual, they would strictly keep confinement for few days. Neither anyone would be allowed to go out from village nor enter into village during restriction days.[13]

Due to lack of any effective social and political mechanism that provides justice to the victims, the retribution action was believed and accepted as to get redressal of justice by the society. This unending retribution raids and counter raids were viewed by the early official explorers as 'savage' or 'wild'. The sense of justice was strongly rooted into the Tagin society. Thus, revenge, murder and counter raids were socially sanctioned and person who killed enemy to avenge for murder was glorified with the status of 'Nyimem' (warrior) and had sole privilege to wear cap decorated with claw of eagle.

The concept of justice by retribution and unending chain of retribution lead to emergence of clan or sub-clan based villages in the modern Tagin society and permanently ended the existence and continuity of some weaker and small clans. However, that clan who could not stand with enemy clans took shelter with friendly stronger clans and lead to emergance of few mixed clan villages in the Tagin society.

NOTES

1. Data collected from field.
2. K.T. Khuma, *Tour Diary,* November-December, 1951, Assam Government Press, Shillong, 1953, p.2.
3. *Ibid.,* p.6.
4. B.C. Bhuyan, *Tour Notes of B.C. Bhuyan, Political Officer,* Abor Hills, Along for the month of September and October.
5. Data collected from field.

6. Interview with late Tadi Riddi (priest) at Village Riddi on July 11, 2001.
7. Interview with late Tomo Bui (expert warrior) at village Bui on August 3, 2000.
8. Interview with late Tate Riddi (lore teller) at village Riddi on November 7, 1997.
9. *Ibid.*
10. Interview with late Tadi Riddi (priest) village Riddi, September 2, 2002.
11. *Ibid.*
12. *Ibid.*
13. *Ibid.*

18

Defence and the Cult of the War Goddess in the Formation of the Dimasa State

Sarah Hilaly

The Medieval Dimasa State as it was integrated into the colonial empire included the Cachar Valley, the North Cachar Hills districts of Assam, parts of Nowgong district, Dayung-Dhansiri Valley in Nagaland and the Jiri Frontier of Manipur. The ethnic composition was varied along the geographical divide. The plains of Cachar was predominantly populated by the Bengali-speaking people; the North Cachar Hills by the Dimasas and the central portion was peopled by the Dimasas, Karbis (Mikirs), Hojais and Lalungs.

S. Endle in his monograph, *The Kacharis*, identifies the Dimasa as an eastern branch of the Bodo family of the Tibeto-Burman linguistic sub-family. The Dimasa or the 'great river folk', according to Endle, once occupied the Brahmaputra Valley and were later driven out of it in historical times.[1] E.A. Gait identifies their habitat in the easternmost extremity of the Brahmaputra Valley. According to Professor J.B. Bhattacharjee the earliest evidence of state formation amongst the Dimasas can be traced back to their stay around Sadiya. The material remains of a copper temple in its vicinity support the evidence of their settlement in that area. This temple was dedicated to *Kachai Kati* (the raw flesh eater), the tutelary deity of the Dimasas and their cognate tribes, which continued to be worshipped even after further formalisation of the state structure took place in Cachar. Endle however regards it as a temple consecrated during the process of Chutiya state formation in that area. Due to the dearth of historical material very little is known about other correlated processes of state formation amongst the Dimasas in that area. Their shifting to Dimapur is attributed to the pressure from Arimatta and Mangal Balahu the legendary princes of Upper Assam.[2]

It was at Dimapur that the beginnings of a polity formation was visible. State formation is a complex process where a range of factors are crucial. It applies differently to varying situations, though a certain cause is accorded centrality. The evolution of bands or lineages into states, both primary and secondary are marked by qualitative changes in the history of a society. A series of interrelated changes occur at many levels of the society. Multiple factors like internal stratification, necessity of irrigation systems, population growth, social circumspection, and war as a factor for stabilizing the leadership contribute to the formation of the state.

Endle refers to a degree of sophistication attained by the Dimasa in contrast to their cognate tribes by virtue of the crystallization of their clan structure. At Dimapur the political structure operated within a defined territory. At that point in time their territory extended along the south bank of the Brahmaputra from Dikhou to Kallang, the Dhansiri Valley and the North Cachar Hills.[3] This phase of the state was sustained by the alluvial plains of the Dhansiri. Here the Dimasas took to plough cultivation in the flat and valley lands that provided resources for the sustenance of the state machinery. They continued with dry cultivation in the hills. No detailed information is available on the structures of the State. There was legalisation of lineages and emergence of a ruling class segregated from the elites and commoners. There were extensive material remains at Dimapur indicative of the strength, the level of technological advancement and the resources of the state. The ruins are spread out over an area of 2.4 miles. Chakradheay the fourth Kachari king is said to have built the city.[4] It was built with bricks. A visible aspet of the ruins is the centrality assigned to fortifications. This feature is amply illustrated in the following passage:

> Dimapur on the other hand was surrounded on the three sides by a brick wall of the aggregate length of nearly two miles, while the fourth side was bounded by the Dhansiri River. On the eastern side was a fine brick gateway, with a pointed arch and stones pierced to receive the hinges of a double door. It was flanked by octagonal turrets of solid brick, and the intervening distance to the central archway was relieved by false windows of ornamental moulded brickwork.[5]

It may be mentioned that a virtual warlike situation with the neighbouring states acted as a very important factor in strengthening the authority of the Dimasa ruler. There were recurring conflicts with the Ahoms.

Conflicts

The first recorded hostilities with the Ahoms was in 1490 AD. In 1526 AD, Suhungmung attacked the Dimasas along the Dhansiri. The Dimasas repulsed the Ahoms by inflicting heavy losses. After a great deal of persistence the Ahoms defeated Khorapa, the Dimasa ruler, and pushed their territory beyond the Dhansiri river. The ruler's brother Khunkhara usurped the throne and renewed offensive against the Ahoms till his defeat in 1531 AD.[6] The State Authority reverted to Dersongpha, son of Khorapha. After initially acknowledging Ahom suzerainty he attempted to regain lost territory. He was defeated and killed in 1536 AD and Dimapur was sacked.

Eventually, a minor son of Khorapa shifted the population to Maibong where it entered a crucial phase of state formation.

Pressure was renewed on the Dimasas under the Ahom ruler Pratap Singha in 1606 AD. The Dimasa garrisons were defeated and they retreated to Maibong. They launched a surprise offensive later, destroying the Ahom garrisons at Raha and continued to retain portions of Nowgong. With the Mughals within sight of the Ahom territory, Pratap Singha did not pursue the Dimasas. Further he instead proposed terms of a friendly alliance, while continuing to address him as Thapita Sanchita (established and protected). The victorious Dimasa ruler assumed the name Satrudaman after defeating the Jaintia ruler Dhanamanik. He changed his name to Pratapnarayan and that of his capital to Kirtipur after defeating Pratap Singha. After annexing portions of Mughal territory towards (Karimganj District) Sylhet, he assumed the name Indrapratapnarayan. He issued coins to commemorate the event as the 'conqueror of Sylhet'.[7] For a short period when the Koch overran the entire Northeast, the Dimasa ruler was defeated in 1562 AD and became its tributary. They occupied a portion of the Cachar valley and established a principality. With the defeat of the Koches by the Sultan of Bengal the Dimasas reasserted their independence. The Dimasas paid an annual tribute to the Mughals in Bengal, but there is no evidence of Cachar ever being a vassal of the Mughals.

In the 17th century the Ahoms were engaged in hostilities with the Mughals and thus avoided any confrontation with the Dimasas. By the end of the 17th century the Ahoms under Rudra Singha insisted on a tribute from Cachar and also sought contribution of soldiers in the confederated army against the Mughals. The rajas of Cachar did not pay tribute for very long. Subsequent correspondences between the two showed that whenever a Dimasa ruler ascended the throne, the Ahoms demanded a tribute, while the ascending ruler demands bribes from the Ahoms. With the decline of Ahom power there was a cessation of conflict between the two. The final phase of state formation was achieved in 1750 AD, following the merger of the Koch principality in the plains of Cachar and the shifting of the capital to Khaspur.

Defence Mechanism and Weaponry

A constant state of confrontation with the neighbouring kingdoms created the necessity for structures for defence. A brick fort fortified Maibong, the capital city. To secure the frontier along the Jaintia kingdom two forts were constructed at Bandasil and Icchamati. After wresting a portion of Sylhet from the Mughals, two forts were constructed at Pratapgarh and Asuratikir. The Ahoms had settled new villages bordering Dimasa territory in Nowgong district to create a buffer. The Dimasas responded by maintaining forts at vulnerable places, which helped them in safeguarding their territory in the Nowgong section of the state.

At Maibong, the Dimasa rulers raised a regular army by enlisting almost all able-bodied men of the state. The chief column of the army was named '*Chandi Paltan*', in honour of the war-goddess, *Ranachandi*. The heir-apparent or Jubraj served as the commander-in-chief of this army.

During the earliest known conflicts with the Ahoms at Dimapur, Gait mentions of initial Dimasa resistance with bows and arrows.[8] This reflects the relative backwardness or lower levels of sophistication in their weaponry and their mode of defence. Pratap Singha defeated the Dimasa at Dharmatika in 1606 AD. He captured a large booty of guns, swords and spears.[9] This reflected a stage of advancement in the weaponry used by the Dimasas from those used in earlier wars. As the process of state formation attained a greater degree of sophistication at Maibong, there was a corresponding advancement reflected in their weaponry. In a war in 1536 AD with the Ahoms, led by Suhungmung, cannons were used by both the Ahoms and the Dimasas.[10] In an account of the conflict with the Ahoms under Rudra Singha, there is a reference of a 'booty taken of a cannon and 700 guns'.[11] The existing data on the Dimasas provides little insight into the techniques of warfare.

Cult of War Goddess

The process of state formation at Maibong crystallized as the Dimasa rulers increasingly came under the influence of Brahminical Hinduism. Brahmins began to occupy positions of eminence in the expanding state machinery. They in turn reinforced the differentiation in status of the ruling elite and the commoners through legitimation, which derived sanction from religious beliefs and rituals. The Brahmins invented myths of origin, which emphasized the separate and special nature of the ruling elite. The Brahmins traced the ancestry of the Dimasas to Ghatotkach, the son of Bhima and the demoness Hidimba. Genealogies were created to support such a claim.

A very significant myth was invented which identified their tutelary deity Kachai-Kati as a form of Sakti. The deity was transformed into *Ranachandi,* the goddess of war. The Brahmins composed hymns and verses for the worship of *Ranachandi* incorporating it into the pantheon of Hindu deities. Further, she was projected as a fierce deity, which corresponded to her original flesh eating form. The Dimasas adopted the rites of Kali in her worst incarnation and identified her with their own female demon/goddess *Ranachandi.*

A legend signifying the association of *Ranachandi* with state power was current amongst the Dimasas. According to the legend, *Ranachandi* appeared in a dream to the first Hindu ruler of the Dimasas, Nirbhoynarayan. He was directed to meet her at the riverside the next day. As directed, he waited there for a long time to find only a snake swimming in the river. Assuming that it was a form of the goddess, he stretched out his hands and seized the snake by its tail, which instantly transformed into a sword that he carried home. That night *Ranachandi* reappeared in his dreams and stated that the sword would bring luck and ensure prosperity for the state.[12]

As the Dimasas were frequently involved in wars, as a protector of the state, the war goddess could easily command loyalty. The success in foiling the repeated onslaughts of the Ahoms on the state strengthened their belief in protecting power of *Ranachandi*. Worshipping her was considered essential for victory. Greater dependence on the war goddess brought the people increasingly under the influence of the Brahmins.

Songs were composed by Krishnachandranarayan and also by Govindachandranarayan during his exile and dedicated to *Ranachandi*. In 1576 AD, Meghanarayan struck a coin proclaiming himself as a worshipper of *Ranachandi*. In 1721 AD Harischandranarayan constructed a temple at Maibong and dedicated it to *Ranachandi*. After shifting their capital to Khaspur, the rulers were accommodated as Kshatriya into the Hindu caste structure, yet they continued to worship *Ranachandi*, along side other Hindu deities like Siva and Vishnu. At Khaspur Harischandranarayan II constructed a *Ranachandi* temple within the precincts of his newly constructed palace.[13]

In the evolution of the cult of the war goddess there was a merging of the temporal state machinery with the spiritual apparatus. While the Dimasas assimilated and absorbed aspects of a new culture, the war goddess provided a space for their traditional belief system to co-exist with it. An appropriation of *Kachai Kati* in its changed form as a goddess into the Hindu pantheon helped in 'integrating the Dimasas into the fold of Hinduism without feeling alienated. The state machinery was successful in expanding into newer territories and retaining existing territory in the face of recurring external aggression supported by their belief on *Ranachandi*.

Conclusion

The transformation of the Dimasa polity from its indigenous tribal formation into statehood was achieved due to various factors. It was primarily through the syncretic adoption of Hindu symbols. The myths of origin provided legitimacy to the ruling clan and stressed on their divine descent. Rituals reinforced their special position. On the other hand the state maintained control over its population by military strength. Attaching importance to a war goddess reinforced this aspect. Warfare played a predominant role in strengthening the stabilization of the states and ensuring the dominant position of the ruling elite.

NOTES

1. S. Endle, *The Kacharis,* First published 1911, Reprinted 1975, New Delhi, 1975, p.xvi.
2. J.B. Bhattacharjee, *Social and Polity Formation in Pre-Colonial North East India: The Barak Valley Experience,* First published 1991, New Delhi, p.136.
3. J.B. Bhattarcharjee, *op. cit.*, p.137.
4. Sukanya Sharma, "A Study on the Dimapur Ruins of Nagaland", *Bulletin of the Assam State Museum,* No. XIV, 1998, p.10.
5. E.A. Gait, *A History of Assam,* Second Edition, 1926, p.299.
6. J.B. Bhattacharjee, *op.cit.*, p.138.
7. *Ibid.*, p.142.
8. E.A. Gait, *op. cit.*, p.90.

9. *Ibid.*, p. 96.
10. *Ibid.* p. 106.
11. *Ibid.*, p. 172.
12. J.B. Bhattacharjee, *op. cit.*, p.139.
13. *Ibid*, pp. 140, 142, 150.

19

War Dresses and Weapons of the Apa Taniis

Pura Tado

Introduction

The Apa Taniis who inhabit the Ziro Valley and surrounding areas of Lower Subansiri district of Arunachal Pradesh are surrounded by the Nyishis and Hill Miris. None of these communities achieved state formation. Moreover, there was no head hunting system prevalent among these communities. The Nyishi and Hill Miri settlements were scattered and far between. The Apa Taniis in contrast were settled in seven compact villages of Hiija, Duta, Miidang-Tage, Michi Bamin, Haangu, Hari and Biila. These villages are compact, very large and are located very near to each other, the longest distance between two Apa Tanii villages being two and half kilometres. Some of these villages have more than thousand households. Moreover, the houses are constructed in very congested way where eaves of two houses touch each other. On top of it the Apa Taniis have a highly developed agricultural economy. In such a situation the need for war was very minimal. In case of the Nyishis and Hill Miris, the distances between villages did not allow for protracted war campaign. In case of Apa Taniis they cannot afford to wage a war to disturb their tranquil. Hence, occasional raids were used for settling disputes among themselves. During these raids the raiders used to wear typical war dresses. To make their raids successful, in a short time period, they used many types of war weapons also.

War Dresses

Byopa (cap)

To protect their head the Apa Taniis wore a cane cap called *Byopa* locally which fitted the wearers head tightly. This cap is made of fine splits of long canes found in dense jungles. This finely split cane is used as warp while much thicker cane splits shaped into cylindrical is used as weft. The weft is started from one end is tightly tied by the warp. As the circumference of the weft increases, the shape of the Byopa or cap increases and it takes the shape of a head. The ends of the weft and warp are made to taper at the back of the Byopa like shape of an ear of a barking deer. It looks very aesthetic and is handy for removing the Byopa or the cap.

It is decorated with two or three long tail plumes of jungle cock called Parsing in Tanii or of common domestic fowl. Usually long and curved tail plumes of male are used. Sometimes the forelimb of an eagle is also tied in the middle of the cap, its tail on pointing, towards backside of the wearer. The tallon of the eagle is said to ward off the evil spirits and dominate the enemies. Thus, the cane cap acted as a helmet protecting the wearer from any head injury by any war weapons.

Lampru (muffler)

The *Lampru* or the muffler is wrapped tightly around the neck. This *Lampru* was usually made of coarse woollen material. The coarse wool was usually imported from Tibet. It is then washed well after mixing with ash of hearth very thoroughly and dried. It is then spinned into thick woollen threads, its warps are kept as per the neck measurement of the wearer. It is woven in a small loom held in the loin.

Its warps and wefts are woven very tighty so that an arrow or a spear or lance or for that matter any sharp edged or pointed weapons may not penetrate and injure the neck. Thus, it protects the neck of the wearer from any sharp-edged weapons.

Jilya Pulye (silk/endi cloth)

The body is covered with a long silk (*endi*) cloth called *Jilya*. The *Jilya* cloth is folded into two and wrapped around the body in such a way that two ends of the cloth joins on the chest. It is held tight by the help of pins made of bamboo. The other way to wrap the *Jilya* cloth is to tie the one end of the cloth diagonally on shoulder. Likewise the other end of the *Jilya* is to be similarly tied across other shoulder. The middle portion of the cloth is held tight to the body by help of a belt. The *Jilya* fibre is so strong that the pointed or sharp-edged weapons hardly penetrate it.

Hupo

A *hupo* is type of band made of hides. Usually skin of buffalo or mithun is used for making a *hupo*. It covers the body from below armpit to groin. Thus it protects the stomach and half of the chest. It is made in such a way that it fits the body of the wearer perfectly and does not in anyway impede the movements of hands and legs of the wearer. The skin is well tanned before it is used for making a *hupo*. Thus the *hupo* protects the stomach and half of the chest of the wearer.

Hurin

Hurin is a large ring made out of two split long canes, which is used as weft of the ring. The warp is made out of fibres of giant ferns. The fibres of the giant fern is wrapped round very tightly around the two split canes in such a way that the canes cannot be seen from outside. This *hurin* is made in such a way the circumference is neither too loose nor too tight for the wearer. It is worn in many numbers so that the stomach and groin are covered. The *hurin*, thus, protects the stomach and groin of the wearer. It directly protects the wearer from injuries by weapons like swords and other sharp-edged weapons.

Lahii (wrist band)

Lahii is a wristband usually worn on the left hand for right handed persons and on the right hand for the left handed person. It is made out of long hairs of human being. The fallen hair while combing is collected and made into yarn by spinning. Then it is artistically made into a thick rope with some symetrical designs. Sometimes, a piece of well-tanned skin is also fashioned into armband and wore. This armband is necessary to protect the hand from being hurt by the string of the bow while shooting arrows to enemies. This also protects the vulnerable wrist from injuries by the enemies.

Laake (finger band)

Laake is a ring made of small strip of split cane fashioned as finger band. This is worn on the fingers covering all the four fingers of the hand. It keeps all the four fingers in one place so that it becomes very good platform for gripping the bowstring with arrow. It helps grip the arrow tightly with the thumb on one side and fingers on the other side and shoot the arrow well.

As pointed out earlier the Apa Taniis neither had a long war with their neighbours nor could afford a war among themselves because of the very nature of the their economy, habitation and village settlement pattern. Neither the Apa Taniis knew about the use of gun powder and guns. Hence, the weapons of war used by them had been very simple and very few.

Weapons of War

Ilyo/Chirih (dao/tibetan sword)

The chief weapon of defence as well as offence of the Apa Taniis had been the *Ilyo* or the *Chirih. Chirih* is a special type of *dao* imported from Tibet through Nyishi people. It is longer than the ordinary *dao* of the Apa Taniis. Its breath is much narrower than the usual *dao* but lighter and very sharp. This *dao* is costly and everyone cannot afford it. It is also used in ceremonies and festivals. There are three types of *chirihs*. They are (a) *Shah,* (b) *Pinji* and (c) *Huluh. Shah* and *Pinji* are costlier than the *Hulu*. There are mythological reasons behind it.

There are many types of Ilyos. However, they are mostly divided into two categories: (a) ordinary Ilyo and (b) *Pare Sala*. Any *dao* of iron is called *Ilyo* and it is used by an overwhelming majority. On the other hand *Pare Salas* are special type of *Ilyos*. They shine better and their sharpness is much greater than other *Ilyos*. Hence its capacity to cut is much higher than that of any ordinary *Ilyo*. Its quantity is much less and hence it is much costlier. Now-a-days it is very rare to see them.

Adang/Iidang (spear)

This is a piece of sharp iron weapon. Its shape is like spade in the playing card. The tip and sides are sharpened so that it inflicts maximum injures to the enemy. It is attached to a long hard and well-seasoned stick. At Ziro; a species called *Tai-hlang* stick is used to hold a spear. The stick is seasoned well by keeping it over hearth for many months before the spear is attached. The length of the stick is usually from six to seven feet.

Punyang (javelin)

This is pointed iron instrument to attack the enemy with. This is also attached to a well seasoned stick like the spear. The stick used for attaching a punyang is also same as for the spear. This particular weapon is used for attacking enemies who are within well protected walls or in bunkers.

Hu-lyuh (bamboo javelin)

Hu-lyuh is a javelin of bamboos small in girth but matured bamboos. These are usually first or second generation bamboos of newly raised bamboo garden. These are used while fighting a battle near the villages among Apa Taniis. Young children and women bring them to fighting men who hurl them towards the enemies. These are never used in a raid far away from the Apa Tanii village. This is used only during the feuds between Apa Tanii villages as they are very close to each other.

Apu (arrow)

Arrows are made either from the matured bamboos of Ziro or bamboos found in Nyishi areas. Bamboos with long girth are usually used for making arrows. Arrows are of two types. One is ordinary bamboo arrow. Another type is called Morto Apu. In this type of arrow a sharp iron piece in the shape of spade as in a playing card is used. When this type of Morto arrow pierces the body, it cuts through the flesh. When one pulls it out it further cuts the flesh and the wound inflicted is very deep and painful. Sometimes aconite (*iimyo*) is attached to a Morto arrow. The aconite or *iimyo* is a type of poison, which is collected from very high altitude mountain ranges. Many restrictions are observed during collection, preparation and storing of *iimyo* (aconite). Once the aconite enters the body, it is absorbed in the blood and the person or animal dies of poisoning.

Siitin (shield)

Siitin is a shield usually measuring three feet by five feet. It is made out of skin of either buffalo or mithun. The well tanned *Siitin* can withstand impact of any sharp or pointed weapons of war. This shield is used as an item in certain rituals also.

Since the Apa Taniis cannot afford to disturb their peace frequently, they did not really fight any war. Sometimes they are used in fighting between two or more villages in the open paddy field. Both the sides used to fight in the manner the battle was fought during *Mahabharat.* Once, anyone from either side is killed, the battle used to break up and disperse.

In certain cases when a grievance is to be vent out against a village or an individual by other villages, a demonstration of war called *Gyambo sonii* was performed. In this *Gyambo sonii* the group will demonstrate exactly how they fight a battle. In the process some crops and fences of vegetable and bamboo garden may be damaged.

In these battles the *Buliang* or members of the Village Council plays very important role. Even at the thick of the battle if a *Buliang* comes with his *Buliang Dangkho* or *Panyih* raised in the air the warring parties have to cease fighting and listen to him. He may take the responsibility to settle the dispute to the liking of warring groups. Nobody usually disobeys a *Buliang* (Village Council's) decision. Thus the *Buliang* restores peace and tranquility in Ziro Valley.

20

Military Activities in North East As Uniting Force

Bharat Kalita

Assam or in broader term the present North East Frontier region of India has been a museum of anthropology due to the presence of multiple races of various ethnic stocks. Besides Austric, Dravidian, Aryan and Mongoloid, there emerged scores of sub-races both in the hilly tracts and Brahmaputra and Surama valleys. Intermixing of blood between the main stocks perhaps resulted this multiplicity of sub-races developing into a political and territorial sectioning of the area. Presently many races have put up their claims both in plains and hills as the original inhabitants of the region in order to bargain territorial and political authorships. Without raising the questions whether these claims to be accepted or rejected it may be put that it is certainly an unhealthy omen if historical course of the region is not given a go-by.

Tribal States

Many a time it appears that the tribal divisions of people as may be found in the region was not a creation by man alone but to a great extent an imposition by nature or geographical factor. In the hills one tract is separated from the other by natural barriers as watertight compartment where a group of people living years together in this tract develops a separate identity from the other. This compartmentalization was extremely minimum in the plains where geographical barrier was much less. In other words lack of communications between all sections of the people happened to be the main dividing line thereby creating scores of racial political units in the hills.

A question may be raised why then in historical period so many political kingdoms existed in the Brahmaputra valley where communication hurdles were less? In ancient time entire Brahmaputra valley was united though there might by some feudal landlords having their autonomous jurisdiction in some limited areas. In those days when divergent groups of people took shelter in Assam entering both from the east and west this arrangement of relegation of powers to certain heads suited well. Aryan Hindu dynasty was ruling in Assam till the attempted invasion of the country by Ikhtiyar Uddin Yuzback (about 1256-57 AD). The king who defeated Yuzback was one Hindu Aryan King Sandhiya Prithun (if Gurucharita of Ramacharan Thakura is to be believed). After this campaign he shifted his capital from Kamrup to Kamatapur. It is difficult to ascertain the cause of this shifting. But when the capital shifted from the centre of power to one corner of the kingdom it gave indulgence to the petty clannish chieftains to declare independence in their fiefdom. It can be convincingly assumed that this situation gave birth to the rise of the principalities like Bhuyans, Kacharis, Dhekeris, Koches, Khasi-Jayantias, 18 Hill Rajas like Rani, Dumaria, Beltola, etc., in the Brahmaputra plains. At the same time Ahoms entered in Assam in 1228 AD and they were gradually rising to power defeating the rulers of these principalities as well as subjugating the tribes in the high hills like Nagas, Khamtis and their kinsmen, the Naras. They fought for about 400 years, Muslim invaders being their main enemy. Finally, they emerged out to be most powerful political authority with the absence of which Assam's present political unification perhaps would have been something different. One advantage which the Ahom enjoyed was the spontaneous demand for the presence of a powerful political authority to defend the region from Muslim invaders because in place of many weak and small kingdoms one powerful kingdom was certainly more effective for strategical and tactical reasons. Ahom capitalized this situation by strengthening their defensive capability with offensive action wherever it was found to be expedient. Probably without the Turko-Afghan and Mughal expeditions turn of events in the political history of Assam would have been different. Unfortunately these ugly heads of clannish survivalism is again spearheading the Assam politics since last four decades after the splits in 1963, 1972, 1973 when Nagaland, Arunachal Pradesh, Meghalaya and Mizoram took birth respectively as separate states inside the Indian Union dividing the existing unity of the region.

Live and Let Live

Internal rivalry and warfare in-between the tribal groups happened to be the normal condition of life in the medieval period. For a trifle cause they used to pick up quarrel and fought. Whatever might be the cause of warfare, it is certain that all the contacts between the tribes used to be through this military confrontation. In the hilly tracts victory of one side did not mean merger of one's country with another. They fought to punish each other for some fault. Once this aim is fulfilled 'Live and Let Live' principle was followed. This finally resulted the survival of almost all the races and tribal groups. Even the Ahoms also adopted the policy of 'let others also live' once they secured the recognition of their overlordship. After the occupation of the region the British imperialism also followed the same pattern of policy by leaving the tribal peoples of their own by making the latter believe that there was a superior power over their head.

Significance of Military Contacts

In the life of North East Frontier the role of the Brahmaputra valley has been always significant. This is the most fertile and resourceful region where ratio of population is much more than the hilly regions. This valley was first Aryanized—though the date of Aryanization cannot be accurately determined. Many scholars are of opinion that the Aryan-Kshatriyas (present Kalitas of Assam considered to be their descendants) settled down in the Brahmaputra valley and ruled the region for hundreds of years. They maintained the Aryan culture, which ultimately influenced even the Ahom invaders. Though they were defeated politically and overthrown from power yet Aryan culture—with Hindu religious rituals, Sanskritized Assamese language and other polished norms of life remained as permanent features to be accepted by all sections. During Ahom period import of scholarly Brahmins from Kanauj by the Kings further served the cause of Aryan cultural superiority. Indeed the Aryan culture unhesitatingly accepted the good conducts of life and society as was existed in the non-Aryan system. Until military confrontations took place between ancient Pragjyotish-Kamrup with the rest of India this Aryan culture was the only common link. In the prehistoric period there are accounts of war between Kamrup and rest of India. Lord Krishna with his Jadava Bahinis first defeated king Bhismak of Kundilnagar (Eastern Assam) to secure the Krishna-devoted daughter of the latter as his wife. Lord Krishna also attacked king Bana of Sonitpur (present Tezpur in middle Assam) to rescue his grandson Aniruddha along with his consort Usha—who was the daughter of Bana. King Bhagadatta joined the Mahabharata war on the side of Kaurava and died in fighting. King Ghatotkach of Dimapur (now under Nagaland) fought on the side of Pandavas and fell in the battle. King Shankaladipa in pre-historic period advanced upto Pundarvardhana and Samata thereby creating a sea outlet in the Bay of Bengal. King Bhaskarvarmana in seventh century AD joined Harshavardhana in defeating Sasanka of Bengal. Subsequently, he joined the religious conferences of King Harsha in Kanauj and Prayag. The point can be drawn from these accounts is that ultimately it was the military contacts which established link with Assam and rest of India and this process continued throughout the ages.

After Invasions

Attempt of Muslim subjugation of Assam started from the beginning of the thirteenth century with Bakhtiyar's expedition to conquer the land. But the attempt was a failure. Several others Turko-Afghan attempts and subsequent Mughal attempts also became failure. Some limited parts of the region close to the Muslim frontier of Bengal were brought under the administration of the Muslims for short duration. But surprisingly the repeated Muslim attacks on Assam from 13th century to 17th century AD could not significantly influence in the social and political system of the region. To quote Dr. P.C. Choudhury: "While almost whole of India was subjugated by the Muslims, their invasions of Assam, beginning with that of Bakhtiyar, met with total failure. Muslim culture in fact was kept at arm's length until comparatively late times, and the western culture crept into her body politic only during the middle of 19th century AD. Nothing perhaps better explains this independent character of Assam's history than an appeal to her geography and none can draw a true picture of the character of the Assamese and aesthetic sense in particular, without due emphasis on the surroundings in which they live. This independent nature of the people, distinguished by a sense of patriotism, if it may be so called, is a contribution to the fundamental cultural unity of India."

One important political development of Assam can be noted from the arrival of the Ahoms in Assam since 1228 AD. They had conquered the country by inches after fighting about 400 years. Though all the tribal neighbouring chieftains could not be brought under their direct administrative control, yet they put them down depriving the tribal chieftains' attempt to dominate over any part of Assam. This undoubtedly helped the formation of the present Assam as a united country amidst the greatest amount of racial diversities in the region. In the plains of the Brahmaputra valley they brought all sections under full-scale subordination not only by the use of military strength but also using their wise policy of total merger with the geographical, cultural and popular environments. Ahoms even showed their catholicity by rehabilitating quite a significant section of Muslim population who came as soldiers but was trapped in the land after getting defeated. This Muslim community still is contributing greatly in the Assamese culture and tradition. In the district of Nowgong there is a village named Lanka inhabited by Sikh community. Except their Sikhism, by custom, tradition and language they are Assamese farmers. The ancestors of these people came as Mughal soldiers. They were rehabilitated in Assam. They intermarry with the Assamese high caste claiming themselves to be Kshtriyas. Ahoms followed surprisingly the same policy of Sakas, Hunas, Bactrian Greeks, Kushanas, etc., of getting fully absorbed in Indian culture and tradition forgetting their foreign identity thereby becoming local people of the land.

Muslim cultural impact in Assam is quite negligible. Even in present Kamrup and Goalpara where they established sarkar and pargana, except the religion followed by a limited section, nothing identical to be found worthmentioning of Mughal or Turko-Afghan culture. When visited a Muslim village of Dalibari in the district of Kamrup I found in all families only Hindu system of hospitality and food. Kabab, Pulao are unknown to them. Yet they claim that their ancestors came with Raja Ram Singha to fight against Assam. But after the defeat of Ram Singha they decided to stay on. This village is in the close proximity of Alaboi where a severe battle was fought between Ram Singha and Lachit Barphukan with heavy loss on Assamese side.

The Ahoms took another intelligent step of increasing their population in the country. This they did by intermarriage with the local clans and admitting them to their own faction and by using other conciliatory method. The king and royal family even married into the families of Kamatapur, Koch Behar, Jayantia. With their bridal trains came Hindu priests, artisans and other skilled hands.

After their victory against the Pathans and Mughals in several battles they captured huge store of cannons, muskets and other firearms to strengthen their position. Ahoms also manufactured their own guns and subsequently they used skilled hands of the captured soldiers. With the increasing confrontations with the Muslims, Ahom's gun-powder had attained a near perfection.

Weak Points

The weak points of the Assamese cannot be neglected. One major defect of their system may be said the lack of skill in the art of government in earlier time. The king generally did not enjoy supreme power unless he was tactful and ambitious. The administrative machines used to be left in the hands of a few jealous and intriguing ministers and officers. This resulted interregnums and court rivalry and even occasionally leading to the full control of the country by unscrupulous officers like Debera Barbaruah. Debera even managed to kill three kings in quick succession. Sometimes even in the hands of over-ambitious officer wise and great persons of the country had to be victims. One glaring example was Atan Buragohain. Atan Buragohain was one of wisest ministers of Assam contributing greatly for Ahom victory against the Mughals. He even refused the crown, which was offered to him at a very critical juncture declaring that the crown belonged only to royal blood. But, finally, he was imprisoned and executed inhumanely by unscrupulous officer.

There was great laxity in the law of primogeniture, which the kings followed. This led to serious dispute for succession after the demise of a king. Besides, there was no proper training for the would-be king as many a time selection of a king could not be determined till the death of the sitting monarch. Another drawback which could be observed was that a weak king used to be flattered by self-seeking sycophants. Even the queens were not exception in this business thereby causing instability, chaos, and interrognum in the country. The Ahom principle was that a prince could not succeed to the throne if certain limbs of his body got mutilated. When an unscrupulous prince would occupy the throne, he used to adopt harsh measure to get other princes' body mutilated so that no attempt could be made by anyone to replace him. This method deprived the chances of many able princes to become king.

The Assamese army no doubt deserves praise for their valour, patriotism and truly martial characteristics. But the greatest drawback to the army was the absence of a good leader to command them more often. Lachit Barphukan for a short duration could offer the benefit of his leadership. But in the rest of the fighting scenes a terrible dearth of this quality was visible. Without the dynamic guidance of a supreme leader in the battlefield men, arms, ammunitions and provisions did not prove to be of much avail.

The defection amongst Ahom commander in-charge of important positions was another drawback. Even there are examples of king's father-in-law rebelling and passing secret informations to the invaders. General like Baduli Phukan betrayed the cause of his country and sold it for his meagre personal gain. Muhammedan inhabitants of Assam were trusted by the kings and even were given responsible position in the state affairs. But many of them betrayed the trust and passed on secret informations to the Mughals when entered into Assam.

The Muhammedan campaign created a new chapter in the relation of Assam and Bengal. In ancient time we have references that Assam King could expand his territory occupying a large part of Bengal territory. Powerful rulers of Bengal also occasionally tried their best to expand their realm incorporating part of Assam. But this chapter did not create much of misunderstanding between the people of the two neighbouring countries. At the time of Muslim expeditions quite a large number of Bengali soldiers used to accompany the Muslims. Many of the Hindu Zamindars of Bengal after becoming vassals of the Muslim ruler played leading role in the war against Assam. Raja Sattrajit was one of them who played an important part in the Mughal victory in Assam.

An unhealthy feeling in Assam that the land was outside the Indian mainland throughout the courses of the Indian history can be treated baseless. In this vast Indian subcontinent military expeditions happened to be the main linking factor between the peoples. Assam in that way, used to draw attention from the ruling authority of Delhi more prominently from 1200 AD onwards besides their link in ancient past.

21

War and Art Tradition of the Wanchos of Arunachal Pradesh

Sarit K. Chaudhuri

Head hunting had existed in many parts of the world like among the aborigines of Formosa, the Dyaks of Borneo, the Wa of Burma, Marings of New Guinea, Iban people of Sarawak, Maories of New Zealand and many other communities across the world. In the context of Northeast India some of the Nagas, Kukis as well as the Wanchos come in immediate reference. Taking examples of the Ao and Konyak Nagas Mills (1935) tried to find out their ethics of head hunting. Haimendorf also wrote on various aspects of head hunting (1938, 1969) on the basis of his work on the Konyak Nagas. Julian Jacobs *et al.* (1990) discussed different aspects of Naga head hunting in their latest work on the Nagas. It appears from the existing literature that various beliefs are associated with such practice, such as, concept of fertility cult[1], bringing good fortune on both the taker and the whole community, getting slave in the next world, removing sickness, protection of crops, cattles or even environmental compulsions (Archer, Vayda 1876). Mills (1935 : 178) writes, "The fact that head hunting is not merely the sport of irresponsible criminals but the pursuit of persons of otherwise estimable character, even by our standards, shows that it plays an important part in the lives of those who practice it". He (*ibid.*) adds, "The head hunter is not, therefore, from his point of view, a blood thirsty savage. He naturally loves to win applause and the right to wear the ornaments of a warrior, but deep down there is a feeling that he is a patriot, ready to risk his life for the benefit of his fellows."

However, present paper neither tries to explore such rationale behind head hunting nor try to romanticise the practice of head hunting. Rather it makes an humble attempt to show how head hunting worked as a stimulus to generate some of the art forms of the Wanchos and then what about the fate of such art forms in the emerging context of Arunachal Pradesh.

The Wanchos[2] represent one of the major tribes of Arunachal Pradesh inhabited southwestern tip of the Tirap district with a population of 50,128 as per the 2001 Census report. This area is surrounded by Tissa river in the east, Mon district of Nagaland in the west, Patkai hills in the south and the Sibsagar district in Assam in the north. They are basically agriculturist and obviously shifting hill cultivation still plays the pivotal role in their economic life. Chieftainship is one of the most significant features of the Wancho social structure. Of late, Panchayat system is also introduced. Besides existence of dormitories (both boys and girls), rich art traditions as well as previous practice of head hunting are some of the identity markers of the community. During colonial period they came into prominence in 1875 when they killed Lieutenant Holocombe and 80 other men of his survey party at Ninu village (Elwin 1959:70-85).

Undoubtedly, the Wanchos have carved out a unique space in the art history of this frontier state and some of these art forms such as tattooing, woodcarving and war dance are essentially linked with the practice of head hunting. Present paper focuses solely on the first two forms. I have tried to build up my arguments on the basis of the available published works (Dutta 1990, Srivastava 1970, Elwin 1959/1988) as well as my involvement with the Wanchos of Senua, Zedua, Pumao etc. since last few years.

Tattooing

According to Thomas (1995 : 100), "The word tattoo is like taboo, in a small but culturally significant group of European words derived from Polynesian languages, the original term being tatau in both Samoan and Tahitian". Tatooing is one of many forms of irreversible body alteration including scarification, cicatrisation, piercing and branding, and it is probably the oldest and most widespread of these. Physical evidence for the practice survives from the late fourth millennium BC in Europe and from about 2000 BC in Egypt and tattooing can be found virtually all parts of the world at some time (Caplan 2000 : 1). Tattooing which is locally known as Hueh or Huehtu, is one of the most significant events in the life of both men and women [3]. Apart from being a most admired and cherished decoration, tattoo with them is of important social significance. These body marks symbolise the stages in women's life and the social status and achievements of a male individual (Dutta 1990 : 50)[4]. Dutta mentioned (*ibid.* 53),"Male tattoo is more serious business. It is related to war and only those who could establish their bravery by taking trophies of heads and bring them to the village for prosperity could aspire to it. Along with it, they went up in special estimation and girls would give their highest choice to those with this insignia of heroism".[5] He quotes from Peal (1896),"The man who brings in a head is no longer called a boy and can assist in council of state.... The head he brings is handed to the Raja, who confers the *ak* or right of decoration by tattoo, at which there are great feasting and pigs and cows or even buffaloes are killed, and no end of *maod* or fermented bear is drunk. Those who are not tattooed, when old enough, make a party and lie in wait for stragglers, men, women or children, anybody in fact, with a head on him, and as cover is plentiful, they can get on the enemy's land and lie in ambush alongside his paths, never breaking cover unless certain of success and getting clear off. All those who get heads, get the *ak* (tattoo) on the face; those who get hands and feet, get marks accordingly for the latter on the leg". It needs to be remembered that female tattooing has nothing to do with the war tradition. A Wancho woman tattoos at different parts of her body as per their cultural norms but never tattoos their face, which their counterpart does. Generally male members tattoo on their face and chest after a successful headhunting by the tattoo specialist who must be a *wancha* (chief's wife). Such a head hunter is called *Nowmaipa* and during tattooing his family used to arrange great feast by sacrificing pig, buffalo etc., to mark the ritual. Depending on the position each tattoo has its own nomenclature, such as, *Thaanhueh* (on face), *Khahhueh* (on chest) etc. However, such tattoo designs have clan as well as village specificity which leads to the wide heterogeneity of forms at the community level.

In fact, this form of body art is so prominent and profuse in nature that it had attracted the attention of most of the colonial writers like Woodthrope (1878), Badgely (1875) etc. To quote S.E. Peal (1896) again,"As long as social position depends on tattooing, as here, and can only be got by bringing in the head of an enemy, so long shall we have these wars and consequent isolations of clans".

Interestingly such an pervasive tradition gave rise to the specialist tattooists who are essentially women attached to chief's family and who need to observe certain taboos and wear leaves of wild plant on the ear and enjoy certain special privileges in terms of receiving foods and drinks during the tattooing operation.

Wood Carving

It is evident that head hunting was one of major events in Wancho lives, which had multiple implications. Traditionally a successful head hunter was not only supposed to be tattooed—may be on the face or even on the chest but also he is supposed to wear the replica of a human head or the hand and as a result he himself may carve by utilizing his understanding and skill. As these woodenheads are associated with the head hunting, the Wancho carver gives more attention to the head while carving of such items. Of course, other parts of human figures are also they carve with realistic image. Some wood carving are still available comprising of head at one side and impression of hand along with distinct fingers on the other side which a head hunter can insert within the hair just below the headgear. Except such individuals no one in Wancho society can use it for hair dressing.

Dutta (*ibid.* 239) reported, "Head hunting has left its impress on the Wancho culture, specially on their dress, wearing on the back of their heads carved hands of wood, often dyed red. Sometimes the hands have one head or more carved in the palms. If several men attacked an enemy, only the first to strike had the privilege to bring the head and afterwards of wearing a brass of woodenhead on the chest or basket. The second man would amputate the hand and bring this home, thereby earning the right to wear a wooden hand, the actual hand being hung in the morung. A third man might remove the foot and he could attach a wooden foot to his basket".

Such wooden body parts may be carved by the warriors themselves or by other villagers and may be gifted by the chief as a mark of their successful mission which again involves rituals, sacrifice etc. as per their traditional norms.

It may be added here that the heads thus taken in different raids are kept in the chief's dormitory as trophies. But in case of chief's head or any member of his family, a hole made in the roof of the skull and tufts of dyed goat's hair were inserted to distinguish them from the commoner's heads. Such heads are fed during annual festivals.

It may be mentioned here that the art of woodcarving is associated with mainly male's dormitory (*Pa*) and hardly it has any significance with the female's dormitory, which does not have any separate formal structure. In male's dormitory the most important items of wood carving is the log drum. Log drum is popularly known as *kham*. It is astonishing to see that they have developed their collective fertile imaginations to create the biggest musical instrument—drums—out of wood. It is the source not only for pleasure but also more importantly for communication and cultural exchange which this paper tries to underscore. In fact, its construction and installation inside the dormitory, which involve a series of sacred and secular activities, can also be perceived as the reflection of their local wisdom. This drum is an excellent piece of their traditional craftsmanship, which is gradually fading out. But the most significant aspect of it is the variegated sounds, which are context specific and having tremendous implications in relation to their traditional social system. Such context specific sounds, which do not reveal any social reality to a non-Wancho individual, have crucial ramifications to articulate available social spaces of the Wanchos. Rhythm emanates out of beating such drums by a group of expert Wancho male members, communicates special message at the cognitive level of the community, which in turn triggers up corresponding intricate social interactions at the empirical level. Such collective wisdom, which transcendent from one generation to another, helps their social system to adjust or to negotiate with the emergent social situation (Chaudhuri, 2001).

Tattooing and Woodcarving in the Changing Context

In comparison to the initial phase of post-independent period, which Elwin (1957, 1966, 1959/1988, 1959) had observed, the tribal situation in Arunachal Pradesh has undergone a tremendous change due to various historical, social and induced forces in spite of the special constitutional provisions it enjoys even today. The changing status—starting from erstwhile NEFA to Union Territory and finally, statehood, have a great socio-political significance for the tribal people of Arunachal Pradesh who have started a great deal of interaction with the different ethnic groups and have gained almost absolute control over decision making processes. This has culminated in a real dent in their overall socio-economic life by initiating a series of changes in response to new opportunities and specially, articulation with wider market economy and flow of new world views. Such induced forces of change may also be perceived in the form of modernization, westernization, industrialization and welfare measures in the form of state's interventions.

As a sequel to such politico-historical happenings and greater administrative penetration the tribal people of Arunachal Pradesh have been compelled to cast aside many of their socio-cultural traits and at the same time new elements are sipped into their emerging socio-cultural matrix. Interestingly, the resultant nature of tribal transitions varies from one tribe to another depending on their proximity to above forces of change. And this very process also made them aware of the various elements of their identify formation.

Like many other tribes of Arunachal Pradesh the Wanchos are also in transition. The tradition of head hunting is no more traceable as the context that had promoted head hunting has changed. Naturally the art of woodcarving as well as tattooing which to a large extent associated with such tradition has lost its sacred implications and social sanction.

The institution of dormitory (*pa*) is not only the treasure house of different items of woodcarvings but it is also the centre from where such skill gets transmitted from one generation to another as a part of their local wisdom.

This institution of the Wanchos under the cross roads due to the impact of modernization as well as penetration of the alien religious ideological flows, particularly the Christian missionaries, who looked up them as the centers of immorality or heathen institutions which should be condemned and shunned. During my field visit it was noticed that in the villages where majority are converted to Christianity, the girl's dormitory (*Zip-ham*) is wiped out through banning and the male's dormitories are also at the decaying stage as the alien cultural frame or religious behaviours which Christianity impose does not conform with the tradition emanates from *pa* or *zip-ham* of the Wanchos. Besides, Christianity such institutions also surfaced some basic problems to cope up with the emerging social reality.

So, with the rapid fade out of the male's dormitory not only the existing woodcarvings are decaying due to deliberate negligence but such skill or 'local wisdom' is getting eliminated from the mass which is more important to notice.

Woodcarving in the form of funery images of the successful head hunters or warriors or important individuals are also loosing importance due to commission of Christianity. This is because of the fact that installation of such image involves a series of ritual practices with the intervention of their traditional priests. Of course, this practice is not yet completely wiped out as the practitioner of such indigenous faith still persist and the social stratification or the chieftainship or the importance of Wangham clan still have functional value though rigidity have got diluted to a great extent.

However, Elwin rightly pointed out that such funery tradition itself has inherent destructive impact on the art tradition in general. In his own words (*Ibid.* 8), "Death destroys not only an individual, but a tradition".

As mentioned earlier that the art of tattoo had a great social value as it symbolizes not only different stages of human life but also intricately linked with the tradition of head hunting among the Wanchos. Dutta (*ibid.* 53) mentioned, "The day of inter-tribal war no more but still the social value of the tattoo associated with it lingers. So to win the decoration mock battles are staged". He (*ibid.*) quoted Elwin, "The Wanchos still have the custom of preparing wooden dummy, which is hidden in the field of some hereditary enemy; the young men hunt and 'kill' it and after they have returned in triumph, they can be tattooed as an essential preliminary to marriage". But such a love for tattooing which had indulged another form of art (carving wooden dummy) is rarely traceable today. However, tattooing or body art is gradually diminishing from the Wancho society though not yet wiped out completely in spite of a resolution taken by the Wancho Student Union to ban such form of body art.

Conclusions

In the changing context educated youth or Wancho elites are conscious about their rich tradition of wood carvings as they feel that this has became a unique component of their identify marker[6]. Though any significant conscious effort at the community level or individual level are yet to be found to think and rethink about the fate of such art. Emergence of craft centres has multiple implications in relation to the art of woodcarving. This may be perceived as an attempt to preserve and promote such vanishing art tradition of the Wanchos. But at the same time woodcarving became a special knowledge restricted to a few individuals in contrast to it previous cognition where every Wancho village had their own woodcarvers.

De-contextualization of such art form has its roots in the historical process as well as emerging socio-political reality in Arunachal Pradesh, which has reflected in the nature, items as well as the technology associated with woodcarvings. Now it became an item of showpiece or may be gaining ground because of an interest in recreating traditional art forms looking at the emerging context of neo traditional craft production for tourists in Arunachal Pradesh. Now what will be the item and form of woodcarvings by and large determined by the consumers or follows the basic rules of market—demand and supply.

Naturally, there is a great improvisation in the type of the tools presently used by the instructors or trainees inside the craft centres. Of course, such craft centres are also suffering with multiple constraints due to lack of innovative measures and proper planning to grab wider market opportunities. Though there is a general tendency to replicate certain specific items, mostly Wancho male or female in traditional attires and obviously males with war weapons. But some amounts of experiments are going on by carving popular heroes or choosing subjects from local history or popular folktales. Wancho boys who received training in craft centre failed to sell their products due to lack of buyer in the village areas or even in semi-urban areas. As a result, survival of this art form gets absolutely depended on whatever created within the four walls of craft centres. There are cases where some expert wood carvers started doing some other business or carpentry works to earn bread and butter. Some of their creative imagination gets reflected through a few woodcarvings traceable in their houses, which do not have, any linkage with their traditional values that Wancho woodcarvings used to emanate.

Evidence of carved woodenhead from Zedua village symbolizing 'Jesus' and incorporation of many motifs which are related to Christianity perhaps explain the relation between changing tribal art forms and emergent social reality. Such an understanding about art as a cultural symbol perhaps may help us to re-affirm one basic understanding that culture may be conceptualized as a process of negotiation.

NOTES

1. Linkages between fertility and head hunting have a critical dimension. Jacob (1990:121-22) cited some of the observations of Archer and J.P. Mills.

   When asked, the Nagas themselves were very clear about why heads were important. 'Since head-taking was stopped, Wanching has got smaller. Formerly when illness swept through the village, we took a head, offered it and the illness stopped. Now-a-days we cannot offer heads and the sickness goes on and on. Man after man falls ill and dies, and there is nothing we can do. The fields too have gone off and we do not get the crops we did.... Another Konyak put it thus: 'If we do not get a head every year, the crops will be bad, the pigs and cattle will not increase, our children will get ill...By equating soul with the 'fertility' idea, thus making the skull as the receptacle of the soul, act as a sort of fertilizer, causing prosperity in the village and in its crops. The problem is that the Nagas do not really make this link.

2. Etymology of the term Wançho is perceived in different ways as reported by the Ralonghaaam (2004:11). According to the versions of elderly members of the Wanchos, Wancho is derived from local term Wancho which means the Hillman or Wang follower or Hillman living under the domain of King. A few other opined that the word Wancho means follower of Wangham (King), whereas some mean Waan—means to live under the law of village formulated by the forefather. Other said that the common practice of rang-wan-to could be a probable origin of the word. They celebrate annual festival with the worship of rangwań, i.e. use of long bamboo with its branches or leaves on a platform during Oriah festival.

3. Available local words for 'Tattoo' varies, such as Huhtu (Pansa 2004:17), Huhtu (female) and Zanhuhtu (male) (Wangpan 2004 : 22), Hu or Chu (Dutta 1990:51) etc. It need to be mentioned here that dialectical variation is traceable among the upper and lower Wanchos.

4. I have a collection of good number of photographs showing the various designs associated with both males and females and specially tattooing of some of the head hunters with whom I was able to meet during my fieldwork.

5. Tattooing as such and specially on face is not in practice in general except in three villages, namely Senua and Niaunu and Niausa. With the establishment of the Wancho Youth Association in 1975 this art form is almost prohibited. In 1990 they took a resolution to abolish such art form from the above mentioned villages though Senua people are still continuing but in a much lesser scale.

6. It can be noted that other performing art forms, such war dance and songs associated with such dance are also important components of their cultural identity, which do not come under the purview of the present paper. Dutta (1990: 191-92) mentions, "Dance amongst the Wanchos was mainly connected with martial exploits. In the old days dance by warriors was a regular part of warlike expeditions. Now a days the main occasion does not occur: yet the dance continue to be performed. They now perform some of the rituals in symbolic forms during such dances. Before the dance starts the braves tattoo their faces and are fully equipped with war weapons such as dao, shield, spear and gun. As they dance and old man sings songs narrating the glorious exploits by ancient

heroes". In fact, Wanchos are called in different cultural programmes and even during the visit of political heavyweights as state guest to show their war dance. In one such occasion in 2004, I had a chance to see how the young Wangcho members perform such dance and I did extensive photography.

REFERENCES

Adam, L. 1949. *Primitive Art.* Penguin Books, Middlesex.

Archer, W.G. - Notes, papers of W.G. Archar, private collection of Mrs. Mildred Archer, cited from Julian A. Jacobs, A. Macfarlane, S. Harrison and A. Herle, 1990. *Hill Peoples of Northeast India The Nagas: Society Culture and the Colonial Encounter,* Thames and Hudson, London.

Caplan, J. 2000. Introduction *in Written on the Body : The Tattooing in European and American History* (ed) J. Caplan, Reaktion Books, London.

Boas, F. 1927. *Primititive Art,* Oslo.

Badgeley, W.F. 1875. Report of the Treacherous Attack made by the Nagas, *General Report on the Topographical Survey of India for the Season 1874-75, Calcutta.*

Burland, C.A. & J.T. Hooper 1953. *The Art of the Primitive People,* The Fountain Press, London.

Chaudhuri, S.K. 2001. *Beating the Drums and Weaving through the Social Spaces.* Paper presented in a Seminar on "Indigenous knowledge system of the Tribes of North East India: Implications and emerging Issues" held on 15-16 February, 2001 organized by the Department of Tribal Studies, Arunachal University.

Collingswood, R.G. 1938. *The Principle of Art,* Oxford.

Duara, D.K. (1992): *The Monpas of Arunachal Pradesh,* Directorate of Research, Itanagar.

Dutta, P.C. and S.I. Ahmed,1995. *People of India: Arunachal Pradesh,* Vol. XIV, Seagull Books, Calcutta, pp. 400-405.

Dutta, P.C. 1990. *The Wanchos,* Directorate of Research, Itanagar.

Dutta, P.C. (1990): The of Wood carving in Arunachal Pradesh, *in Handicraft of Arunachal Pradesh,* Directorate of Research, Itanagar, pp. 53-56.

Linton, R. & P. Wingert. (1941) *Art of the South Seas*, New York.

Elwin, V. 1958. The *Art of the North-East Frontier India,* Directorate of Research, Itanagar.

Elwin, V. 1957. *A Philosophy for NEFA,* Directorate of Research, Shillong.

Elwin, V. 1959. *The Tribal Art of Middle India,* London.

Elwin, V. 1959. *India's North-East Frontier in the Nineteenth Century,* OUP, New Delhi.

Elwin, V. 1966. *The Democracy in NEFA,* Directorate of Research, Shillong.

Haimendorf, C.V. F. 1969. *The Konyak Nagas,* New York.

Haimendorf, C.V. F. 1938. The morung system of the Konyak system of Assam, *Journal of the Royal Anthropological Institute,* LXVIII.

Jacobs, J., A. Macfarlane, S. Harrison and A. Herle, 1990. *Hill Peoples of Northeast India The Nagas: Society Culture and the Colonial Encounter,* Thames and Hudson, London.

Mills, J.P. 1935. The ethics of headhunting, *Discovery,* June.

Pansa, K. 2004. Tattoo: The Mark of the Wanchos, in *Wanchonu,* Souvenir, 29th Oria festival in 2004.

Peal, S.E. 1896. Eastern Nagas of the Tirap and Namtsik, Sibsagar, J.A.S.B.,Vol. LXV.

Ralongghaam, M., 2004. *Origin and Migration of Wanchos,* in Wanchonu, Souvenir, 29th Oria festival in 2004..

Srivastava, L.N. 1973. Among the Wanchos of Arunachal Pradesh, Directorate of Research, Shillong.

Thomas, N. 1995. *Oceanic Art,* Thames and Hudson Ltd., London.

Underwood, L.1948. *Masks of West Africa,* Alec Tiranti Ltd., London.

Vyada, A.P. 1976. *War in Ecological Perspective,* Plenum Press, London.

Wangpan, S. 2004. The Wanchos of Arunachal, in *Wanchonu,* Souvenir, 29th Oria festival in 2004.

Wood Thorpe, R.G. 1878. *Report on Topographical Survey in India, Assam Survey,* 1877-78, Simla.

22

Thang-Ta
The Traditional Martial Art of Manipur

Sristidhar Dutta

Manipur, in the words of Pandit Jawaharlal Nehru 'A Jewel of India'[1], is a small border State of India in the northeastern region of the country. Manipur can broadly be divided into two geographical regions—the Valley and the surrounding Hills. Of the total area of the present State of Manipur, the hill areas cover 20,513 sq. kms. and the valley area constitutes of only 1,843 sq. kms. This Valley area known as Manipur Valley or Imphal Valley is surrounded by hills on all the sides.[2] It is a land-locked state connected with the neighbouring areas with a long border line, of which 352 kms. are international borders with Myanmar (erstwhile Burma) on the east and Chin Hills of Myanmar on the Southeast. At present the remaining 502 kms. connect her with other neighbouring sister States of India.

The indigenous population of Manipur can be classified broadly into two groups—the hill people and the people of the valley area. Later on many people from outside Manipur like the *Pangals* (Muslims) and the Brahmin groups came to Manipur, settled here and became a part of the greater Manipuri population. Among the different ethnic groups of people of Manipur, the Meiteis of the Valley area are the most dominant one and are considered to be a very advance community.[3] The Meiteis were divided into seven clans who in the beginning had their independent principalities in different regions of Manipur. The Mangang or Ningthouja clan in course of time established supremacy over the other clans and absorbed them all. Thus they came to be commonly known as the Meiteis. Pakhangba, who founded the Ningthouja dynasty in 33 AD, was the first known king of the history of Manipur,[4] and after him a series of kings ruled over the kingdom of Manipur establishing a powerful kingdom consolidating many neighbouring areas.

During the historical period the geographical areas of Manipur fluctuated from time to time depending on its political strength. Its geographical areas increased at the time of powerful rulers but decreased on the frontier during the reign of weak rulers. R.B. Pemberton states, "The territories of Manipur have fluctuated at various times with the fortune of their princes, frequently extending for three or four days journey east beyond the Ningthee and Khyendwon rivers and west to the plains of Cachar".[5] William McCulloch also wrote, "to the northeast and south, the boundary was not well-defined and would much depend upon the extent to which the Manipur Government might spread its influence amongst the tribes in those directions".[6] James John Stone also states that sometimes the political boundaries of Manipur were extended upto Chindwin river and put a considerable territories under their rule and at other times Kabaw valley was the only boundary of Manipur.[7]

From these fluctuation of boundaries, it can be surmised that Manipur, in the words of C.J. Lyall "an Oasis of Civilization and Organized Society"[8], in course of its evolutionary history had to wage constant warfare for the survival as an independent kingdom. But the ancient Meiteis did not have an official system of a reserved group of soldiers like standing regular army to fight the invaders. It was, therefore, customary for every male person above the age of 16 to serve the country[9] as and when their services were required by the state. They had to render service for ten days out of forty days according to the needs and decision of the government. This system of allotment of duties was called *Lallup*,[10] which is a combination of two words *Lal* and *Lup*. *Lal* means war and *Lup* means group. Thus during wartime or during critical period of national emergency and importance, the people had to be grouped into batches to proceed to the battlefield or to do the other works of urgencies of national importance.

Incidentally almost a similar system like the *Lallup* of Manipur was prevalent in medieval Ahom kingdom known as the *Paik* system. In order to mobilise the strength of the entire population of the State against the Mughals, the Ahom King Pratap Singha introduced in 1609 AD a system known as the *Paik* on the procedure of exacting compulsory manual labour from every adult male member of the state in the age group of 16-50, with the exception of the Brahmanas, the religious preceptors and the nobles. Four *Paiks* formed a unit called *got*; one member from each *got* was to be always available for state service. In times of emergency two and sometimes even three *Paiks* were recruited from each *got*. The *Paiks* were further organized into *Khels*, which were both occupational and territorial. There was a gradation of officers to control the movements of the *Paiks*.[11]

As mentioned earlier, the long and incessant power struggle among the feudal clans and frequent wars with Burma and other neighbouring kingdoms quite often brought Manipur to a point of devastation. In the words of Rajkumar Sanahal Singh, "Foreign aggressors cannot be sent away by pious talks or sweet and reasonable words but by physical force only."[12] This hostile atmosphere, in case of Manipur, proved to be a blessing as it gave rise to a classic and skilfully evolved martial system known as *Thang-Ta*. Because the Meiteis had to organize themselves into a well-trained armed groups or

Lallups trained in *Thang-Ta* to repel foreign aggressions. Thus *Thang-Ta*, like any other tradition of Martial Arts, although has its universal character but there are certain traits and trends specific to the Manipuri *Thang-Ta* rooted in her historical past.

The term martial-art refers to those combative skills of attack and defence applied with or without weapons. The indigenous combative art of *Thang-Ta* is a kind of armed martial art because in the combat *Thang* (sword) and *Ta* (spear) are used. Historically, it is presumed, the different forms of unarmed combative arts and some other forms of games and sports acted as preliminary to the evolution of *Thang-Ta*. Of the unarmed combative arts of the Meiteis, the most important are *Mukna* and *Sarit Sarat*. In *Mukna* two male competitors holding the loincloths of each other, try to throw down the opponent by using their strength, the dexterity of hands and legs. One who is capable of throwing the other on the ground and top over him is declared the victor leaving no second chance to the loser.

The origin of *Mukna* is considered as old as the mythological origin of earth according to the belief of the Meiteis. Old manuscripts, such as, *Leithak, Leikharol* and *Pudin*, which are revered as *Puyas* (chronicles), account for the fact that this art of *Mukna* has its origin in mythological events. The rich traditions of *Mukna* and other unarmed forms of combative arts prove that the people of this ancient small kingdom had an innate and gifted knowledge of self-defence even when they were unarmed. In *Mukna* a number of techniques were used to overcome the opponent. These techniques are popularly known as *Lou*, a short form of the Manipuri word *Loushing*, which means wisdom. Techniques and skilful implementation of these techniques are considered as the vital matters in this unarmed combat. A *Mukna* expert can easily defeat a man stronger and bigger than him. So this could be the reason why during the medieval days everybody practiced *Mukna* as a military art along with the *Thang-Ta*. Apart from being a game in its true sense, *Mukna* is also closely associated with the great ritualistic festival of the Meiteis like the *Lai Haraoba*.[13] A *Lai Haraoba* festival can never come to its end until a game of *Mukna* performance is done as a ritual item on the final day of the festival.[14] Thus it has been deeply rooted in the cultural world of the Meitei society of Manipur.

Sarit-Sarat is another combative form of martial art. It was and still now necessary for a *Thang-Ta* player to master this art of *Sarit-Sarat* to perfect his skill in *Thang-Ta*. An expert of this art can tackle a number of assailants single-handedly. *Sarit* literally means evading or defending from an unarmed or armed assailant. *Sarat* means counter-offensive move to hurt the attacker. In short offence in defence is the basic principle of this martial art. One cannot master this art prior to his training in *Thang-Ta* or *Mukna*, because the fundamental techniques of *Sarit-Sarat* were derived from the basic movements of *Thang-Ta* and throwing techniques of *Mukna*. It is very difficult to know about the origin of this art as there are hardly any *Puyas* or manuscripts which give an authentic account of its origin and evolution, excepting some passing references about this art found in some *Puyas*.

But the most important of the armed martial art tradition of the Meiteis is the *Thang-Ta*, with the help of which they could win many battles and survive as independent people. *Thang* and *Ta*, although invented by man, had to be firmly situated in the mythological world because the Meiteis attribute all their creations to the heroes of their primordial time who are revered as their progenitors. So there is a number of mythical lores explaining the circumstances leading to the origin of *Thang* and *Ta* in different *Puyases* like *Pudin*, *Thanglon Thangchat, Karthong Lamlen*, etc. Another ancient manuscript called *Thengourol* supports the lore of *Pakhangba*, who became the king of Manipur in 33 AD, as the originator of *Thang-Ta*. Ancient Meiteis linked the origin of *Ta* (spear) also to the mythological lores and considered it as a sacred object or a gift given to them by their ancestors who were deified.

There are various references about the origin of Meitei clans, which are seven in number. Though various myths were invented to mystify the origin of different clans of the Meiteis, still the names of the clans in all these myths are same. These seven clans or *Salais* had different swords. These swords of different nature are even now compulsorily included as a ritual item during functions related with ancestor-worship. Thus *Thang-Ta*, besides being weapons of war, have also indelible relationship with the spiritual life of the Meiteis. The swords are of different shapes and sizes with specific names and characteristic of each of them. Most of the ancient Meitei kings who ruled successfully in Manipur also used to decorate themselves with swords of their choice. Such a chosen sword was a compulsory ritual item in the coronation ceremony of the king.

Meiteis attributes the origin of *Thang* and *Ta* to their ancient heroes who reigned supreme during primordial time. They consider *Thang* and *Ta* to have been invented by their progenitor and gifted to them to ensure their living safely althrough the tiresome journey of life. The myths they *weave* regarding the origin of *Thang* and *Ta* clearly place these two weapons in a spiritual context. This undoubtedly is the reason why the Meiteis consider both *Thang* and *Ta* as an embodiment of spiritual power given by their forefathers.

There are various forms of *Ta* in Manipur. Like *Thang* (sword), *Ta* is a universal weapon used by the people of Manipur since antiquity. Ancient Manipuri people called it

Timen, which *Chung,* an elongated shield associated with this *Ta* is called *Marung*. The *Ta* may roughly be featured as a weapon having a long shaft of hard wood or bamboo, tipped with different shapes of iron points on both the ends of the handle. In short it is a weapon, which can advantageously be used in thrusting man and animal alike with either end of the *Ta*. The front tip is called *Tamang* and the other tip is called *Taning*. There are different forms of Ta, such as, *Lambu-Ta, Lang-soi-Ta, Sagol-Ta, Thongal-Ta, Khang-ning-Ta,* etc.

In early days there was a customary ritual to initiate a student to the training in the art of *Thang-Ta*. For this an auspicious day was chosen. It should be a day when a healthy and unbridled star known among the people as *Thawan Michak Achangba* was located in the clear sky by the astrologer. The auspicious day normally preferred by the people is *Thangja* (Saturday); as the people believe that it is a day closely associated with weaponry. A child between the age of five and seven was normally considered to be the most appropriate period to start the training in *Thang-Ta*. On the auspicious day the customary ritual of initiating a student into the real of weaponry of *Thang-Ta* was observed and this ritual is called *Ojah Bariba*.

The lessons in *Thang-Ta* are a splendid course of exercises meant for promoting all round physical development. The exercise system also helps to develop agility, flexibility, balance and coordination in the body and thus promote a profound coordination of body and mind. A world of moral codes of conduct, all bound to a belief system, was involved on the part of the warrior and the warrior had to strictly follow the laws set by the tradition.[15] Any breach of these traditional laws could bring harmful effect to the warrior or to his near and dear ones or even to the entire community. Wild animals were equally considered as enemies so far the application of the mode of conduct is concerned. A warrior well versed in the art of *Thang-Ta* is one who is equally well versed in the codes of conduct set by the tradition and taught by the *Gurus*.

Successive kings of Manipur institutionalised an educational practice and training to its officers and citizens who could show merit in war or in catching wild animals like elephants and tigers. They were rewarded with some high official posts in the royal court. Further, the kings also quite often betrothed their daughters to such heroes irrespective of caste and creed. It has been recorded that during the reign of Maharaja Goribniwaj (1709-1748) one Thangjaba Chekes Chakrapani, who showed excellent merit in the war against Tripura, was married to the king's daughter Sana Tampha though Chakrapani was a low caste man by birth. Thus knowledge and skill possessed in the field of martial art was not only a crucial factor in the historical evolution of Manipur but this was also considered to be of highest social and cultural importance during the feudal period of the Manipuri Society and Polity.

Since the Meitei state was formed in the 15th century, the state was administratively divided into four territorial divisions or *Panas*. These divisions had severe competition among themselves through native games and warlike form of exercises. Each *Pana* used to present specific forms of *Thang* and *Ta* performance during certain ritual celebrations.[16]

Spectacular developments took place in the art of *Thang-Ta* and other methods of warfare during the reign of king Khagemba (1597-1652). Khagemba fought against a horde of Mayang invaders led by his own younger brother Shanongba, won the battle and arrested one hundred *Pangals* (Muslims), eighty elephants and one thousand guns. He introduced some reforms in polo game as well as in the forms and techniques of the martial art particularly in the use of sword and spear. In fact it is said that the traditional combative art of *Thang-Ta* reached its height of perfection during the reign of Khagemba.

The intricacies of the art of *Thang-Ta* was fully used during the numerous wars fought against the Burmese. The real test of strength, skill and courage of the Manipuri warriors was proved in the wake of the expansion of the Burmese kingdom when not only Manipur but many of her neighbouring kingdoms had to bear the brunt of Burmese invasions. It was mostly because of *Thang-Ta* and intricacies of the other methods of Manipuri warfare that they could launch counter attacks by intruding and raiding deep into the interiors of the Burmese kingdom with the help of famous Manipuri cavalry. Massive successes of the Meitei Kings very often to repulse the huge Burmese army and penetrate deep into the territory of a giant and powerful kingdom like Burma during the 18th century was, of course, also due to the efficiency of horsemanship and skilfulness in using Arambai (a kind of weapon) and other weaponry like the *Thang-Ta* by the Manipuri cavalry.

Another important event, which is crucial in tracing the martial tradition historically, is that of the fiercely fought Anglo-Manipuri War of 1891, after which Manipur lost its independence to the British imperialists. A significant aspect which prominently featured in the history of the war are the details of heroic exploits of Paona Brajabashi, a Manipuri hero, in the field of *Thang-Ta* and other techniques of warfare. While giving a report narrating the historic battles the Gurkha Rifles fought, General Manek Shaw made special mention of the Anglo-Manipur war. He stated that among all the battles the Gurkha Rifles fought in its history like the First and the Second World Wars, the battle fought at Thoubal Athok Pam in 1891 was the most 'dreadful and fierce battle'. He further reported that largest number of Gurkha soldiers were killed in the battle of Thoubal.[17] Captain F.M.Tundull of the 4th Gurkha Regiment mentioned in his letter that soldiers who had fought in the Anglo-Manipur war had reported to him that they had never experienced such a 'determined and stubborn resistance'.[18]

Immediately after the British defeated Manipur in the war, the British government issued orders banning possession of firearms and swords. If any person was found guilty of breaking the standing order he had to be penalized with death or deportation. So strictly was the order enforced that no one was allowed to move even with a stick on the road. Henceforth the practice or teaching of *Thang-Ta,* which was a regular traditional feature at home of the Meiteis, came to an abrupt end.

Today the practice of martial art like the *Thang-Ta*, which was once meant strictly for field application during wartime, has been transformed into a performing art in altogether a different context. *Thang-Ta*, in its new incarnation of decorative form as a performing art, has of course been tremendously successful in attracting the national and international attention since the decade of 1970s. It has now become customary to include an item of *Thang-Ta* performance in most of the State sponsored programmes held within the country or abroad. At present there are a good number of institutions in the Manipur valley that impart knowledge of Manipuri Martial Art specializing in the traditional use of the *Thang-Ta*. Some pioneer organizations of *Thang-Ta* have even opportunity to perform or demonstrate *Thang-Ta* in various National and International forums and festivals. There is also no dearth of official and public patronage for the revival of this traditional art and there are enough talents in Manipur to take advantage of this patronage.

Thus even though *Thang-Ta* has lost its historical significance in the changed situation because of change of mode of warfare and weaponry, the strong sense of love and passion of the Manipuris for this traditional martial art form along with policy of the State and Central governments for preserving this rare form of art, have given a new lease of life not only for its preservation but also in its continuation with more creativity. Reputed National Bodies like the Sangeet Natak Academy and the Government of India have been encouraging the growth and preservation of this art by acknowledging it in the form of giving prestigious national awards. The State government has also included *Thang-Ta* in the school-syllabi of class IX and X in Physical Education.[19] It is hoped like the recognition of identity of Manipuri talents in the cultural activities and games and sports in the international scenario, *Thang-Ta*, the traditional Martial Art form of Manipur, also one day will get international recognition.

NOTES

1. Media sub-committee, 5th National Games: Introduction to Manipur, 1999, p.1.
2. M. Bhattacharyya, *Gazetteer of Manipur State,* Calcutta, 1963, p.1.
3. Gangmumei Kabui, *History of Manipur: Pre-Colonial Period,* New Delhi, 1991, p.12.
4. L.Ibungohal Singh and N. Khel Chandra Singh (eds), *Cheitharol Kombaba,* p.1.
5. R.B. Pemberton, *Report on the Eastern Frontier of British India,* Reprint, Delhi, 1979, p.21.
6. W. McCulloch, *The Account of the Valley of Mannipore and Hill Tribes,* Report, New Delhi, 1980, p.1.
7. James Johnstone, *Manipur and Naga Hills,* Reprint, New Delhi, 1987, p.81.
8. T.C. Hudson, *The Meitheis,* Introduction by C.J. Lyall, p. XXI, Reprint, New Delhi, 1975.

9. *Ibid.*, London, 1980, p.56; Johnstone, *op. cit.*, p.113.
10. Rajkumar Sanahal, *Satjal* (Pt. I), Imphal, 1970, p.8.
11. S. Dutta, *The Mataks and Their Kingdom,* Allahabad, 1985, p.74.
12. Rajkumar Sanahal, *op. cit.*, p.3.
13. S.N. Parrat and John Parrat, *The Pleasing of Gods, the Meitei Lai Haraoba,* Delhi, 1999, p.17.
14. L. Kokngang Singh, *A Historical Study of the Traditional Manipuri Martial Art (Thang-Ta),* Ph.D. Thesis (Manuscript) 2000.
15. *Ibid.,* p.35.
16. L. Ibungohal Singh and N. Khelchandra Singh, *op. cit.*, p.110.
17. Translation from *Doinik Vishwamitra,* April 14, 1956.
18. Correspondence relating to Manipur, London, April 13, 1891, p.54.
19. The author of this paper specially acknowledges the help taken from the Ph.D. Thesis *A Historical Study of the Traditional Manipuri Martial Art* (*Thang-Ta*) of L. Kokngang.

The Contributors

A. Nshoga

Research Scholar, Department of History and Archaeology, Nagaland University, (Kohima)

A.S.W. Shimray

Principal, Christian Patkai College, (Nagaland)

Amarendra Kr. Thakur

Lecturer (Selection Grade), Tirap Govt. College, Deomali, (Arunachal Pradesh)

Ashan Riddi

Senior Lecturer, Dept. of History, Rajiv Gandhi University Rono Hills, Itanagar, (Arunachal Pradesh)

Bharat Kalita

Former Reader in History, National Defence Academy, Pune

Byomakesh Tripathy

Head, Department of History, Rajiv Gandhi University, Rono Hills, Itanagar, (Arunachal Pradesh)

D. Nath

Professor, Dept. of History, Dibrugarh University, Dibrugarh (Assam)

Jahnabi Gogoi Nath

Professor, Department of History, Dibrugarh University, Dibrugarh (Assam)

N.K. Das

Anthropological Survey of India, Kolkata, (West Bengal)

N.T. Rikam

Senior Lecturer, D.N. Govt. College, Itanagar, (Arunachal Pradesh)

P.C. Sarma

Director, Research Council, Vivekanda Kendra, Institute of Culture, Guwahati (Assam)

Punyadhar Gogoi

Lecturer, Garhgaon College, (Assam)

Pura Tado

Reader, Dept. of Political Science, Rajiv Gandhi University, Rono Hills, Itanagar, (Arunachal Pradesh)

Ramesh Buragohain

Scholar Gauhati

Ritu Bhat

Research Scholar, Bomdila, (Arunachal Pradesh)

Sangkima

Principal, Govt. College, Aizawl, (Mizoram)

Sarah Hilaly

Senior Lecturer, Dept. of History, Rajiv Gandhi University, Rono Hills, Itanagar, Arunachal Pradesh

Sarit K. Choudhury

Senior Lecturer, Dept. of Tribal Studies, Rajiv Gandhi University, Rono Hills, Itanagar, (Arunachal Predesh)

Satyadeo Poddar

Head, Department of History, Tripura University, (Agartala)

S.K. Dash

Lecturer, Govt. College, Bomdila, (Arunachal Pradesh)

Sristidhar Dutta

Professor, Dept. of History, Rajiv Gandhi University, Rono Hills, Itanagar, (Arunachal Pradesh)

T. Nyori

Registrar, Rajiv Gandhi University (formerly Arunachal University), Rono Hills, Itanagar (Arunachal Pradesh)

INDEX

Abortion, 19
Abor War, 93
Abu Tani, 114, 115
Accessories, 97
Adang/Iidang (Spear), 225
Adi foothills, 89
Adi Weapons, 90-92
Administration system, 125-26
Agreement (*Dapo*), 96
Agricultural production, 43
Ahoms, 105
  administration, 70
  armed forces of, 70
  garrisons, 214
  language chronicles, 122
Akbar, 153
Allen, B.A., 164
Allen, B.C., 197, 198
Angamis, 4, 10-12, 18-20
Ani sacrifice, 24
Angami head-taker, 62
Anglo-Manipur war, 259
Aos, 19, 62
  social order, 29
Apa Tanis, 222-27
  weapons of, 220-26
Apu (arrow), 226
Archer, Kayda, 237
Arthasastra, 142
Artillery, 99-100
Arunachal Pradesh, defenc[illegible]logy, 179, 184-86
  economic evolution of, 179-80
  martial tradition, forts—indicatory of, 195-200
  pre-historic artifacts in, 177-78
  technology and sociey, 170-78
  tribes of, 243-45
  village defence technology, 190
Army, composition of, 141
Aryan Culture, 231
Aryan Hindu dynasty, 229
Aryan-Kshatriyas, 231
Askasa Yuddha, 143
Assam, attempted Muslim invasion of, 153
  espionage system, 77
Assam Rifles, 119
Assamese Art, War Scenes in, 149-50
Assamese Chronicles, 72, 85-86
  weak points of, 234-35
Astronomy, 173
Asukuda-phi, 66
Asvamedha sacrifice, 139
Atan Buragohain, 155, 235
Aurangzeb, 80, 84, 153, 158
Awkpaka, 130

Bachadar artillery, 99
Bachelor's Chamber, 29-30
Bali Gadh, 108
Bamboo baskets, 17
Bamboo matting, 22
Bangladesh, 28
Bargaon grant, 142
Barganga rock inscription, 139
Battle betwean Chutias and Ahoms, 99
Battle of Saraighat, 76-80, 153-60
  significance of, 159-60
Battle strategy, 105
Bawhbel, 130
Bhagavatapurana, 147

Bhandagarika, 146
Bhang, 85
Bharat Kalita, 153
Bhatt, Ritu, 195
Bhattacharjee, J.B., 211
Bhismaknagar Forts, 199
Blood feud, 17, 25
Blood-thirsty, 33-34, 37
Bodo-family, 211
Boka Gadh, 109
Bomdila, 188
Brahmaputra Valley, 195, 196, 197, 198, 211, 229, 253
Branch longs, 40
British administration, 5, 24
British operation against Singphos, 182
Brown, R., 14, 21
Buliang, 227
Bungriang-Bungta, 117
Buranjis, 102
Buragohain, Romesh, 121
Buruz, 106
Busar Sonam, 117
Butler, J., 8, 15, 22, 23
Butler, J.K., 13, 14

Cachar Valley, 211
Cannons, 99-100, 105
Captured enemies, 53
Capturing of Men/Women, 88
Ceremonies, 95
Ceremonial dresses, 47-48
Cessation, 43
Chakrapani, Thangjaba Chekcs, 258
Chakravarty, L.M., 196
Chakravarty, S.K., 148
Chalcolithic societies, 171
Challenges, 14, 53, 138
Chandi Palton, 215
Chang Nagar, 9, 24
Chao-Lung-Siu-ka Pha, 121
Chatterji, M., 127
Chaudhuri, Sarit K., 237, 242
Chaudhury, P.C., 232
Child bearing, 46
China, 28, 204
Chokpe, 90
Chonyu-phe, 65
Chopping head, 38-39
Chorbachas, 71-73
Chors, 71
Christian missionaries, 244
Chutiyas, 187, 212
    dynasty, 200
Clans, 5-6, 16, 58-60, 74, 88-92
    areas, 3-5
Communication, 54, 87, 197, 229
Compartmentalization, 228
Confrontation, 214-16
Constraints, 174, 246
Corruption, 32-119
Counter-attacks, 44
Cowries, 62-65
    ornaments, 18
Culture, 112
Customs, 47, 67, 112
Customary allegience, 4
Customary religious performance, 157
Cyclones, 46

Daga yuddha, 81
Daos, 57-58, 64, 131
Darwin, Charles, 125
Das, D.M., 198
Das, M.K., 1, 3, 4, 7, 8
Dash, Sasikant, 195
Davis, A.W., 11
De-contextualization, 245
Declared war, 34
Defence Mechanism, 146-47, 161-67, 215-16
Defence Organization, 93-94
Defence technology, 171, 176, 180-82
Defence Weapon, 97-100
Deodhai Asam Burani, 71
Dhansiri Valley, 212
Dhanya Manika, 162, 163
Dhatura, 85
Dibrugarh University, 81
Dimasa State, War goddess in, 211-17

Dimasas, plough cultivation, 221
Dimasa garrisons, 214
Dispute settlements, 5
Divorce, 34
Dolu paanamn, 95
Doobi grant, 144
Dormitory, 2
    importance of, 24-25
Dresses, 14-15, 97-98
Dress and attires, 47
Dress and Ornaments, 47-48, 62-65
Drum, types of, 145
Dubi Copper plate, 144
Dutta, P.C., 238, 239, 241
Dutta, Sristidhar, 251
Dzu, 17

Elwin, Varrier, 8, 9, 13, 14, 15, 17, 18, 20, 39, 183, 238, 243
Employment, 135
Encountered, 55-56, 95, 131, 154
Encroachments, 29, 34
Endle, S., 211
Enemies, Wooden models of, 52
Environmental problems, 196
Erap-Tenam, 95
Errors, 90-91
Espionage system, 70-78
Ethios of war, 146
European Travellers, 173-75
Exchange of War Weapons, 40
Expeditions, 52, 56, 63

Female slaves, 19
Female Tattooing, 240
Fertility, 44-45
Feuds, Causes, 88-99
    economics, 89
    political, 88
    social, 88-89
Feuds between clans and villages, 88
Fighting, arms and mode of, 20-21
First Anglo-Naga War, 7-8
Foreign policy and diplomacy, 145-46
Fortifications, 187-89, 213
    elements of, 180-81
Fortresses, 104
Furer Haimendorf, C.Von, 3, 29, 32, 237
Gadh, 106
Ghatotkach, 216
Ghorachowas, 75
Glory to Ahoms, 155-56
Gluckman, M., 4
Gogoi, Punyadhar, 97
Goliathic War, 34
Governance, modern system of, 113
Green leaves, 37-40
Guerilla fighting, 80-85
Guerilla tactics, 43, 84, 85
Guerilla warfare, 55, 116
Gurkha regiment, 119
Gurkha rifles, 259, 260
Gyambo Soni, 226

Haki, 25
Hamilton, A., 91
Harshavardhana, 232
Hastibandhake, 142
Hastyayurveda, 142
Heads, disposal of, 19-20
Head-chopping, 32
Head-hunters, 31
Head-hunting, 23-24, 32
    customs of, 12
    mode of, 1-2
    occurrences of, 7
    philosophy of, 10-12
    practice of, 8-9, 238
Head-taking *genna,* 64
Head-taking competition, 57
Head-taking rituals, 12-14, 81-82
Helmets, types of, 92
Hilaly, Sarah, 211
Hillaidharias, 102
Hill miri settlements, 220
Hilltop ramparts, 107
Hindu Zamindar, 236
Hitewar Barbarua, 99
Homogeneity, 2
Hookas, 85

Horse sacrifice, performance of, 139
Hospitality, 41
Hostalities, 87, 125, 213
 cessation of, 96
Hostile expedition, 51
House defence technique, 208-08
Howraghat Copper plate, 140
Hu-lyah, 225
Human sacrifices, custom of, 19
Hussain Shah, 162
Huttom, J.H., 3, 5, 9, 10, 11, 12, 31

Illegal head-taking, 34
Ilyo, 224
Imphal Valley, 251
Indian agricultural technology, 172
Industrial technology, 174-75
Industrialisation, 243
Infighting between Abo Tani and Weyis, 114
Inner line regulation, 7
Insignias, 65
Inter-tribal disputes, 7, 58
Inter-Village land dispute, 47
Irfan Habib, 147
Irrigation system, 212
Itafort, 186, 196-198, 200

Jacobs, Julian, 237
Jai Jawan Jai Kishan, 123
Jaintias, 105, 164-66, 174
Jakhama Village, 6
Jhums, 20
Johnstone, J., 18
Jones, William, 173
Joint operation, 53
Juda-phe, 65
Jural community, 4-6
Jural obligation, 25

Kachaikati, 211, 218
Kachari, 105
Kachari Buranji, 74
Kachcha Nagas, 20
Kalidasa, 142
Kalikapurana, 146
Kalita, Bharat, 228
Kamarupa, 138
Kamata Kingdom, 72
Kamayun Hillai, 101
Kame-Panam, 95
Kamrupa Buranji, 82
Kataha Gadh, 107
Katakis, 72-73
Kautilya, 144, 188
Kebang, 92
Kebora Gadh, 110
Kepsi Simat War, 89
Khamptis *Dhaos,* 182-85
Khanda Yuddha, 143
Khargharia Phukan, 101
Khels, 58
Kidnapping, 88
Kinship lieage, 2
Kipuchie, 12
Koch-Ahom powers, 82-83
Kanyak Nagas, 10
Koth, 106
Kukis, 7, 164-65

Labyrinths, 110
Lai Haraoba, 255
Lallup, 253
Lalthangliana, B., 132
Land of the Dead, 48
Langta baragi, 74
Late Medieval Assam, defence strategy of, 104-10
Lavakusar yuddha, 149
Leeping, 61
Lengta, 62-64
Lewin, T.H., 127
Linking-Mimiang, 95
Live and let live, 230-31
Log drum, 38, 57, 242
Logphong, 40
Lord Krishna, 149, 187, 231
Lothas, 4, 58, 62
Loushing, 254
Luhupas, 21

Lunar dynasty, 161
Lyall, C.J., 252
McCulloch, William, 252
McMahon line, 204, 205
Mahabharata, 112, 138, 141, 142, 147, 226
Maharaja Goribniwaj, 258
Manifestation, 43, 44, 48
Manipur, traditional martial art of, 251-60
Marriages, 57, 88
Marriage market, 33
Material Culture, 14-15
Mayonrin, 41
Medieval Assam, War Weapons in, 97-100
Meiteis, 253-55, 256-58
Migration, 3, 179, 190
Military activities, 228-36
Military administration, 148
Military Barracks, 130
Military Contacts, significance of, 231-32
Military operation, 13
Military organization, 12-13
  aspets of, 138-50
  nature of, 126-28
Military training, 24-25, 53
Military and economic activities, 2-3
Militia peasants, 7
Mills, O.P., 12, 25, 32, 45
Minhaj-ud-din-Siraj, 81
Mir Jumla, 75-78, 80, 82-84, 99, 113
Mithaholong Zop, 99
Mithun, 56
Mizo Society military system, 125-35
Moamariya revolt, 77
Modern military system, 135
Modernization, 243
Molamah Naga, 14
Mongoloids, 28
Mortality role, 44
Morungs, 1, 10, 12, 24, 59
Morup Kas, 92
Mud forts, 200
Mughal expedition, 153
Mughal soldiers, 83
Muhammedan Campaign, 236
Mukna, 254
Mung-Mao, 121
Mugical instruments, 242
Muslim policy, 153
Muslim subjugation, 232
Myanmar, 28, 281

Nag, R.C., 32
Naga-British Conflict, 6
Naga-dormitory, 29
Naga head-hunting, 8-9, 43-44, 237
Naga Log-Drum, 31
Naga offensive weapons, 21-22
Naga political systems, 1-25
Naga war, Causes of, 34-35
Naga Warfare, 34-35
  arena, 60-61
  mode of, 45-50
  nature of, 31-32
Naga Warriors, 55
Napoleonic War, 134
Nath, D., 80
Nath, Jahnobi Gogai, 70
Natural Calamities, 46
Natural defence mechanism, 196
Natural transformation, 67
NEFA, 243
Nehru, Jawaharlal, 251
Neolithic Culture, 3
  stage, 177-79
Nidhanpur Coppar plate, 139
Ningthouja dynasty, 252
Nowmaipa, 240
Nshoga, A., 43
Nyele Donam, 118
Nyimok (raid), 204
Nyishis, 220
  martial qualities, 118
  martial tradition of, 112-18
  systems, 198
  warfare techniques, 113
Nyishi Regiment, 119

Oakhirai, 165
Obligations, 47, 61
Occupations, 2, 19-20
Offensive Organization, 94-96
Offensive Weapons, 97-100
Ogik, 90
Ojah Bariba, 257
Ornaments, 58-60

Pachala Gadh, 108
Padam-Panggi and Minyong war, 89
Paik system, 253
Paleolithic tool-making technology, 170
Palestine Giant Goliath, 38
Panas, 258
Pancha mahasabha, 145, 164
Panchayat system, 238
Pandey, B.B.,198
Pangals, 251
Parvi Gadh, 109
Panjies, 15, 23, 92, 180
Pangsa areas, 7
Pasu Chuchik, 89
Peace emissary, 41
Peal, S.E., 240
Pembertor, R.B., 252
Piriya Pinam, 117
Pitch battle, 56
Poddar, Satyadeo, 161
Political hegemony, 175
Politcal structure, 4-5
Pragjyotisha, 138
Pragjyotishapura, 147
Pratap Singha, 73-74, 85-86, 214-16
Prisoners of war, treatment of, 20
Provocation into Raid, 46-47
Pukhareila, 36, 37, 39
Punyang (Javelin), 225
Puyases, 255
Pyke Milita, 123-24

Quick-firing rifles, 134

Raid, 46-47, 56-58, 132
Raikar, Y.A., 196
Raja Udayaditya Singha, 113
Ramparts, 105-07
Ranachandi, 215-18
Rape, 39
Raypa, R.S., 9
Reang Chakdiras, 166
Redcliffe Brown, A.R., 6
Regular army, 128-29
Regulated interrelationship,1, 25
Relationship against enemy, 59
Relationship between soul and fertility, 46
Rengmas, 4, 62
Reservation, 37
Resource mobilization, 195
Rice-bear, 56
Riddi, Ashan, 204
Rigveda, 142
Rikam, N.T., 112
Ripunjoy, 101
Rituals, 53-55
Ritual and Divination Defence Technique, 208-09
Riyan, 41
Robbery, 34
Robinson, W., 12
Rukmininagar Forts, 199
Russian Winter, 81

Sacrification, 239
Sacrifice, 11, 33-35, 117
Sangeet Natak Academy, 261
Sangkima, 125
Sangtam Nagas, 10
Sarit-Sarat, 255
Sarkar, J.N., 85
Sarma, P.C., 104
Sema Community, 9
Sema head-dresses, 63
Shahjehan, 153
Shakespear, J. 94, 134
Sharma, T.C., 176
Shihabuddin Talish, 81, 82, 102
Shimong-Tangam war, 89
Shimray, A.S.W., 28, 32, 35

Shimray, R.R., 39
Shimray, Y.K., 32
Siitin (shield), 226
Sikh Guru Teghbahadur, 158
Sikh regiment, 119
Sikhism, 233
Singimuri kar, 98
Single Combat, 34, 38-39
Singph-Dapo Dingnam, 118
Slavery, 19-20
Smith, W.C., 3
Social Constraints, 174
Social evolution, 170
Soppit, C.A., 20
Sotung-Tamu, 117
Spear, 91-92
Spices Inland, 105
Spikes, 133-34
Stone Age, 28
Stone, James John, 252
Surma Valleys, 228
Sylhet, 214, 215
Symbolic message, 53

Todo, Pura, 220
Tagin's traditional villges, defence techniques of, 204-08
Tai-Ahom Martial Traditions, 121-23
Tai Nyori, 87
Taka Lakbu, 91
Tangkhul Long, 40
Tangkhul warfare, 36-38
Tatooing, 66-67, 239-45
  ceremony of, 14
Technology and Society, 170-72
Tengima Angamis, 5
Terracotta panels, 149
Teri Phiketsu, 65
Territorial Organisation, 6
Terrorism, 123
Terror tactics, 122
Tezpur Rock inscription, 140, 148
Thakur, Amrendra Kr., 170
Thang-Ta (Martial system), 253-55, 256-62
Thawan Michak Achangba, 257
Thomas, N., 239
Torture, 39
Traditional Customary laws, 32
Travener, J.B., 98
Treaty, 96
Tree Trunk Barricades, 108
Trespassing, 89-90
Tribal Council, role of, 92-93
Tripathy, Byomakesh, 138
Tripura, defence mechanisms of, 161-66
Tsungkotepsu, 66
Tuensang area, 7
Tughril Khan, 162
Tundull, F.M., 260
Turko-Afghan expeditions, 230-34
Tusnim yuddha, 143

Uncentralized political system, 4
Undeclared war, 34, 37-38
Uniethnic settlement pattern, 2
Upa Min (Prime Minister), 127

Vallabhavadeva, 140, 142
Valupa, 128-30
Vawklu Vuakthalaka, 132
Vendetta, 17
Vengeance, 1, 13
Victory against Pathans and Mughals, 234
Vijayasri, 141
Village Assembly, 33
Village defence mechanism, 1,15-16, 206-07
Village fortifications, 131
Village settlements, 30
Violation, 31, 36, 41
Visnupurana, 142, 147
Voksa, 90

Wade, John P., 99
Wanchos, 237-45
  war, art and tradition of, 237-48
Wancho Student Union, 245

War, Ahom tactics of, 70-78
War Council, 40
War dresses, 220-27
War expedition, 54
Warfare, methods of, 131-32
  mode of, 51-82
War Goddess, cult of, 216-17
War helmets, 14-15
War implements, 90-92, 143-45
War like qualities, 138-40
War mechanisms, 1, 12, 28-40, 87-95
War Music, instruments of, 44
War of Challenges, 36-37
War preparation, 156-57
Warrior's Status Symbol, 61
Warriorship, 66-67
War time, dress in, 134-35
War weapons, 29, 116, 224-27
  types of, 221
Water barrage, 109
Waterlogged areas, 104
Weapons, 14-15, 49-50
  categories of, 97-98
  gathering and sharpening of, 94
  types of, 133
Weaponry, 215-16
Wild animal, 22
Wood carving, 241-45, 247
Woodthrope, R.G., 240
Worshipping, 217

Yalung Barek, 118
Yalu (feud and dispute), 204
Yelling, 59
Yogini Tantra, 147
Yuan Chwang, 142, 143
Yudhisthira, 140
Yuzback, Ikhtiyar Uddin, 229

Zawlbuk, 125, 138
  groups, 128-30
Zig-Zag pattern, 63, 65
Ziro valley, 220, 227
Zohdimi, 4
Zounus-keyhonuo Mage Tribe, 3, 5
Zumho, 12